C000181860

An English empire

The Ecclesiastical History of the English People by Bede is one of most influential contemporary sources for our understanding of Britain in the early Dark Ages. This book, the second in N. J. Higham's Origins of England trilogy, takes Bede as the starting point for a fascinating investigation of the nature of power in early seventh century Anglo-Saxon England.

The author shows how Bede made efforts to legitimise the English domination of his own day by comparing it to the Roman rule of Britain in the past. He examines and reinterprets the principal literary sources for an English 'empire': Bede's famous list of 'overkings' in *Historia Ecclesiastica*, and the Tribal Hidage. He argues that a comparatively stable and long-lived pattern of regional 'overkingships' existed in early England, and he describes in detail King Rædwald's career as a king and 'overking'. The book closes with an account of relations between the Anglo-Saxons and Britons in early England which provides highly original insights into the structure of rural society in the age of Bede.

An English empire reveals the milieu behind the early Anglo-Saxon kings' exercise of power. Its radical reinterpretations are required reading for all those interested in the history and archaeology of Dark Age Britain.

N. J. Higham is Reader in Medieval History at the University of Manchester

For Naomi

An English empire

Bede and the early Anglo-Saxon kings

N. J. HIGHAM

Manchester University Press
Manchester and New York
Distributed exclusively in the USA and Canada by St. Martin's Press

Copyright © N. J. Higham 1995

Published by Manchester University Press
Oxford Road, Manchester M13 9NR, UK
and Room 400, 175 Fifth Avenue, New York, NY 10010, USA

Distributed exclusively in the USA and Canada
by St. Martin's Press, Inc., 175 Fifth Avenue, New York,
NY 10010, USA

British Library Cataloguing-in-Publication Data
A catalogue record for this book is available from the British Library

Library of Congress Cataloging-in-Publication Data
Higham, N. J.
An English empire/N. J. Higham.
p. cm.
Includes index.
ISBN 0-7190-4423-5. — ISBN 0-7190-4424-3 (pbk.)
1. Great Britain—Politics and government—449-1066. 2. Anglo—Saxons—Kings and rulers. 3. Imperialism—England. 4. Monarchy—England. I. Title.
DA 152.H53 1995
942.01—dc20 94-23921
CIP

ISBN 0 7190 4423 5 *hardback*
0 7190 4424 3 *paperback*

First published 1995
99 98 97 96 95 10 9 8 7 6 5 4 3 2 1

Typeset in Hong Kong by Best-set Typesetter Ltd.

Printed in Great Britain by Bell & Bain Ltd, Glasgow

Contents

Figures

Abbreviations

AC: *Annales Cambriae* or 'The Welsh Annals', in *Nennius: British History and the Welsh Annals*, ed. and trans. J. Morris, Chichester, 1980, pp. 85–91.

DEB: *De Excidio Britanniae*, or 'The ruin of Britain', in *Gildas: the Ruin of Britain and other documents*, ed. and trans. M. Winterbottom, Chichester, 1978, pp. 87–142.

FC: *Famulus Christi: Essays in commemoration of the thirteenth centenary of the birth of the Venerable Bede*, ed. G. Bonner, London, 1976.

HB: *Historia Brittonum* or the 'British History', in *Nennius: British History and the Welsh Annals*, ed. J. Morris, Chichester, 1980, pp. 50–84.

HE: *Historia Ecclesiastica gentis Anglorum*, or 'Ecclesiastical History of the English People', in *Bede: Ecclesiastical History of the English People*, ed. and trans. B. Colgrave and R. A. B. Mynors, Oxford, 1969.

Orosius, *Histories*: Paulus Orosius, *Seven Histories against the Pagans*, ed. and French trans. M.-P. Arnoud-Lindet, Paris, 1991, in 3 vols.

Acknowledgements

I would like to express my gratitude to Dr. Simon Keynes who read chapters three and six in draft, at a time when it was intended that they should be published as discrete articles, to Dr. Alex Rumble for his helpful criticisms of chapter four, and to both him and MUP for permission to publish this chapter (which has long been placed in *The Defence of Wessex* volume) herein. My thinking concerning this period has benefited enormously from an entire generation of Extra-Mural students and several groups of third year undergraduates at the University of Manchester, yet the ideas offered herein are my own, as too are any errors. My greatest debt is to my daughter, who has repeatedly reminded me of the richness of life which lies beside and beyond the computer keyboard. This book is for her.

Introduction

This volume, which focuses on the political systems operating in southern Britain between *c.* AD 597 and 633, is offered as the first of two companion volumes to *The English Conquest: Gildas and Britain in the fifth century*, which was published in the summer of 1994.[1] It might be objected that there already exists a plethora of published work of excellent quality on the subject of Germanic kingship in general,[2] the government of sub-Roman Europe,[3] and – more particularly – the kingships of early Anglo-Saxon England.[4] What, however, distinguishes this book from others is its commitment to exploring the several suggestions which emerged from my own earlier work, in the context of the next tranche of relevant written sources which are available to us – primarily from the seventh and eighth centuries.[5]

The recognition that Gildas's *De Excidio Britanniae* (*Concerning the Ruin of Britain*) was highly allegorical in style opens the door to a far wider exploration of his purposes and attitudes, and a far better understanding of the context in which he wrote, than has proved possible on the basis of comparatively literal interpretations of the text. In brief, my own study proposed a significantly earlier date for the *DEB* than has hitherto been conventional,[6] and argues in favour of its localisation in west-central, southern England.[7] Having placed the text in a novel chronological, and more certain spatial, context, it further proposed, on the basis of detailed attention to the author's introduction and use of biblical references, that it was written in a political context which differed markedly from that to which it has conventionally been apportioned,[8] namely that its author was concerned to protest at the Saxon domination of his own people (the Britons) in the present, rather than solely to offer a diatribe on the Britons' moral inadequacies.[9]

Key elements in this re-interpretation include recognition of Gildas's use of the analogy of Jeremiah's lament concerning the Babylonian sack of Jerusalem and its temple and the ensuing captivity of the Israelites, with the fate of the Britons in the present.[10] They include also previously unnoticed references to Saxons in the text of the *DEB*: this is largely through the exploration of a series of metaphors and allegories which Gildas seems to establish in the course of his description of the Saxon arrival and revolt;[11] they include also his recognition of some contemporary *dux* ('military leader' or 'general') more powerful even than Maglocunus, the mightiest of the British kings to whom he referred by name.[12] If his purpose in so doing was to test the moral credentials of such British *duces* as potential leaders of the British people in a grand and divinely sanctioned push to expel the Saxons, then his failure to identify and consider this anonymous but greater warrior-king necessarily implies that he was a Saxon; this interpretation finds support from recognition that Gildas referred repeatedly to the Saxon pagans of his own day by such terms as 'gentiles', 'lions' and 'devils';[13] that he was mindful of a particular Saxon warrior-leader or king is necessitated by his repeated use of the phrase *pater diabolus* ('father devil') in a context which placed such a figure alongside the five British kings as if a patron of the British clergy in the present.[14] Similarly, analysis of the various roles of kings, 'governors' and 'tribute' in contemporary Britain may imply that there then existed a wide-ranging Saxon domination over the bulk of southern Britain. Re-examination of the brief reference to a Saxon conquest of much of Britain in the 'Gallic Chronicle of 452' provides valuable support to this reading of Gildas's text.[15]

The thesis put forward in *The English Conquest* therefore, is that the 'War of the Saxon Federates' occurred in southern Britain (or at least not exclusively in northern Britain[16]) and that it was won by the Saxons, leading to the inception of a peace which was dependent upon a formal treaty, or *foedus*. The principal result of that treaty was the subjection of all southern Britain, excepting only the five kingships named by Gildas, to Saxon control or lordship, and the payment of tribute by many local communities to the same Saxon overlords. In return, the Britons obtained long-lasting security from Saxon attack and protection from other barbarians. In short, the treaty to which Gildas so often referred established a Saxon protectorate or dominion in lowland Britain which performed many of the same central functions as had the Roman protection, domination and exploitation of Britain up to *c.* AD 410. To that extent, the treaty to which Gildas (and perhaps also the Gallic Chronicler) referred established a 'Saxon Empire' in Britain.

It is that concept to which we return, therefore, in this present volume, via a much later body of written material. It immediately becomes apparent that this concept was close to the heart of England's leading ideologue in the early eighth century – the venerable Bede – when writing his own *Historia Ecclesiastica*.[17] There is, therefore, considerable scope to pursue these themes into a much later era, and their reappearance at this later date tends to sustain the foregoing interpretation of Gildas's comments in a much earlier context.

In pursuit of this objective, this volume begins with a detailed analysis of Bede's notion of *imperium* (literally 'empire'), both in the Roman contexts from which he derived his vision of empire and also in those English ones in which he applied it with a degree of originality.[18] Since it remains the most significant source for widespread 'overkingship' which is independent of Bede and his clerical peer group, there follows a comprehensive analysis of the Tribal Hidage,[19] a list of peoples and hides which unfortunately now exists in no form earlier than the single late tenth- or early eleventh-century vernacular copy, known as Recension A, in the British Library.[20] This re-interpretation offers a precise context and date for the two lists therein, on the basis primarily of information deriving from Bede's *Historia*. With this in mind, it is suggested that the conflation of these two sources provides an opportunity to examine the geographical context of those *imperia* to which Bede and his contemporaries made passing reference.

It must be recognised, however, that Bede's comments are extraordinarily subtle as regards the level of interpretation appropriate to them – as one might perhaps expect from the greatest exegete of his day.[21] There remain considerable difficulties as regards the history of the early seventh century in distinguishing reality – or reality to the extent that that was perceived a century or so later – from the rhetoric developed by Bede and other of his contemporaries to sustain his own, highly contemporary and dialectical purposes.

At issue is the very notion of *Britannia*, or the *Britanniae* ('Britain' or 'the British provinces'), and the nature of *imperium* therein, in the present (i.e. the early eighth century), as much as in the more distant past. Bede was familiar with several uses of the term *imperium*, or cognate terms: firstly, his readings in several Church Histories provided him with a battery of usages in an antiquarian context from which he was then able to draw;[22] secondly, the dating mechanism used by successive seventh-century popes depended on the regnal year of the emperor of the day,[23] and Bede certainly made use of this convention in his own work;[24] thirdly, Bede was familiar with what seems to have been the official transcript and record of Archbishop Theodore's synod at Hatfield, wherein the term *imperium* was applied to four English kings, two of whom were arguably more powerful than the remainder, in a context which implies that Theodore had in mind the collegiate imperial system of the late Roman Empire;[25] and fourthly, he was familar with, and himself used, the language of *imperium* in the context of instructions issued by senior clergymen.[26]

In general, Bede used the terminology of 'empire' comparatively sparingly. He seems to have considered it more appropriate to Christian than pagan English rulers, so presumably had some notion of divinely sanctioned legitimacy as a precondition of *imperium* (but not kingship in general or military leadership for which he variously used *rex* and *dux*). The principal exceptions are the pagan *imperium*-wielding kings of book two, chapter five, whose brief appearance was arguably necessary to his purpose of bolstering the reputation of that somewhat nondescript first Christian king of the English, King Æthelberht of Kent.[27] Furthermore, excepting only Bernician kings,[28] Bede's 'overkings' (and therefore kings wielding *imperium*) tend to be conquerors – so men with their own military reputations – as well as patrons of Christianity (as were Pippin in Frankia and Cædwalla of the West Saxons[29]). These themes will be explored below through an analysis of the sources relevant to Rædwald of the East Angles, whose greatness arguably posed special problems for Christian writers and whose career therefore offers an exceptional perspective on both *imperium* itself and on the rhetorical and dialectical responses of Bede to a post-Conversion, pagan ruler.

To the extent that Bede portrayed the English as the legitimate successors of Roman *imperium* inside Britain,[30] so was his concept of *imperium* a universal one, encompassing both the English and the Britons (and even the Scots and Picts), and his rhetoric certainly sustains this image. The English, *in toto* and in the generic sense, were portrayed as exercising *imperium* over the Britons, and they were in that respect being portrayed as an imperial race to match the Roman people.[31] So too were the English in Bede's perception a people chosen by God to rule in Britain. The Britons were, by contrast, damned as obstinate heretics,[32] albeit impotent ones in the present, being subject to the power of the English as well as an unyielding and anglophile God.[33] Their current servitude could be portrayed as a punishment from and by God which was appropriate both to the resistance of the 'older inhabitants' of Britain to the messages brought by St. Augustine from Rome, and to their earlier immorality, of which Bede had read in Gildas's work.[34] So too did Theodore proclaim his title as 'archbishop of Britain', as much as of Canterbury,[35] so denying the existence of any sector of Christianity not subject to himself throughout the length and breadth of Britain. Such rhetoric had a sound base in Gregory's delegation of authority to Augustine but there was surely a substantial gap between that rhetoric and the reality of power to which it laid claim, albeit it had significant parallels in the secular world of English *imperium* on which Theodore's power was ultimately founded. Bede was not, therefore, the sole originator of the rhetoric which he employed, albeit his remains the fundamental source through which we can today examine it.

Bede sustained his perception of the English as an imperial race by numerous rhetorical devices, among which an interesting example (not discussed elsewhere in this work) is his careful manipulation of several different dating systems. One which he used very sparingly was the by now antique count of years from the foundation of Rome, which occurs herein solely in the context of the Roman conquest of Britain (*HE*, I, 2) and the eventual collapse of that same control *c.* 410 (*HE*, I, 11). Such dates were used in this text, therefore, exclusively to bracket the period of Roman *imperium* in Britain. In what can only have been an attempt to construct a rhetorical parallel, Bede established for himself a notional and approximate date for the arrival of the English in years before the present, and then offered calculations for the dates of the arrival of Augustine's mission and of Northumbria's initial conversion in years from that same *adventus* ('arrival') of the English in

Britain.[36] Thereby Bede offered to the more thoughtful of his own audience the message that English (and particularly Northumbrian) history since the *adventus* was that of an imperial race worthy of comparison with the divinely sanctioned 'empire' of the Romans in antiquity.

There is, therefore, both the rhetoric of *imperium* and *imperium* itself available for examination by the historian with an interest in early England, but these issues must necessarily be placed in the intellectual and historiographical context appropriate to them. That context is centrally that of interactions between Britons and Saxons in the fifth century, the consequences of which are only again available for study in the seventh and eighth centuries. It is, therefore, Gildas's vision of a Saxon (so in Bede's terms, 'English') domination of the bulk of (at least southern) Britain which has precipitated the present volume, which attempts to carry forward the process of re-interpretation, as already begun in *The English Conquest*, to the next major corpus of written evidence which is available. The principal imperative is to explore thereby the nature of *imperium* as that was understood by Bede and his contemporaries and applied to a series of seventh-century English kings, and so examine the insular domination of the English and the unequal relationships then existing between Britons and Anglo-Saxons, in contexts which are both generic and individual. This new study is offered, therefore, in the hope that it will make a positive contribution to our understanding of early British and English history. As such, it may attract the attention of both historians and archaeologists with an interest in this period, and perhaps also help to illuminate, and even reinvigorate, what is already a debate of some antiquity concerning the ethnic or racial origins of the population of Britain.

Notes

1 *The English Conquest* is published by Manchester University Press. It is proposed that the third and final such volume will re-examine the English conversion to Christianity.

2 See, for example, in English, J. M. Wallace-Hadrill, *Early Germanic Kingship in England and on the Continent*, Oxford, 1971, *passim*; H. A. Myers, *Medieval Kingship*, Chicago, 1981, particularly pp. 1–14, 59–97; S. T. Driscoll and M. R. Nieke, edd., *Power and Politics in Early Medieval*

Britain and Ireland, Edinburgh, 1988.

3 E.g., R. Van Dam, *Leadership and Community in Late Antique Gaul*, Berkeley, 1985; J. Drinkwater and H. Elton, *Fifth Century Gaul: a crisis of identity?*, Cambridge, 1992; I. Wood, *The Merovingian Kingdoms, 450–751*, Harlow, 1994.

4 S. Bassett, ed., *The Origins of Anglo-Saxon Kingdoms*, Leicester, 1989; B. Yorke, *Kings and Kingdoms of Early Anglo-Saxon England*, London, 1990; D. P. Kirby, *The Earliest English Kings*, London, 1991.

5 *Bede: Ecclesiastical History of the English People*, ed. B. Colgrave and R. A. B. Mynors, Oxford, 1991; *The Life of Bishop Wilfrid by Eddius Stephanus*, ed. and trans. B. Colgrave, Cambridge, 1927; *The Earliest Life of Gregory the Great by an anonymous monk of Whitby*, ed. and trans. B. Colgrave, Kansas, 1968; *Two Lives of St. Cuthbert*, ed. and trans. B. Colgrave, Cambridge, 1940; D. N. Dumville, 'The Tribal Hidage: an introduction to its texts and their history', in Bassett, ed., *Origins*, pp. 225–30.

6 See, for example, D. N. Dumville, 'The Chronology of *De Excidio Britanniae*, book I', in *Gildas: New Approaches*, edd. M. Lapidge and D. N. Dumville, Woodbridge, 1984, pp. 61–84; K. R. Dark, *Civitas to Kingdom: British Political Continuity 300–800*, Leicester, 1994, pp. 258–66.

7 This view is now becoming less controversial, as see *ibid* above, but my own treatment of the issues in *An English Conquest*, pp. 90–117, remains by far the most substantial exploration of the evidence.

8 See particularly E. A. Thompson, 'Gildas and the History of Britain', *Britannia*, X, 1979, pp. 203–26, which presented several interpretations which much affected, for example, the perspectives adopted by Dumville, as in note 6 above.

9 Contrast, for example, the perception of Gildas's attitudes towards the Saxons in P. Sims-Williams, 'Gildas and the Anglo-Saxons', *Cambridge Medieval Celtic Studies*, VI, 1983, particularly pp. 25–30, and my *English Conquest*, *passim*.

10 *Ibid*, particularly pp. 67–89.

11 *Ibid*, pp. 53–8.

12 N. J. Higham, 'Medieval "Overkingship" in Wales: the earliest evidence', *Welsh History Review*, XVI, 1992, pp. 156–7, and *English Conquest*, pp. 183–4.

13 *Ibid*, pp. 53–6, 161–2.

14 *Ibid*, pp. 160–1, 191–3; *DEB*, LXVII, 3; CVII, 3; CIX, 3.

15 *Chronica Minora*, I, Berlin, 1892, ed. T. Mommsen, p. 660; *English Conquest*, pp. 172–4.

16 As proposed most trenchantly by Thompson, 'Gildas', pp. 214ff.

17 See below, pp. 37–9.

18 See below, pp. 21–34 and pp. 11–17, respectively.

19 See below, pp. 74–99.
20 British Library, MS, Harley 3271.
21 See, in general, *FC*.
22 See *HE*, I, 2–11, 32; II, 1; IV, 1; V, 16, 21, 24. Many of these denote the use of *imperator*, which Bede used exclusively in a Roman context.
23 *HE*, I, 23, 24, 28, 29, 30, 32; II, 18; V, 7.
24 E.g., *HE*, IV, 12; V, 24.
25 *HE*, IV, 17.
26 *HE*, I, 17; IV, 27, 29.
27 See below, pp. 47–52.
28 *HE*, V, 18, 19.
29 *HE*, V, 10, 7, respectively.
30 See below, pp. 15–17.
31 See below, pp. 37–40.
32 E.g., *HE*, II, 2, but see Bede's use of Gildas's *DEB* in the latter part of I, 22.
33 *HE*, V, 23.
34 *HE*, I, 22. St. Augustine's endeavour 'to bestow his pastoral care upon the older inhabitants of Britain' recalls and probably derives from Bede's account of the Augustine's Oak conferences in *HE*, II, 2.
35 *HE*, IV, 17: 'by the grace of God archbishop of the island of Britain and of the city of Canterbury'.
36 *HE*, V, 24; II, 14, respectively.

1

Bede and *imperium*

Bede's standpoint

Our perception of England in the very late sixth and early seventh centuries has been shaped primarily by Bede's attempt to write a history of the English Church. We are, therefore, very much at the mercy of his priorities and of his success in identifying sources appropriate thereto. More particularly, we find ourselves constrained by his editorial judgements, his purposes as an author and his prejudices: although Bede has often been portrayed as a disinterested – even humble – scholar writing in comparative seclusion for primarily idealistic motives,[1] those currently involved in the re-evaluation of his purposes are united in the view that he wrote in response to imperatives which were current in 731 and, in part at least, political as well as ideological. His work is both less even-handed, and more politically charged, than has often been imagined. In particular, his oft-claimed humility, modesty and detachment should be viewed as indicative of a particular style of writing – that is the style known as the *sermo humilis* – rather than as indicative of his own personal character.[2] Bede could be, and often was, mischievous. He was also writing within a particular literary and intellectual environment so far distant from our own that it is a risky business to describe him by such words as 'historian' at all. Bede was an exegete of the first rank and expert in the allegorical skills which that required. His *Historia* should be read as a narrative obedient to his own very peculiar and distinctly developmental imperatives, and with such facts continuously in mind.

Bede's perceptions can be explored as regards the material which he incorporated but that which he elected to omit is almost entirely lost to us. As an introduction to this problem, it is worth recalling that he offered a partial list in his preface of his sources for the state of the English Church in the present, and the recent past. His southern material came primarily from Kent and Rome (via Nothelm, his 'dearest brother' and fellow cleric who was then at London but destined to become metropolitan at Canterbury in 735). These sources were supplemented by information on specific local matters obtained from Bishops Daniel of the West Saxons and Cyneberht of Lindsey, and the otherwise unknown Abbot Esi who was probably resident in East Anglia, if only because his communication refers specifically to that province.

Aside from his recognition of bishops in Mercia and districts west of the Severn at the time of writing, Bede discussed the Mercian Church only via the testimony of the Lastingham community (in north Yorkshire, so Northumbrian), whose information pertained to the heady days when successive ministries to the Mercians operated under the ultimate patronage of Lindisfarne and its regal protectors, the Northumbrian kings of Bede's own native Bernician dynasty. The omission of further material pertinent to Mercia and most of its numerous satellites (as of 731) testifies to Bede's own prejudices as much as political tensions still existing between Bernicia (so Northumbria) and Mercia at the time of writing. He was, after all, writing as a member of that Bernician political community which had, within his own lifetime, been worsted in a century-long struggle with the Mercians for the dominance of all Britain, yet at a date when Mercian supremacy may still have seemed vulnerable to renewed challenge from the north. Perhaps Mercian sources were inaccessible to Bede, so producing an unavoidable bias in his text: more probably he sought none, preferring to minimise references to Mercia which might be deemed complimentary within the providential context in which he wrote, so inevitably and purposely detracting from the virtues, legitimacy and authority of Mercian *imperium* in the present.

The *Historia Ecclesiastica* has a comparatively clear agenda in this respect: the apogee of English kingship in Britain occurred, in Bede's perspective, under King Oswiu of Bernicia, once he had defeated Penda of Mercia, extended his hegemony over the Picts and united the Irish and Roman branches of the English Church; his unique position passed to Ecgfrith, his son, but was bitterly contested by both the Mercians and the Picts; and Ecgfrith's disastrous defeat and death at *Nechtanesmere* was seen by Bede as the turning point of recent history and the beginning of the decline which characterised the present: 'From this time the hope and strength of the kingdom of the English began to "ebb and fall away"' (*HE*, IV, 26). Although he gamely used the term *imperium* for both Aldfrith and his young son Osred (*HE*, V, 18, 19), Northumbrian claims to hegemony in the south were in abeyance, at best. In the official transcript of the Hatfield synod, Bede was using sources which recognised that several kings, including Æthelred of Mercia, wielded *imperium* in Britain alongside Ecgfrith *c.* 679, rather as if they constituted a college of four emperors, with two senior and two junior partners, on the model of fourth-century Rome.

Bede jealously guarded the Bernician claim to *imperium* at least so long as Oswiu's dynasty survived: for example, he emphasised the independence of the West Saxon Cædwalla from Mercian control by recognising his rule over the defeated subkings of the region as an *imperium*, while in the same chapter (*HE*, IV, 12), using Ecgfrith's 'years of *imperium*' as a dating mechanism; Æthelred, *rex* of the Mercians was, by contrast, damned for the ravaging of Kent and its churches at the head of a 'malignant army'. This is providential history (that is, the unfolding of God's design for his people) at its best, but even Bede seems to have found himself constrained by the realities of power politics in the present, recognising, in his ultimate chronological summary, the 'imperial years' of Æthelbald of the Mercians. Mercian supremacy over much of England was a present fact, therefore, if not one which Bede and his audience could be expected to either applaud or consider fully in accord with the divine plan for the English race.

As regards earlier eras, but in retrospect, he directed his considerable intellectual and rhetorical skills to the task of undermining Mercia and promoting Northumbrian kings. For Bede it was the latter who wielded *imperium* over other insular kings, and so implicitly stood comparison with the virtuous and divinely appointed Roman rulers of the world. At most, southern kings were *subiecta sunt* – 'made subject' – to King Æthelbald of the Mercians (*HE*, V, 23), which is a form of words which is at best neutral but at worst hints at the use of force without the moral sanctions appropriate to *imperium*. No Mercian king prior to Æthelred (675–704) was recognised by Bede in imperial terms, and he only in the chronological summary which closes the *HE*.

Such partiality is likely to have been intentional. Bede's pronounced Northumbrian-Kentish – and to an extent East Anglian – bias mirrors the several political accords between Northumbrian and south-eastern kings during the seventh century which had been the bedrock of the attempts of such northern kings as Edwin and Oswiu (but not Oswald) to contain and control the Mercians.[3] Bede never compromised his belief that Bernician hegemony over Britain was a matter of divine will. Even the collapse in 685 of Ecgfrith's attempts to sustain Northumbrian expansion and power was explained by Bede (in IV, 26) in the light of divine anger at his attack on the harmless Irish in the previous year, and so in terms which were personal and easily reversible. Ecgfrith had angered God, yet Bede was careful even in this context to depict Oswiu's heir as the legitimate ruler of the *regnum Anglorum* ('kingdom of the English'), with all that that might imply in equally Anglian Mercia. That Ecgfrith's struggle with the Mercians had divine support is implicit in Bede's deployment of a pro-Bernician miracle story in his description of Ecgfrith's defeat by the river Trent. Until Wilfrid's fall from royal favour, the author of his *Life* (XX) was at least as keen to portray Ecgfrith's supremacy as divinely sanctioned.

Particularly in instances where Bede had reason to treat a Mercian ruler generously, he remained staunchly committed to his consistent advocacy of Bernician supremacy. This comes over most clearly in his treatment of King Coenred of Mercia (*HE*, V, 19), whose rule over Mercia he described as *nobilissimus* and who then even more nobly renounced his throne and journeyed as a pilgrim to Rome, where he ended his days as a monk. Although this passage begins the chapter, it merely prefaces an unusually lengthy treatment of (or elegy for) the Northumbrian bishop, Wilfrid, whose career featured numerous links between England and the papacy and between the several English kingships and dioceses. Coenred's virtues are, therefore, carefully overlain by a far longer, Northumbrian-centric account of contacts with Rome which begin, significantly enough, with Wilfrid's education at Lindisfarne – a religious establishment of which Bede was himself a keen advocate.

What is more, Coenred's departure for Rome was dated not in terms of his own regnal years – which Bede certainly believed he knew (*HE*, V, 24) – but by 'the fourth year of the *imperium* of Osred', the boy king of Northumbria. The contrast between Osred's *imperium* and Coenred's *regnum* is a compelling one which was surely designed to diminish the undoubted stature of the Mercian kingship and at the same time to enhance the status of the Bernician crown.

The *Historia Ecclesiastica* was offered to the Bernician king of Northumbria as a narrative account of the first century of English Christianity, the primary function of which was to explain and contextualise the present. This is apparent from the first sentence of Bede's preface, in which he spelled out his perception of it as an *Historia gentis Anglorum ecclesiastica* – an 'Ecclesiastical History of the people of the English'. Since this preface was self-evidently written after the completion of the remainder, this was necessarily Bede's considered opinion of his *Historia*, arrived at in retrospect – or at least it was how he then wished it to be perceived.

It was, however, a far more subtle work than this might imply and obedient to imperatives which went far beyond this grandiose but simple design. As already noted, it was transparent in its Northumbrian bias: indeed, it fell little short of propagandist in this respect, particularly (one suspects) as regards what Bede chose to omit. Within Northumbria, it was Bernician, rather than Deiran, in focus, rendering valuable support to the status of Lindisfarne, and so to King Ceolwulf who identified himself closely with that community and eventually retired there: Bede's partiality for the Irish-originated Church of his own people is as clearcut as is his ambivalence towards St. Wilfrid,[4] who was almost certainly a Deiran, and whom, by contrast with the *Life of Wilfrid* (which was written by one of its hero's closest associates), Bede damned by the faintest of praise.[5]

Although the reader encounters it at a later stage, Bede's description of his work which he incorporated in the final chapter of book five was actually written before his preface. Herein he stated that he had:

> arranged this concerning the ecclesiastical history of the Britains, and particularly of the race of the English, according to ancient writings, the tradition of the majority or from my own knowledge.

When he came to list his *Historia*, he described it as:

> The ecclesiastical history of our island and people in five books.

It was only in his final phrase, with which he closed his great work of providential history, that Bede shortened this to: *Historia*

Ecclesiastica gentis Anglorum – 'Ecclesiastical history of the people of the English' – which is the form of words which he then adopted in his preface and which thereafter became, in various translations, the title by which the work would be known.

Precisely what Bede intended by his fuller descriptions is heavily dependent on the meaning attached to 'Britains' here: if he was referring specifically to the provinces of erstwhile Roman Britain then this was primarily, in the present, the English and British churches; if his vision of the 'Britains' extended far beyond this (as, for example, in *HE*, I, 11), then it necessarily incorporated also the Pictish and Scottish churches in the north, and the interest which he displayed in Scotland in his geographical introduction would seem to sustain this view. Undoubtedly, *Britanniae* is a collective term for the *provinciae* of Britain, and Bede certainly used this term in reference to the Picts. He used the word *Britannia* far more commonly in the singular, and clearly often meant by it the entire island of Britain. His reference in the second of these quotations to 'our island' seems to confirm that it was the wider insular context which he considered appropriate to his own work.

There is, therefore, reason to suppose that he intended his work to be seen as a history of Christianity in Britain, rather than just in England. The universality of this vision was perhaps sustainable in Bede's own mind by virtue of his comments concerning the Scottish and Pictish Churches, and particularly their recent adherence to the Roman method of dating Easter, but his treatment of even the English dioceses was heavily weighted, and the British Church hardly referred to other than as an object of brutal condemnation, particularly once Archbishop Augustine was dead. His claim to a universal relevance for his work (at least as regards Britain) – albeit a conditional claim – was therefore flawed from the beginning, and obviously so. To make a claim for the universality of so partial an account may itself have been an important feature of the mechanics of Bede's own, very subtly developed, ideological position, within which illustration of the damnation of the Britons, in particular, was a clearly stated objective. We can be sure that a British text written about this same date concerning the 'ecclesiastical history of the Britains' would have offered a very different perspective on the relative merits of the English and British Churches and their traditions, reversing the several claims (both implicit and explicit) to moral virtues, and the accusations of heresy, which Bede deployed. Bede, however, could exploit Gregory's delegation to Augustine of authority over the British clergy, and Theodore's claim to be 'archbishop of Britain'. In the light of such claims, Bede found the justification necessary to enable him to dismiss the rival claims of the British clergy as perverse. That the English Church could be portrayed as dominant throughout Britain was a viewpoint which could be made to sustain the vision of an 'English Empire' throughout the same insular context.

The complexity of Bede's purposes in this respect are to an extent revealed in the opening few books of the *Historia Ecclesiastica*. Given that he intended his *Historia* to focus on the English Church, it must be worth noting that, out of its 278 pages of text,[6] the first seventeen pages of book one contain almost no mention of the Angles or Saxons,[7] and we are kept waiting a further eleven pages before the arrival of St. Augustine.[8] In all, there are twenty-nine pages of text which are entirely devoid of discussion of either the conversion or the English Church – that is in excess of ten per cent of the total.

It would be churlish to deny that some scene-setting was necessary – and Bede was apparently inspired by such earlier writers as Orosius and Gildas to conform to classical stereotypes and proffer a 'geographical' introduction to his 'History'[9] – but the allocation of such a high proportion of the total text to this purpose suggests that Bede was here pursuing some important but subsidiary purpose, which required an extended introduction to his central theme prior to its introduction and subsequent development.

Bede's text throughout this introductory section depended heavily on pre-existing Latin literature, even to the point where in places it seems to be little more than a 'mosaic of quotation', but it is never entirely unoriginal.[10] He rarely copied out long sections from pre-existing texts: he regularly altered vocabulary, syntax and word order or redrafted existing material to accord with his own style of presentation, and his own meaning; he obviously exercised considerable discretion in selecting and ordering even his longest blocks of material,[11] and frequently inserted comments which adapted information extracted from pre-existing writings to his own current perspective and value-system concerning the past. He was no disinterested copyist but a scholar who continuously interacted with his sources in ways which were obedient to his own imperatives – and these too differed in detail from the purposes being pursued by the authors of the texts from which he borrowed, be they continental Church Histories on the one hand, or Gildas's *De Excidio Britanniae* on the other.

Bede shared the philosophy of history which he found in Rufinus, Orosius and Gildas: his was a providential work, at the core of which lay relationships between man and God, good and evil, Christian and pagan.[12] He wrote, however, in a very different political, cultural and racial context from those of his precursors and it was his unique task to adapt the providential nature of history which he found laid out and defended in these works to accord with the specific needs of the comparatively youthful Church of the English, as well as the political system which sustained it. This, in very general terms, seems to have been his primary purpose in writing a lengthy introduction as a preface to the English conversion, which placed the English people themselves, their eventual conversion and their Church, in a moral and providential context which was appropriate to their triumphant seizure, even while still pagan, of much of Britain from the Christian Britons.

It was the self-awareness of the English,[13] as much as their neighbours,[14] of their immigrant, barbarian and heathen origins that threatened the very foundations of Bede's own belief – which was presumably widely shared by his compatriots – that the English were a race chosen by God.[15] This opinion was obviously not one which was shared by the Britons at the time of writing, whom Bede recognised still retained an 'ingrown', but impotent 'hatred' towards the 'people of the English'.[16] He diagnosed that very impotence as evidence of their evil:

> nevertheless they cannot obtain what they want . . . being entirely constrained by divine and human virtue in combination. Indeed, although they are in part under their own laws [or 'their own masters'] nevertheless they have in part been sold into servitude to the English.

That the English had triumphed over the Britons, even to the extent that many were, at the time of writing, their slaves and the remainder impotent to retaliate, was in itself sufficient to justify Bede's retrospective interpretation of Anglo-British relations through time: if the Christian God be accepted as the ever-present adjudicator of human affairs, then the triumph of the English over their neighbours was necessarily divinely sanctioned and the

English a people chosen to rule – much as the Romans had been in the distant past.

There still remained, however, the problem of reaching this Anglo-centric perception of history in the present, via a narrative which necessarily depended on late classical texts for its starting point. In this respect, there was little assistance to be had from pre-existing literature: as far as Orosius was concerned, the Saxons were just one of the several savage, heathen and barbaric peoples who infested the coast of the Christian Empire or attacked Roman and Christian Gaul;[17] to Gildas they were 'an enemy more savage than the first', 'the very ferocious Saxons, whose name was abominable, detested by man and God',[18] and it was in his view the Britons, and certainly not the Saxons, who were God's chosen race.[19]

It was with such unpromising – indeed, contradictory – material at his disposal, that Bede set himself to justify both the English seizure of wide lands in Britain (for the seizure was an obvious *fait accompli* by Bede's lifetime) and his own perception of his countrymen in the present as a race specifically picked out by God for special favour. His difficulties *vis-à-vis* Latin literature *may* be one reason he preferred the term 'Angles' to that of 'Saxons', which was used exclusively in his several sources, while making it quite clear from the beginning that he considered them interchangeable when used in a generic sense (as *HE*, I, 15).

At the same time, these dialectical imperatives required that the Britons be demoted from the status of a chosen race (a view which Bede confronted in the *DEB*, XXVI, 1) to that of iniquitous heretics and rebels against God – as was only appropriate given their servitude to the English and impotence in that regard in the present. The resolution of this dialectical difficulty was to be a major function of Bede's narrative of the pre-Augustinian history of Britain, being introduced very subtly as a theme in chapter one and brought to fruition only at the very end of chapter twenty-two, immediately prior to the introduction of Pope Gregory – the so-called apostle to the English – and his mission to England in chapter twenty-three. This whole section of the *Historia Ecclesiastica* should be read, therefore, very much as a dialogue between the English present and the classical and sub-classical past, the primary purpose of which was to develop, contextualise, justify and explain an English perception of their own superior virtues in the present, *vis-à-vis* the

Britons, so justifying English *imperium* as much as the British *servitio* ('servitude') which was its essential antithesis.

The 'geographical' introduction

In his first chapter, Bede offered a 'geographical' account of Britain which opens with a mass of quotations from pre-existing classical authorities, but moves rapidly to a far more original perspective on Britain which is ethnographic as much as geographical in content. He noted the correspondence of the five languages spoken in Britain with the five books of divine law, so claiming, albeit implicitly, that the presence of the English – the last arrivals – was necessary to bring some divinely sanctioned equilibrium of relevance to the entire island to fruition. That his own *Historia* was contained in five books may owe something to this schematic vision and he may additionally have been mindful of Gildas's reference (in *DEB*, I, 4) to Jeremiah's lament in four alphabetic songs, to which the addition of an English song might have been thought to make five.

Bede then commented on the origins of the several peoples present within the island, stressing his opinion that every race – and not just the English – was immigrant. The Britons were (necessarily) the first to arrive but Bede incorporated what he claimed to be hearsay information (*ut fertur*) that they had come from Armorica, whence they had 'seized' (*occupaverunt*) the southern part of the island. Such a story is most unlikely to have derived from a British source: it is certainly not founded in the *De Excidio Britanniae*, wherein Gildas offered no origins myth for the Britons of any kind, although he did distinguish the virtues of an Eden-like Britain from its inhabitants in a fashion which might (but need not) imply that he believed the Britons to have once been immigrants to a previously uninhabited land.[20] Gildas's implicit allusion to the story of Adam and Eve has Britain as the Garden into which chosen humans (so the Britons) were then placed by God; nor is this opinion shared by the *Historia Brittonum*, which offered classically inspired origin myths for the Britons which wrapped them in the borrowed clothes of Roman virtues and tied them into a chronology which was founded in, and empowered by, the Old Testament, even while adhering to a similar opinion that they were the first people to inhabit the island.[21]

Bede's opinion laid no claim to literary precedents, although such did exist, albeit unbeknown to him.[22] His may have been a view then circulating in (northern) English circles and based on nothing more than (presumably well-known) cultural similarities between eighth-century Wales, Cornwall and Brittany. It did, however, enable Bede to avoid portraying the Britons as aboriginal, with any residual, natural rights to land and self-governance which that might have implied, and it may be that his incorporation of this piece of gossip was neither innocent nor disinterested. He may even have been responsible for it himself. Just like the English, he implies, the Britons were immigrants who had 'seized' Britain. So did Bede begin the gradual process of challenging – and ultimately undermining – British perspectives then presumably current on the relative virtues of Britons and Saxons, and adjusting the moral stature of each to conform with his own prejudices.

English rule over the Picts was also a matter of considerable interest to Northumbrian kings, and thence of significance as regards Bede's own perception of English *imperium*. Bede was to show considerable interest in the Bernician conquest of parts of southern Pictland and the temporary development of an English diocese in the region. The Picts were, therefore, likewise depicted as immigrants and portrayed, as regards their settlement in Britain, as in some respects dependent on the Irish. The latter were consistently the less dangerous of Northumbria's northern neighbours in the late seventh and early eighth centuries,[23] and Bede's portrayal of their respective settlements in Britain offered some dialectical advantage to his own countrymen, since the victories of the Picts over the Northumbrians in and after 685 were thereby robbed of any special moral status which might have attached to them had they, in turn, been portrayed as aboriginal, or even as independent in their settlements of the Irish. The Picts were, however, at peace with the Northumbrians at the time of writing,[24] and several factors enabled Bede to sustain a generally favourable perception of them throughout the latter part of his *Historia*, which was not marred by his references to Ecgfrith's fall at *Nechtanasmere* – which he depicted as a consequence of divine displeasure at Ecgfrith's activities rather than as an expression of divine support for his opponents *per se*.

Of all the non-English immigrants, the Irish of Dal Riata were portrayed in the most virtuous light, having obtained lands among the Picts 'either by friendship or the sword'. They, too, were not considered by Bede to be a danger to his own people at the time of writing,[25] and he was content to boast of Ireland's fabulous, or miraculous, properties – which in turn tended to reinforce his favourable perception of its people and the tradition of Northumbrian Christianity for which they would ultimately be responsible. That had, of course, been centred in Bernicia and sustained by the active patronage of its kings. In the light of his comments on Bishop Aidan and the Irish mission to Northumbria, this philo-Hibernian stance is transparently Bernician as regards its propagandist inferences.

By 731, both the Irish and Pictish Churches had acknowledged, and converted to, Roman practices as regards the dating of Easter and this factor, combined with the peace of the present, enabled Bede to treat both peoples with considerable sympathy in his *Historia*. The Irish strand of his narrative had combined with that of Canterbury and Rome at the Synod of Whitby in 664, enabling Bede to portray these two traditions of English Christianity as twin pillars sustaining the edifice of the present, Northumbrian-orientated and Canterbury-centric, insular Church. That this reconciliation of Roman and Celtic traditions was seen by Bede as something of great importance is clear from the detail with which he treated of these matters (*HE*, V, 21, 22) and it was with this achieved that he brought his great narrative to a close just two chapters later.

It was the Britons for whom Bede reserved his most scathing strictures: it was they who still, in the 730s, resisted Roman practices and the authority of English bishops but Bede's virulent hostility goes well beyond this *casus belli*; it was their land which the English had conquered, reducing the inhabitants to servitude, so it was the Britons, beyond any other people, whose virtues as a Christian race must be utterly destroyed if the current position of the English people was to be rendered morally sustainable. Bede was engaged, therefore, in a fundamentally ideological conflict with the Britons. Since current British hatred of the English was necessarily sustained by their own version of providential history, it was to the historical roots of the current Anglo-British antipathy that Bede himself turned.

These foundation myths are not, therefore, any more free of current political influences than are the retrospectively conceived genealogies of early medieval kings. On the contrary, it is possible to identify subtle nuances in Bede's treatment of the folk origins of the different peoples of Britain which relate to other manifestations of his several attitudes to them, even up to the present. By replacing British views of their own origins with his own, Bede severed them from the virtues attendant on either a classically inspired origin myth or an aboriginal status which might have been fortified by reference to the Old Testament, and began the lengthy process of undermining and refuting British historical perspectives on the present. With that in hand, he apparently set out to face down British perceptions of the English as barbarian land-grabbers whom God would one day expel from Britain, so restoring the Britons at last to their rightful birthright. That no such British texts survive from his generation does not mean that such ideas were not then in circulation.

The 'historical' introduction

With his geographical and ethnographical introduction brought to completion, Bede turned to pre-existing Church Histories – primarily those of Orosius – to provide himself with the raw materials from which to produce a narrative history of Britain before the English conquest. His selection was carefully controlled as regards content: the majority of the works available to him were universal, rather than insular or diocesan, in scope but he selected material primarily in consideration of its relevance to Britain; the principal theme which he developed was that of the relationship between Britain and the Roman Empire and the material he marshalled was almost entirely directed to this aspect of the past, at least until that relationship collapsed early in the fifth century. His interest focused on the nature of Roman *imperium*, *per se*, and more particularly on its specific application to Britain and the Britons.

It was his need to place the 'English Settlement' in a suitable moral context which led Bede to offer such an extended narrative concerning Roman Britain, developing his own text backwards into the distant past in search of an intellectual, historical and causal framework appropriate to his perceptions of the English superiority of the previous century, and the present. Bede explored and laid out for his audience the Roman domination of Britain and its inhabitants, therefore, so as to provide a morally unassailable analogy for an English *imperium* over Britain which spanned the conversion period, and so justified his interpretation of the English supremacy as God-sanctioned.

Bede's use of the term *imperium* throughout his *Historia* is central to the current process of reassessment of early English kingship and 'overkingship'.[26] It is likewise crucial to our understanding of relations between the Anglo-Saxons and other peoples in Britain: it was not merely English kings whom Bede portrayed as ruling over Britons (in particular) but the very 'English people' – the *gens Anglorum*. It was that *gens Anglorum* to whom Æthelfrith made the Britons tributary;[27] it was likewise the Angles as a race to whom the servitude of the Britons had been transferred, or sold as if chattels – by implication by divine agency and from the Romans.[28] Likewise, King Edwin subjugated Man and Anglesey to the *imperium Anglorum* (*HE*, II, 9) and the Picts were similarly subjected by Oswiu to the 'imperial rule of the English' (*HE*, IV, 12). Bede offered, therefore, an account which sought to justify his vision of an English empire in Britain by analogy with the Roman Empire of the past, of which he wished it to be thought a legitimate, but insular, heir.

Bede used the term *imperium* with reference to the power exercised by some, at least, of the greater English kings of the late sixth to early eighth centuries but he first explored and so established its meaning in his introductory chapters, courtesy of the Roman Empire. That process may have been very necessary if his contemporaries had no word in the vernacular capable of expressing *imperium* (imperial rule), as opposed to *regnum* (kingship).[29] The *imperium*, or 'overkingship', of which he wrote was merely Anglo-Saxon kingship taken to the furthest extent of its logical development, so not an institution or office separate from 'kingship' and requiring a distinctive terminology. In his attempts to distinguish the greater kings from their lesser neighbours, Bede may have been among the first to equate Latin *imperium* with the powers wielded by them,[30] to our general confusion, but his assumption that such kings, like the Roman emperors, ruled over a variety of provinces, and different peoples or races – and particularly the Britons – is fundamental to his use of the term.

That Bede made repeated use of *imperium*, *imperator* and various cognate terms in the opening chapters of his *Historia* when referring to Roman emperors and their rule,[31] offers us the opportunity to establish the meaning which he attached to it in a secular setting. He explored its use in a moral context which was borrowed from Orosius and Gildas, who both portrayed universal Roman rule as legitimate, so divinely sanctioned, and opposition to that rule as illegitimate, at least so long as Roman emperors forebore to persecute the Church.

Britain was, in Bede's version, initially conquered by Julius Caesar,[32] but had to be subdued thereafter on account of a British insurrection.[33] From the very beginning, therefore, British resistance to Rome was characterised by Bede (as by Gildas) not as the legitimate self-defence of a community resisting aggression but as rebellion, so morally bankrupt. When Cadwallon, for example, was later to fight against English *imperium*, Bede afforded him comparable treatment, describing him as a 'wicked rebel'.[34] The inherent virtues of the Roman Empire were associated with that universal peace which coincided with and facilitated the birth of Christ, and so of Christianity,[35] so were sanctioned at the highest level possible. Bede's exploration of Roman *imperium* and his juxtaposition with it of the Anglo-Saxon rule of Britain reflects his concern to deploy those same virtues on behalf of the English.

Even so, *imperium* and its derivatives were in some passages used by Bede in a context which would have been readily understandable and uncontentious even in Roman Britain: Claudius's regnal years were *sui imperii*; *imperio* was to 'rule imperially' or to 'rule the empire' and *imperium* was 'imperial rule'.[36] *Regnum* could be used as an alternative for that imperial rule,[37] as commonly occurred in Bede's Latin sources, but not the reverse.[38]

More revealing of Bede's purposes were his comments on Claudius *imperator*, with whom he associated earlier but anonymous wars and victories and who was then depicted as the leader of a great expedition to Britain. His universal conquest of the island was characterised not by great victories over the Britons but by their uncontested recognition of his supremacy: he 'received in surrender the greatest part of the island without any fighting or bloodshed within a few days'.[39] He even added the Orkneys to the *Romanum imperium* without ever journeying anywhere near them,[40] so their voluntary surrender to his protection provided clear proof of the magnitude of his reputation. But as Orosius had made clear, Claudius did not warrant portrayal as a great general, so the assumption that he was a war leader with a proven record of achievement already before his expedition to Britain depended on

Bede's own highly retrospective assumptions concerning *imperium* in general – so that of English kings in particular. His treatment of Claudius is therefore capable of providing valuable insights into Bede's vision of *imperium* in an Anglo-Saxon context.

Vespasian, who *imperavit* after Nero, subjugated the Isle of Wight to Roman rule as an agent of Claudius,[41] though whether or not Bede supposed him to have achieved this by the sword he did not state.[42] A great *imperator* could, therefore, conquer even through some third party operating on his behalf: just so did several layers of kingship characterise seventh-century Britain and various *duces* and *praefecti* fight on behalf of Northumbria's kings during Bede's own lifetime – and it is noticeable that Bede used *imperium* of the rule of these same recent northern kings even despite their loss of the Southumbrian hegemony to the Mercians.

By contrast, Nero 'dared no military activity whatsoever'. As a direct consequence, he presided over innumerable injuries to the Roman *regnum* among which was his near loss of Britain, where two 'very noble towns' were captured and destroyed.[43] Military incompetence and the total lack of a warlike reputation were, therefore, entirely incompatible with Bede's perception of an *imperium*-wielding king.

The Britains

Severus, the victor in Roman civil wars, was 'drawn into Britain through the defection of almost all the allies (*socii*)'. Bede's use of the plural *Brittanias* – 'the Britains' – derives from that of Orosius,[44] but his subsequent comment on Severus's recapture of southern Britain makes it clear that he thought of these 'allies' primarily as the Britons still within the Roman part of Britain, rather than the tribes beyond the Wall. That he should follow Orosius in describing the intra-mural Britons as the *socii* of the Roman emperor tells us much concerning the nature of the relationship which he assumed to have existed between the Roman *imperator*, the Roman people, and the Britons. This usage was sustained by a second reference to 'allies' – *socii* – which he had already come across in Orosius as pertinent to southern Britain,[45] but it seems to have led Bede into a series of mistakes as regards his interpretation of Roman Britain: the *Britanniae* were transformed in his version from the Roman provinces of Orosius's text into putative tribal communities which were still under British kings, of like kind to those with which Bede was himself familiar as the separate kingships and tribal peoples of contemporary and near contemporary Celtic and Anglo-Saxon Britain.

With this perception in mind, references to the British *socii* of the Romans become closely analogous with Bede's later reference to the battle near the river *Winwaed*,[46] wherein he described Penda's power in terms which recall an *imperium*-wielding king while always withholding this prestigious accolade from such a detestable and Mercian pagan: his army contained thirty *legiones* led by thirty *duces regii* ('royal generals') who had come to his aid (*auxilium*) – as if from his *socii*. These same *auxilii* ('allied troops'), alongside Æthelhere's East Anglian *milites* ('warriors'), were reputed casualties of the battle. Although he did not mention it, Bede may have been familiar with the story found in the *Historia Brittonum* that had the Welsh present in Penda's forces until the eve of the battle, when they deserted him.[47] If so, by ignoring their departure before the battle, Bede squeezed the maximum moral benefit from the tale on Oswiu's behalf – and this was probably in large part his purpose in recounting it. Once again, therefore, Bede seems to have been interpreting his sources for Roman Britain by reference to his own perceptions of *imperium* in the recent past in an English-dominated Britain.

Bede's meaning in this passage is made clearer by a second reference to British leadership under Roman *imperium*. The curious and apparently apocryphal story of Lucius reached Bede from the *Liber Pontificalis*, a Rome-centric, Latin source which is not in this context contemporary.[48] He described this Lucius as *rex Brittaniarum* – 'king of the Britains'. By implication, Bede perceived British-ruled Britain under Roman *imperium* as a group of tribes or peoples, analogous with those with which he was familiar in the seventh and eighth centuries. Bede regularly termed such local kingships *provinciae*, using that term in a way which differs dramatically from its standard usage in late classical texts – even including the entry for 441 in the Gallic Chronicle of 452 and Gildas's use of it in *The Ruin of Britain*.[49] There is no evidence that Bede recognised the novelty of his own usage. Given that the supposed *obit* of the apocryphal Lucius lay in the third quarter of the second century, when Britain was still in reality a single province,[50] Bede's *Britanniae* cannot refer to provinces in a contemporary context. Instead it necessarily carries his own idiosyncratic and very different use of *provincia* in an English context back into the lost world of Roman Britain, which he apparently envisaged as something which would stand comparison as regards its administrative style and geography with the English-dominated Britain of the present and recent past. His use of *provincia* does, therefore, seem to have been consistent across his entire text and represents a significant, but unwitting, departure from its use in his classical sources. That departure arguably resulted from his mistaken interpretation of earlier writings on the basis of inappropriate assumptions derived from the present: what Bede failed to recognise – indeed had no reason to know – was the vast gulf as regards political organisation which separated Roman rule of Britain and the Britons in antiquity from the *imperium* of the *gens Anglorum* of his own lifetime.

Bede believed therefore that Roman Britain contained numerous British peoples who were the 'allies' of the Roman *imperator* of the day, and of the Roman people, to whom he imagined that his sources were referring when they used terms such as *Brittaniae* or *provinciae*. Just as those of the Britons of the present who were free of direct English rule were often subject to a single, Welsh 'overking',[51] so too were the *Brittaniae* of the second century collectively subject to the kingship of the British king Lucius. Given the complex relationships between subsidiary and superior kings which characterised the political structures of Britain in his own day, Bede may well have shared the assumption which was later to be found in the *Historia Brittonum* that Lucius, *Britannicus rex*, was an 'overking' of the Britons, from whom the other *reguli* – 'petty kings' – took their cue as regards religious policy.[52]

To Bede, Lucius was a British king, therefore, who was responsible for ruling the Britons under Roman *imperium*, rather than a Roman governor. When the peaceful Christianity which he had instituted was disturbed by the persecutions of the pagan Diocletian, St. Alban was the victim of *perfidi principi* – 'treacherous princes'[53] – the term *princeps* being one which was otherwise used as an alternative to *subregulus* – 'underking', or 'ealdorman' in eighth-century England. Bede himself used it in this context, among others, referring for example to Peada, Penda's son and the underking of the Middle Saxons, as a *princeps*.[54] It was, therefore, the contemporary hierarchy of kingship overlying an English-dominated Britain which Bede had in mind when writing of Roman

Britain and it is fair to conclude that he recast the relationship between Romans and Britons – which he had no reason to understand in its own terms – in the light of his own knowledge of the Anglo-British interface of his own times.

The authority of rulers

These examples provide a clear indication of Bede's vision of relations between the Romans and the Britons during antiquity: a successful *imperator* (like Claudius) was one whose military prestige was sufficient of itself to ensure that others – even kings and entire peoples – submitted to his *imperium* without fighting. In direct contradiction of Orosius (who made it clear that his invasion of Britain was Claudius's sole expedition[55]), Bede portrayed the latter's imperial prestige as stemming from a plethora of successful, but anonymous, military actions previous to his invasion, and the reputation as a general which he had earned thereby. It is implicit in Bede's account that he had not been opposed in Britain due to insular respect for that very prestige. The military conquest of numerous individual peoples was rendered unnecessary by their recognition, unfought, of his *imperium*, and their near universal submission made that *imperium* in turn near universal. In support of this interpretation, Bede was able to marshal examples of even the most distant peoples who were so impressed by the military resources and reputation of a truly great *imperator* that they actively sought his protection. Claudius's rule was made effective even over off-shore islands – *imperium* over which was apparently deemed particularly noteworthy by Bede;[56] the means by which that *imperium* was extended to the distant Orkneys differed from that which secured Wight,[57] but unequal alliances were as much an attribute of the Bernician *imperia* of the recent past as were actual conquests. Both instances to which Bede was able to refer could, therefore, be reconciled with his own present assumptions concerning the nature of Bernician and English *imperium* within Britain.

Claudius therefore provided Bede with a stereotype for divinely sanctioned 'overkingship' in Britain which could be exploited as an analogy which legitimised subsequent, and (necessarily) equally virtuous, English kingships. The uncontested nature of Claudius's new, insular *imperium* was such that Bede felt obliged to justify it by reference to his pre-existing personal reputation as a successful military leader, so clothing Claudius in the ill-fitting clothes of an English warrior-emperor, such as King Oswald.

The antithesis of this virtuous and successful imperial ruler was encapsulated in the example of Nero, whose primary failing in Bede's version was his total military inactivity. In consequence he lacked military prestige, so the peoples subject to him (in this context primarily the Britons) lacked the respect which was an essential prerequisite of *imperium*. Bede could safely assume that his aristocratic and Bernician audience would appreciate that the *imperium* of such a ruler over subject kings and peoples would be fragile in the extreme.

The figure of Lucius and his relationship with Rome provided a valuable contrast to current relations between the Britons and the Roman pontiff, through his local agent, the (normally English) archbishops of Canterbury. His submissiveness towards Pope Eleutherius provided an analogy which contrasted with the current British adherence to their own customs in defiance of the Church of Rome and its representatives in Britain. Lucius was, therefore, offered as an exemplar of the virtuous British king against which Bede could then proceed to measure later Welsh kings and churchmen, to their disadvantage. So did he sustain his condemnation of the Britons in the present as heretics.

Bede's manipulation of his Roman material has, therefore, an obvious relevance to early Anglo-Saxon England: the prestige which was consequent upon earlier military success was then presumably also a normal prerequisite of *imperium*. Like that of Claudius, that English *imperium* might normally extend to far more peoples – and races – than the unfortunates over whom a victory had been won. The process that Bede transposed back into the Roman period is a simple but subtle one: the pre-eminence of a particular king was heralded by victories over one or more powerful opponents, which established his personal military reputation; his supporters and tributaries were therefore given confidence in his ability to defend them, so deterred from rebellion, while his neighbours were made chary of confronting him, so amenable to his dominion without a struggle. A significant victory won at an auspicious moment over a powerful enemy had the potential to herald in a universal, or near-universal, *imperium*. Without such a victory, *imperium* was difficult to achieve and inherently fragile. The kudos which sustained *imperium* was therefore perceived by Bede as something which was fundamentally personal, rather than institutional or heritable (albeit that he perceived its tenure by successive Bernician kings as especially divinely sanctioned). In this respect, at least, his view surely mirrors that of the pagan world from which Anglo-Saxon kingship was only then emerging.

Such assumptions are more relevant to the political world of Britain during Bede's lifetime and the half century which preceded it than the Roman world to which they are here made to relate. The contemporaneity of Bede's account is in many respects transparent. We should beware of lending to the eighth-century English author our own far more sophisticated knowledge of Roman Britain or the empire of which it formed a part. Bede's perspective was limited to half-understood information culled from a suite of classical texts which was limited in scope, derivative, and highly subjective in content. His work knows little of the institutional apparatus of the Roman Empire, with its governors, professional soldiery and fiscal officers. Instead, his perception of the beginnings of Roman rule rested on a recognition by the various rulers of the British tribes of the military prestige of a particular *imperator*. This procedure could be usefully compared with similarly widespread and rapidly instituted *imperia* in the seventh century. Without any conception of a civil administration, Bede had little option but to assume that pre-existing British hierarchies – which he imagined to be kingships – remained in place throughout the Roman period, beside the insular settlements of the Romans themselves (at Colchester, for example), much as some British hierarchies still survived in the present alongside the Anglo-Saxons.

Unlike Gildas,[58] Bede seems to have been unaware that the Britons were ruled under the Roman *imperium* by governors. His Britons were subject to British kings who were the *socii* of the emperor. His confusion of the *Britanniae* with local tribes implies numerous local rulers. Britain was, therefore, in Bede's view, part of a hierarchical political structure which had a Roman *imperator* at its head but beneath this *imperium* local kings ruling the *Britanniae*, perhaps organised in an insular hierarchy which looked to a single British king who was answerable to the king of the Romans. These *Britanniae* were not (in Bede's imagination) the four or five provinces of the late Roman diocese but something closely analogous to the numerous kingships of seventh-century

England, and so perhaps best rationalised as the tribal *civitates* which were already in place at the Roman conquest – whether Bede knew it or not.

The Britons as rebels

Like Gildas,[59] Bede had a very poor opinion of those who challenged or overturned the unequal relationship existing between the Britons and Rome. The British 'insurrection' which prompted the Claudian invasion has already been noted (above); likewise, Bede followed his Rome-centric sources in judging the Boudiccan rebellion one of 'numerous injuries' to befall the state.[60] Carausius and Allectus were both portrayed as usurpers whose reputations were tarnished by various crimes. Both could be interpreted from Bede's text as Britons,[61] and this was probably his intention. His portrayal of Constantine the Great suffers from this same prejudice: his father, Constantius, was a virtuous man who *regebat* (ruled) Gaul and Spain (as if a subordinate king) under Diocletian, but died in Britain.[62] In a sense, therefore, Constantine's accession (at York) could be portrayed as a British challenge to Roman rule. Bede termed him *imperator* but followed Orosius in stressing his illegitimacy, then ignored his conversion to Christianity and Orosius's claim that his rule was to the general good.[63] In contrast, his association with the rise of Arianism was noted, so tainting him by contact with heresy and spiritual rebellion.[64] The tenor of Eusebius's triumphant description of Constantine's adoption of Christianity as if the climax of history is entirely absent from this English account. Bede therefore selected from amongst the various items of information, and opinions, available to him in such a way as to minimise the virtues of Constantine – or worse.[65] The imperative governing his selections would seem to be the necessity of portraying a rebellion against Roman *imperium*, which stemmed from Britain and which presumably had British support, in the worst light possible.

Magnus Maximus was another *imperator* created by the army in Britain.[66] His otherwise virtuous nature was marred by his breaking of his oath of allegiance,[67] and his rule was tyrannical in consequence. Bede found in Orosius a description of Maximus's relationship with Emperor Gratian as an essentially personal one between two kings of unequal power, one of whom had sworn fealty to the other – a relationship which offered an obvious parallel for one king's personal commendation of himself to a more powerful (probably assuring him of loyalty by oath) in Bede's Anglo-Saxon England. Although he avoided Gildas's vitriolic condemnations of the man, Bede nevertheless left his audience with the impression of a leader whose insular rebellion necessarily rendered his rule morally bankrupt.

Like Magnus Maximus, later British usurpers were *tyranni* and the most successful of them, Constantine III, was characterised as a foolish man without virtue.[68] Their acts in defiance of Roman *imperium* collectively rendered Britain defenceless in the face of barbarian attacks.[69] This wickedness brought its own punishment: in the short term, the *tyranni* met death at the hands of the more virtuous Romans; in the longer term, Britain was lost to the Saxons. Its loss was, therefore, a consequence of British or British-supported rebellions against legitimate and divinely sanctioned, Roman authority, and against God himself. Bede found this argument laid out in Gildas: although he avoided the rhetorical extremes of the latter, the moral which he drew from his account of Roman Britain differed little from that of Gildas, his only insular source. On the contrary, Bede took the opportunity, which Gildas inadvertently provided, to place the Britons in a moral context which was utterly disreputable: it was at this point that he began to paraphrase long extracts from the *DEB* in his own *Historia*. His ultimate purpose was to challenge and destroy the moral and spiritual status of the Britons, as compared with the Angles and Saxons, even down to the present day, so demonstrating that God had abandoned them.

Before taking this road, however, Bede inserted a passage which was designed to highlight, and obtain dialectical advantage from, the moment when Roman *imperium* ceased to protect Britain. He associated that process with an even more cataclysmic event on the continent: the fall of Rome to the Goths in the 1164th year from the city's foundation:[70]

> From that time the Romans ceased to rule [*regnare*] in Britain [*Brittania*], after almost 470 years since Gaius Julius Caesar had entered the island. They had lived [*Habitabant*] however within the *vallum* which we have already noted that Severus had built across the island, as far as the southern district [*plaga*], to which the cities, the lighthouse,[71] the bridges and the roads which they built there testify to

> this day; furthermore they possessed lawful dominion over the further regions of Britain as well as the islands which lie beyond Britain.

This amounts to an elegy, pronounced over the corpse of Roman Britain, but it is neither obviously derivative nor disinterested. Bede referred to three northern walls of various kinds, having found reference to one in Orosius, associated with Severus, and two in Gildas, which were reputedly of a date later than Magnus Maximus.[72] The later of the two referred to by Gildas was stone and linked what he interpreted (mistakenly) as walled towns,[73] so Bede had no doubts that this referred to the Hadrianic Wall.[74] He associated Gildas's earlier wall of turf with the Antonine Wall,[75] and that of Orosius with the Hadrianic *vallum* which runs along the south side of the stone wall. It was this last, therefore, to which he referred in this passage.

It will not have escaped Bede's notice that the settlements of the English were likewise predominantly found between the various Roman walls in the north, on the one hand, and the south coast, on the other, and he took this opportunity to develop his analogy between the ancient Roman *imperium* over Britain and the English rule of the present: he distinguished, for example, the southern extremity of Roman 'settlement' in Britain through a phrase which probably meant something quite specific to his own contemporaries but had no obvious meaning in the context of late Roman Britain: the *plaga meridiana* ('southern district'). This is implausibly imprecise as a reference to the southern Roman province of the third century (of which there is no indication that Bede was otherwise aware) and cannot distinguish one of the four or five late Roman provinces from the remainder since the south coast was divided in approximately equal parts between two of them; it is, however, a meaningful phrase by which to define the 'Southumbrian' Mercian hegemony of the late seventh and early eighth centuries, particularly when used by an author who wished to minimise the kudos attaching thereto – *plaga* is a comparatively neutral term in comparison with *imperium* or even *regnum*.

Bede envisaged, therefore, that the Romans 'settled' both the northern and southern 'overkingships' of the early eighth century. Their *imperium* was, however, closely comparable only with that of those few English kings who had likewise ruled over both the north and the south. This once again has implications for Bede's own use of the term in reference to the several great *imperia* of the Northumbrian kings of the central decades of the seventh century,[76] and for his withholding of the term *imperium* from the Mercian 'overkingship' until the present, since the northern boundary of Mercia lay far to the south of the northern perimeter of Roman Britain.

Bede's reference to lawful dominion over the far north and even the islands beyond was presumably sustained by the Claudian extension of Roman *imperium* as far as the Orkneys but his remarks were once again far from innocent. He was going out of his way to describe Roman *imperium* in Britain in terms to which he would subsequently return when describing the *imperia* of Edwin, Oswald and Oswiu,[77] whose rule he depicted as encompasssing all the English, the Britons and even the Mevanian Isles,[78] and latterly (in Oswiu's case) extending even over the Scots and many of the Picts of the far north. The legality of Roman rule even over the periphery of extra-mural Britain, which he stressed in this passage, seems designed to sustain the right of later English kings to draw tribute from the northern fastnesses of Britain, inhabited by Britons, Scots and Picts. Once again, if this northern dominion could be portrayed as a *sine qua non* of English *imperium*, the Mercian claim to such status in the present was undermined and the Bernician reinforced.

Bede's use of the term *habitare* – literally 'to inhabit' – of Romans in Britain is also significant. He was to use the same word in the context of the conquest of the Britons by the Bernician king, Æthelfrith, whom he was arguably keen to portray as an English equivalent of the Emperor Augustus: just as the birth of Christ coincided with the universal and peaceful rule of the latter, so did the arrival of Roman Christianity in Britain coincide with the conquest of the Britons by an emperor-like, English (indeed, Bernician) king.[79] To this usage we will return: suffice it here to note that Bede was once more imagining the Roman occupation of, and rule over, Britain to have been a carbon-copy of that of the English in the present and recent past. Bede knew that Roman citizens were present as settlers in Britain since some had been butchered by British insurgents (at Colchester and London) during Nero's reign. So too was the *gens Anglorum* now in residence, exercising a corporate supremacy over those Britons who were not 'under their own laws', so were enslaved and subject to the English. The analogy is a powerful one therefore, albeit that the Roman past was being recast in obedience to images derived from the English present.

The ultimate role of Roman *imperatores* in Britain, in Bede's eyes, was as protectors. This is revealed most clearly when that protection was at last withdrawn from Britain, following the series of wicked usurpations: barbarian raids were the consequence. Following Gildas,[80] Bede portrayed two further Roman expeditions as providing temporary protection but that finally failed when Aëtius refused to respond to a third appeal.[81] At this point, Bede found in Gildas an extended and virulent attack on British morality, which the latter had introduced as a providential explanation of the forthcoming Saxon onslaught,[82] and he exploited this to the full, extracting from it the maximum condemnation of the Britons which it afforded, and making subtle changes to enhance the effect.[83] Just as Gildas had proposed, the punishment visited upon the Britons in the form of the Saxons was (implicitly in Bede but explicitly in Gildas) administered by God.

It was the Angles and Saxons who thereafter took up the task of defending Britain, so of protecting the Britons, at the invitation of another British *rex*.[84] In Bede's version, and only in Bede's version, they did so as agents of the Lord. Bede knew from Gildas that the Saxons subsequently rebelled and inaugurated their own *dominatio* of Britain. The Angles and Saxons could, therefore, be portrayed as the legitimate, and divinely-sanctioned, successors of the Romans as protectors of Britain: they had been invited to Britain to undertake precisely this role by the Britons themselves, in the context of the ultimate collapse of Roman protection. Such English kings who satisfied the appropriate criteria could, therefore, legitimately be interpreted as the successors of Roman *imperatores*. It was this analogy between Anglo-Saxon and Roman *imperia* that facilitated Bede's extended justification of the English domination of the present by reference both to providential history and to Roman rule in the distant past. This was the essence of his apology for English – but more particularly Bernician – rule over the various other peoples of Britain.

The Saxons were introduced to Britain by Bede in a passage which looked exclusively to the authority of Gildas's *De Excidio* yet omitted the entirety of the pejorative language with which they were therein invested.[85] Instead, Bede treated them at worst as morally neutral and at best as heroic and valorous, along lines which would later be echoed in his treatment of Æthelfrith, the Bernician 'Saul': he even invested them with a victory over the Picts which was apparently his own addition to Gildas's text. This was (apparently) entirely unjustified as a matter of fact but Bede probably felt that his overall purpose of justifying the Anglo-Saxon supremacy required that the Saxon protection of Britain be seen to be effective even at this stage – so sustaining his analogy between the Romans and the English as successive shields of Britain.

In an extended and apparently original departure from the *DEB*, Bede then described the 'Saxons, Angles and Jutes' as 'three of the stronger tribes of Germany', so comparing them favourably with other Germanic peoples – such as the Franks – who were known to his contemporaries, at least by repute, as great and militarily successful tribes. So did Bede neutralise the moral stigmatisation of the Saxons which he found in both Orosius and Gildas and develop his vision of a valorous and victorious, but still heathen, people, who might appropriately be compared with the virtuous but pagan Romans of the early Empire, to whom God had of old granted the mastery of the whole world.

Before he drew his ultimate conclusion from this dialectic, Bede quoted and paraphrased extensively from a second fifth-century source, the *Life of St. Germanus* by the Gaulish writer Constantius.[86] The material he found therein further assisted his attack on the moral status of the Britons, since it dealt with the efforts of incoming, orthodox, Christian authorities to suppress recurring outbreaks of the Pelagian heresy among the Britons.[87] The missionary zeal of St. Germanus on behalf of the Roman Church offers an analogue appropriate to the later Gregorian mission to the English, that 'people whom God foreknew'. Both episodes contrast with St. Augustine's failure to secure the co-operation and compliance of the British clergy in his efforts to convert the English. St. Germanus's success in the 'Alleluiah Victory' against a combination of heathen and barbarian enemies directly parallels that of several seventh-century English kings, such as Edwin and Oswiu, who had accepted the faith and it redounds to the credit not of the Britons whom he led but of the orthodox (Roman) Christianity, of which he was the representative. British success in war against the English in this episode could therefore be portrayed as conditional on the leadership of a continental saint of the orthodox Church, without whose guidance the Britons repeatedly lapsed into the sin of heresy and so incurred the wrath of God – which was precisely, in Bede's view, their present condition. The obvious contrast is with the battle of Chester, in which Bede portrayed the Britons as punished by God for their obstinacy towards Augustine by the hand of a heathen, but inherently virtuous, Bernician king.

The *Life of St. Germanus* also offered an opportunity to reintroduce the cult of St. Alban – a British martyr whose tale Bede had already plagiarised from Gildas,[88] but whose martyrdom preceded the (supposed) contamination of the Britons by Arianism and other heresies. If Alban was untainted by either Arianism or Pelagianism, then he could be depicted as in the main stream of European Christianity and the veneration of this British saint in the English present could be justified – and Bede committed himself to this view in a brief *addendum* to a Gildas-derived account of his martyrdom. The respect shown his shrine by the orthodox Bishop Germanus facilitated Bede's stance and removed St. Alban's current miracles from the contaminating effects which might otherwise have been incurred by his British origins.

Bede enhanced, therefore, the moral and spiritual condemnation of the Britons which he found in Gildas by reference to St. Germanus's missions to counteract a British infestation of the Pelagian heresy. It was following the second outbreak of that rebellion against God that he reverted to Gildas's characterisation of the present, drawing on it for final proof of the hopeless iniquity of the Britons and now naming Gildas as his source for the first and only time.[89] With divine patience now exhausted, Bede invited his audience to imagine the Britons falling at this stage under a divine displeasure which stretched even to the present, and which contrasted with God's early interest in the English. God was, therefore, portrayed as at this stage abandoning the wicked Britons in favour of the still pagan, but inherently more virtuous, Saxons.

By this construction, Bede had effectively counteracted British complaints concerning the English triumph in Britain by turning on them the rhetorical weapons of their own best-known and most erudite author – Gildas – albeit for purposes which differed dramatically from his own. At this stage and in this context, Gildas's condemnations of his own people and their leaders could be converted retrospectively into an 'own goal', with devastating effect on the ideological contest between Britons and English. Bede's manipulation of his source enabled him to offer a subtle but effective contribution to that contest which firmly established the philo-Roman English of the present as enjoying a monopoly of divine favour.

To this point it was necessarily British opinions and interpretations of the past which Bede considered the most dangerous to his own thesis, so the most necessary to silence and argue down. Although nothing now survives of British polemic which can certainly be dated to his generation, Bede's obsession with the systematic destruction of their case and the construction of an apology appropriate to English claims implies that examples then existed and were circulating, even perhaps within the English Church. That such was the case finds some support from the substantial body of predictive or prophetic British literature still extant, both in Latin (as, for example, certain passages of the *Historia Brittonum*) and the vernacular (as the *Gododdin*, the *Armes Prydein* and the various poems attributed to Taliesin).[90] Only with the British case destroyed could Bede draw to the conclusion of his 'historical' introduction by reference to the unspeakable crimes of the Britons as recounted by Gildas, to which he added one further complaint which was damning in the eyes of his Christian, English audience: that they had failed to preach the Word of God to the English. But the salvation of this 'people whom He long foreknew' was now on hand, via Pope Gregory.[91] He turned thereafter to his principal purpose in writing: that of recounting the birth, and subsequent development to a triumphant climax, of the Church of the English in obedience to Rome.

Rhetoric and ideology

To recap, therefore, Bede's knowledge of Roman Britain was neither great nor profound and his was a retrospective description of Roman *imperium*, which he explored through existing works of providential history but which he manipulated – and sometimes misunderstood – to achieve purposes relevant to the present. He brought to that description his own knowledge and understanding of the royal hegemonies of recent and contemporary England and mistakenly assumed that Britain's subservience to Rome was similar in several respects. The analogy between Roman and Anglo-Saxon *imperium* was essential to Bede's dialectic: he used it as a means to deflect the British-derived accusation implicit in his narrative that the English were a bunch of criminous (even devilish) claim-jumpers who had done much damage to the divinely sanctioned polities of Britain in Late Antiquity and whom God would one day eject; effective opposition to such charges was an essential prerequisite of any Christocentric justification of the present (and by now long-established) Anglo-Saxon domination of Britain.

Bede used Roman Britain also as a framework within which to expound the Anglo-Saxon conversion in the best possible light. Like the Romans, the English passed through a period of paganism, before the conversion to Christianity through the agency of Pope Gregory, Augustine and King Æthelberht. Like the Romans, the English were 'foreknown' by God, preselected as intrinsically virtuous for their 'imperial' role.

As regards the general trend of English history, as well as individual English rulers, Bede drew on Roman and Biblical exemplars.[92] This in turn helped to sustain his analogy between long past Roman and recent English rule over Britain – a device which was much strengthened by the universal acceptance of orthodox (Roman) methods of computing Easter among the English, Scots and Picts (but not the Britons) at the time of writing. That the primary, and ultimately the dominant, mission to the English derived from Rome further sustained the relevance of Bede's allegorical use of past Roman rule over Britain as justification of the Christian, English domination of the present.

Bede did not, however, adjudge all English rulers as morally equal: he used his narrative concerning Roman rule in Britain to construct criteria by which to select *imperium*-wielding kings in such a way as to favour the Northumbrian kings of the recent past at the expense of the Mercians. It was, therefore, in Bede's opinion, the Bernician monarchy which was the true heir of Rome's emperors, while all the English (otherwise his Angles or Saxons and occasionally Jutes) were portrayed as the moral heirs of the Roman people, at large.

Bede's treatment of *imperium* is, therefore, part of the complex web of image and theme which was designed to sustain his own dialectical purposes throughout a text which was both hydra-headed in its purposes and grandiose in its design. His view of Roman *imperium* was not one with which a reader from the old Roman Empire would have totally identified. It owed at least as much to the English world in which he worked as to the Roman world from which he borrowed his terminology. To that extent it is a peculiarly English phenomenon, albeit clothed in the language of the imperial past. We should always remember that it is first and foremost a literary device, adopted for what are essentially rhetorical purposes, which obscures significant inconsistencies between the reality of early English kingship and the nature of Roman imperial rule. Yet Bede's treatment of Roman Britain has the capacity to shed much light on seventh-century England. It is against Bede's perception of Roman *imperium* that we should measure his use of the term when applied to contemporaries, or near contemporaries, of English extraction who controlled large parts of Britain. In particular, the universality of Roman rule in Britain, stretching in his account even to offshore islands and areas never settled by the Romans, has fundamental implications for our understanding of Bede's perception of English *imperium*, which was necessarily over Britons and very extensive in its nature.[93]

By the end of book one, chapter twenty-two, Bede had accomplished his primary aim in writing this great historical narrative: he had argued down whatever British protests were then circulating against the English land seizure in Britain and against the claims of the English clergy to authority over British priests and bishops; he had manipulated his comparatively unpromising literary sources so as to provide a version of insular history which denied the Britons any moral advantage which they might have gained from their primacy as inhabitants and their prior commitment to Rome-centric origin myths; and the virtue inherent in their early Christianity had likewise been undermined by concentration on their repeated rebellions against God and Rome. With the Britons dissociated from the virtues of the Empire and only barely kept within the fold of orthodoxy by the efforts of St. Germanus, Bede was free to exploit Gildas's moral condemnation of his own countrymen to Bede's own advantage.

Bede's repeated imputation of heresy against the Britons during the seventh century – indeed, up to the year of composition – was not a response to minor discrepancies concerning the dating of Easter or the style of tonsure, since such could not sustain his case. Rather, this was a rhetorical device adopted by Bede in order to condemn the Britons as God-forsaken, in contrast with the God-sanctioned English hegemony over Britain. The heresy of which the

Britons were adjudged by Bede to be guilty was disobedience towards God. This condemnation was necessary to sustain his racial (or at least pseudo-racial) perceptions of the present; it was developed by reference to complex relationships between Romans, Britons and Saxons in the distant past and rested on a logic which derived primarily from the Old Testament.

More specifically, it was Gildas's condemnation of the morality of his own British contemporaries which enabled Bede to sustain an even more pejorative view of them and to portray their troubles as self-induced and so deserved. Although his hostility to the British Church has often been noted,[94] the semblance of balance and objectivity which are integral to the style of his text enabled Bede to disguise the excessive partiality of his narrative. In this respect at least, he was a committed ideologue who was developing a specific view of the past for thoroughly contemporary purposes.

What Bede achieved in the early part of his narrative was therefore the progressive demolition of British claims to divine aid; in parallel, he developed the notion of the English as a people beloved of God, and so moving towards an inevitable political, moral and religious supremacy. This was first hinted at in the geographical introduction, then developed through the analogy of Roman government of the island. Via a curiously politically-correct king 'Vortigern', the Roman mantle of divinely sanctioned government and protection passed to the Saxons and the stage was set for English domination of Britain as the heir to Roman rule. Rome's was an impeccable moral authority at the date of composition. Bede's discussion of Roman Britain enabled him to harness that moral authority and transpose it into the past where it could be deployed against the Britons, and so ultimately on behalf of the English.

That Bede felt it necessary, at such considerable length, to thus join issue with the British perspective on the present (and the past) implies that his opponents still commanded a powerful voice as late as the eighth century, a voice which he felt obliged to contradict and condemn. If so, British Christianity and British culture were presumably then still both alive and intellectually active, perhaps not just in the far west where British kings still reigned but even deep inside Anglo-Saxon England. To this issue we will return,[95] but first we should explore Bede's use of the term *imperium* in an English context, in the second book of his *Historia Ecclesiastica*.

Notes

1 See discussion: D. Kirby, 'Northumbria in the time of Bede', in *St. Wilfrid at Hexham*, ed. D. Kirby, Newcastle upon Tyne, 1974, pp. 2–4; G. Bonner, 'Bede and his teachers and friends', in *FC*, pp. 20, 22; P. Mayvaert, 'Bede the scholar', *Ibid*, pp. 56, 62; T. W. Mackay, 'Bede's hagiographical method: his knowledge and use of Paulinus of Nola', *Ibid*, pp. 91, 120; P. Wormald, 'Bede and Benedict Biscop', *ibid*, p. 55; P. H. Blair, *An Introduction to Anglo-Saxon England*, Cambridge, 1977, pp. 325–6; J. Campbell, *The Anglo-Saxons*, London, 1982, p. 84; M. Lapidge, 'The Anglo-Latin Background', in *A New Critical History of Old English Literature*, edd. S. B. Greenfield and D. G. Calder, New York, 1986, pp. 16–22. Bede's characterisation of himself as *famulus Christi* ('servant of Christ') is characteristic of a conventional, rather than a personal, modesty and does nothing to sustain the insufficiently critical treatment which is still all too often accorded him by historians. *Famulus* came to be used generally of a priest in Anglo-Saxon England.

2 R. W. Hanning, *The Vision of History in Early Britain*, New York and London, 1966, pp. 63–90; L. W. Barnard, 'Bede and Eusebius as Church Historians', in *FC*, pp. 106–24; W. Goffart, *The narrators of barbarian history (a.d. 550–800)*, Princeton, 1988, pp. 325–8, but this is by no means the end of this discussion: I for one look forward to the forthcoming comments of Dr. Alan Thacker on this subject.

3 Hence the high profile given his Kentish correspondence in the preface, Augustine's mission and the decision taken at Whitby to unite the Northumbrian and Kentish Churches in obedience to Rome. He was, however, not unacquainted with current affairs within the Mercian Church, which had recently supplied a priest from the monastery at Breedon-on-the-Hill (Leicestershire) to the vacant archdiocese of the south (*HE*, V, 23). Such current information highlights Bede's neglect of potential correspondents who might have enlightened him concerning those periods of the developing Mercian Church which were distinct from Northumbrian influence.

4 As stressed in *HE*, III, 26. See Goffart, *Narrators* pp. 307–20.

5 *The Life of Bishop Wilfrid by Eddius Stephanus*, ed. and trans. B. Colgrave, Cambridge, 1927, *passim*.

6 In the edition edited and translated by B. Colgrave and R. A. B. Mynors, *Bede: Ecclesiastical History of the English Church and People*, Oxford, 1969.

7 Excluding passing references in a contemporary context in I, 1, the 'geographical' introduction.

8 At the start of *HE*, I, 25.

9 Orosius, *Histories*, I, i–ii; Gildas, *DEB*, III; Bede's 'geography' was, however, far more detailed than either of these and drew on several other pre-existing texts as well as his own contemporary perceptions. P.

Mayvaert suggested that it was 'concern for the concrete and fundamental' which prompted him ('Bede the scholar', p. 61) but his purposes were arguably here primarily dialectical.

10 Colgrave and Mynors, *Bede*, p. 14, footnote 1.

11 Which came primarily from Gildas and Constantius: *HE*, I, 12, 14–16, 22 and I, 17–21, respectively. Given the originality of his recasting of these sources, it is unsustainable to claim that Bede's own work begins as late as I, 23: Mackay, 'Bede's hagiographical method', p. 115.

12 Hanning, *The Vision of History*, p. 90: 'From his insight into the workings of providence in his age, Bede re-created the Christian past of his nation, viewing it as the manifestation of a universal order, so harmoniously adjusted by God that every individual act of conversion or accomplishment . . . caused sympathetic vibrations on a national scale. This is Bede's vision of God in history . . .'

13 So, for example, the several transmarine foundation myths incorporated by Bede in *HE*, I, 15 and the *ASC*.

14 *HB*, XXXI.

15 This sub-plot of Bede's text unfurls in the closing sentence of *HE*, I, 22.

16 *HE*, V, 23.

17 Orosius, *Histories*, VII, xxv, 3 (quoted in *HE*, I, 23); xxxii, 10.

18 *DEB*, II; XXIII, 1.

19 *DEB*, XXVI, 1: 'the Lord's latter-day Israel'.

20 Contrast *DEB*, III and IV. I have suggested elsewhere that the Garden of Eden in *Exodus*, II, was Gildas's ultimate inspiration (*English Conquest*, pp. 14–15), in which case he necessarily envisaged the Britons to have been the first inhabitants and Britain as if fashioned for them by the Lord. For general comments on Bede's geographical introduction, see P. H. Blair, *The World of Bede*, London, 1970, pp. 11–30.

21 *HB*, X.

22 As Tacitus, *Agricola*, XI.

23 E.g. Ecgfrith's defeat and death at Pictish hands in 685: *HE*, IV, 26; see also Bede's comments in V, 24. Bede was able to personalise the divine anger implicit in Ecgfrith's defeat and death by arguing that his attack in the previous year on the inoffensive Irish was unjustified, so making the king vulnerable to divine correction, all without damage to the fundamental relationship of God with the English in general and the Bernicians in particular.

24 *HE*, V, 23.

25 *Ibid*; see also I, 34.

26 B. A. E. Yorke, 'The vocabulary of Anglo-Saxon overlordship', *Anglo-Saxon Studies in History and Archaeology*, 2, 1981, pp. 171–200; J. Campbell, 'The Age of Bede and Æthelbald' in *The Anglo-Saxons*, ed. J.

Campbell, London, 1982, pp. 53–4; P. Wormald, 'Bede, the *Bretwaldas* and the origins of the *Gens Anglorum*' in *Ideal and Reality in Frankish and Anglo-Saxon Society*, ed. P. Wormald, D. Bullough and R. Collins, Oxford, 1983, pp. 99–129; D. P. Kirby, *The Earliest English Kings*, London, 1991, pp. 14–20; S. Fanning, 'Bede, *Imperium* and the Bretwaldas', *Speculum*, 66, 1991, pp. 1–26; S. Keynes, 'Rædwald the Bretwalda' in *Voyage to the Other World: the legacy of Sutton Hoo*, ed. C. B. Kendall and P. S. Wells, Minneapolis, 1992, pp. 103–23. Contrast these minimalist reappraisals with the views of F. M. Stenton, *Anglo-Saxon England*, Oxford, 3rd ed. 1973, pp. 34–5 and E. John, *Orbis Britanniae*, Leicester, 1961, pp. 1–63.

27 *HE*, I, 34.

28 *HE*, V, 33.

29 Hence recent discussion of the 'bretwalda' which is based on a later version of the late ninth-century text, the *Anglo-Saxon Chronicle*. This late text has no essential relevance to the terminology in use in the seventh century but seems a valiant enough attempt to render Bede's *imperium* into ninth-century Old English, whatever the precise reading should be. For discussion, see footnote 26.

30 Although Adamnan had already done so: *Adamnan's Life of Columba*, edd. A. O. and M. O. Anderson, London, 1961, p. 200: *Victor post bellum reversus postea totius Brittaniae imperator a deo ordinatus est.*

31 *HE*, I, 3–23.

32 *HE*, I, 2. Orosius used the term *imperavit* of Caesar in the context of his arrangements for a second expedition but not for his authority over the Britons (*Histories*, VI, ix, 3). Bede retained the term but assumed that he had established *imperium* over Britain.

33 *HE*, I, 3: *tumultus*; cf. *DEB*, V–VII.

34 *HE*, II, 20.

35 As so characterised by Orosius, e.g. *Histories*, VI, xxii and see also VII, vi, 8; Gildas, *DEB*, V.

36 *HE*, I, 3.

37 *Ibid.*

38 Fanning, 'Bede', p. 14, *contra* McClure, 'Old Testament kings', pp. 97–8.

39 *HE*, I, 3, quoting Orosius, *Histories*, VII, vi, 10, in turn quoting Suetonius, *Claudius*, XVII.

40 Orosius, *Histories*, VII, vi, contradicting Tacitus, *Agricola*, X, which has the *Orcades* discovered and conquered by a Roman fleet during Agricola's governorship.

41 *HE*, I, 3.

42 Note the parallel with Cædwalla's later conquest of Wight: *HE*, IV, 16, which was depicted by Bede as a triumph for English (i.e. Roman)

Christianity.

43 *HE*, I, 3, based on Orosius, *Histories*, VII, vii, 11: 'there occurred the British disaster in the course of which the principal towns were destroyed with a great and disastrous massacre of Roman citizens and their allies (*socii*)'.

44 Cf. Dio, *Roman History*, ed. E. Cary, London, 1914, vol. IX, LXXVII, xiii, 1, which was Bede's ultimate source, but which placed *Brettania* and the theatre of war beyond the Wall; *HE*, I, 5, based on Orosius, *Histories*, VII, xvii, 7.

45 See above, footnote 43.

46 *HE* III, 24.

47 *HB*, LXV.

48 *HE*, I, 24, based on *Gestorum Pontificum Romanorum I Libri Pontificatis*, I, ed. T. Mommsen, Berlin, 1898, p. 17: *Hic accepit epistula a Lucio Brittanio rege, ut Christianus efficeretur per eius mandatum.*

49 E.g. *DEB*, I, 5: Gallic Chronicle of 452, 441; see discussion in Higham, *English Conquest*, Manchester, 1994, p. 153.

50 The division of the British province into two was the work of either Severus or, more probably, Caracalla. Their sub-division into four, perhaps ultimately five, dates no earlier than Diocletian.

51 N. J. Higham, 'Medieval "Overkingship" in Wales: the earliest evidence', *Welsh History Review*, XVI, 1992, pp. 149–53.

52 *HB*, XXII.

53 *HE*, I, 7. Since Bede based this section on Gildas's *DEB*, X–XI, there may be parallels between the *iudices* and *principes* of *HE* and the *tyranni* and *iudices impii* of *DEB* XXVII; see *Gildas: The Ruin of Britain and other documents*, ed. M. Winterbottom, Chichester, 1978, p. 99. Whether or not, Bede probably imagined that these 'princes' were British sub-kings.

54 For *principes*, see A. Thacker, 'Some terms for noblemen in Anglo-Saxon England, *c.* 650–900', *Anglo-Saxon Studies in Archaeology and History*, 2, 1981, pp. 201–36.

55 Orosius, *Histories*, VII, vi, 9.

56 As in *HE*, II, 5 and II, 9, wherein the offshore Mevanian islands were singled out as the ultimate proof of Edwin's exceptional power.

57 Bede derived this episode ultimately from Suetonius, *Vespasian*, IV, but did not himself refer to the battles noted therein.

58 Higham, *English Conquest*, pp. 151–3.

59 *DEB*, XIII.

60 *HE*, I, 3: *alia detrimenta innumera*; compare Gildas, *DEB*, VI–VII.

61 *HE*, I, 6. Allectus was of unknown origin but Carausius was a Menapian: e.g. S. S. Frere, *Britannia*, London, 1967, p. 376. Orosius (*Histories*, VII, xxv, 3) neglected to incorporate that fact but described

Carausius as 'of base origin but quick in decision and action'.

62 *HE*, I, 8.

63 Orosius, *Histories*, VII, xxv, xxvi; see also xxviii, wherein Constantine was the agent through whom persecution of the Church was ended.

64 Bede had the authority of Gildas for the prevalence of Arianism in late Roman Britain but there is no particularly good reason to think either correct in this respect: *DEB*, XII, 3. He also drew on Orosius, *Histories*, VII, xxviii but ignored xxix in which Arianism was more closely associated with Constantine's successors.

65 Contrast the high moral standing accorded Constantine in Pope Gregory's correspondence with Æthelberht, as quoted in *HE*, I, 32, but which had apparently reached Bede only after the writing of this section of his work.

66 *HE*, I, 9. Bede's treatment of Magnus Maximus was far less caustic than that of Gildas, *DEB*, XIII.

67 Quoting Orosius, *Histories*, VII, xxxiv, 9.

68 *HE*, I, 11: the British *municeps*, Gratian, was a *tyrannus* and Constantine was *sine merito vertutis*. Gildas's invective again looks influential although he referred to neither by name. Bede's primary source was Orosius, *Histories*, VII, xxxvi, xl, xlii.

69 *HE*, I, 12, based on *DEB*, XIV.

70 *HE*, I, 11.

71 Note the singular, which is perhaps specific to the example at Dover as being the only Roman lighthouse then known in Britain: cf. the plural of the translation by Colgrave and Mynors, *Bede*, p. 41. For a discussion of the term 'lighthouse' in Bede's gloss on *Streonæshalh*, see P. H. Blair, 'Whitby as a centre of learning in the seventh century', in *Learning and literature in Anglo-Saxon England*, edd. M. Lapidge and H. Gneuss, Cambridge, 1985, pp. 10–12.

72 Orosius, *Histories*, VII, xvii, 7; *DEB*, XV, 3, XVIII, 2.

73 N. J. Higham, 'Gildas, Roman Walls and British Dykes', *Cambridge Medieval Celtic Studies*, XXII, 1991, pp. 1–14.

74 *HE*, I, 12.

75 *Ibid.*

76 See below, pp. 59–62.

77 For example in *HE*, II, 5.

78 With or without Kent: see pp. 59–60.

79 Goffart, *Narrators*, p. 240, footnote 25.

80 *DEB*, XV–XVI, XVIII.

81 *HE*, I, 12–13; *DEB*, XX. Note Bede's assumption that 'Agitius' should be identified as Aëtius, which has of course dominated his dating of the English *adventus* to the era after 446.

82 *DEB*, XXI–XXII.

83 So, for example, altering the developing moral turpitude of successive kings of *DEB*, XXI, 4 to encompass the entire British community without exception – something which is specifically contrary to Gildas's text in, for example, chapters I, XXVI and CX, wherein a core of true Christians were recognised and carefully segregated from his otherwise universal condemnation. Such were entirely ignored by Bede, presumably since acknowledgement of them would have had profound implications for his dialectic.

84 *HE*, I, 15. Note the divergence here from the *superbus tyrannus* of *DEB*, XXIII. It was essential to Bede's dialectic that this British ruler be legitimate, else the Anglo-Saxon protection which he had inaugurated would have been morally flawed. This subtle shift away from Gildas's text is another small part of Bede's reversal of the moral status of the Britons and Saxons as laid out in *DEB*.

85 *DEB*, XXIII-XXVI; Higham, *English Conquest*, pp. 53–6.

86 Constantius, *Life of St. Germanus*, XII–XVIII, XXV–XXVII.

87 *HE*, I, 17.

88 *HE*, I, 7, following *DEB*, XI.

89 *HE*, I, 22.

90 *The Gododdin: The Oldest Scottish Poem*, ed. K. H. Jackson, Edinburgh, 1953; W. F. Skene, *The four ancient books of Wales*, Edinburgh, 1868, pp. 436–44; *The poems of Taliesin*, ed. Sir I. Williams, Dublin, 1968; for dating, see A. O. H. Jarman, 'The later Cynfeirdd', in *A guide to Welsh literature*, I, edd. A. O. H. Jarman and G. R. Hughes, Swansea, 1976, pp. 115–18.

91 *HE*, I, 23.

92 *FC*, *passim*; J. McClure, 'Bede's Old Testament Kings', in *Ideal and Reality*, pp. 76–98.

93 See p. 27.

94 E.g. Blair, *Introduction*, pp. 235–6.

95 See p. 95.

2
The *imperium*-wielding kings of *HE*, II, 5

Æthelberht of Kent

Bede first used *imperium* in an English context with reference to King Æthelberht of Kent, whom he introduced to his readers as a *rex potentissimus* ('very powerful king'), the limits of whose *imperium* stretched as far as the Humber.[1] Although he never described Æthelberht (nor any other English king) as *imperator*, Bede was consistently keen to emphasise the exceptional status and imperial credentials of the first Christian king of the English. Canterbury, his 'royal *civitas*' was described, therefore, by the exceptional term of '*metropolis* of all his *imperium*'.[2] Bede found in Pope Gregory's letter to Æthelberht an address which conveyed the most profound respect for the Kentish king and which repeatedly referred to him in the most honorific terms, so for example as *uestra gloria*.[3] Gregory's letter referred to *populi tibi subditi* – 'peoples subject to you' – and *reges ac populi sibimet subiecti* – 'subject kings and peoples'.[4]

There can be no doubt that Æthelberht did enjoy a widespread political superiority, or hegemony, over the other kings of southern Britain: otherwise this papal rhetoric would have been unsustainable. It was, for example, presumably Æthelberht's superiority over the West Saxons and Hwicce which gave him the leverage to assist Augustine in organising the Augustine's Oak conference. It was surely significant that that conference took place on the frontier between West Saxon and Hwiccan territory,[5] at precisely that point which symbolised the control exercised by a hegemon or 'overking' over contacts, tensions or alliances between his subordinate kings. Additionally, Bede implies that it was his exceptional prestige that prevailed upon the unwilling Welsh clergy (who probably came from southern Wales, outside his 'over-kingship') to attend on his archbishop. Bede repeatedly insisted that Æthelberht's rule ran as far as the Humber;[6] although this now seems implausible, his comments elsewhere do suggest that Æthelberht's supremacy extended as far as the East Anglian court, so as far north as the Wash.[7]

Bede's next reference to Æthelberht recalls his death and it is to his notice of this event that he attached his notorious list of *imperium*-wielding kings.[8] Like the Roman emperors of Bede's introduction, Æthelberht had held sway over more than one *provincia* (so 'kingdom' in Bede's view) and lesser, tributary kings. Likewise, his intervention at Augustine's Oak suggests that he had exercised influence over peoples of different races – and this was an essential aspect of Roman rule of Britain, which was exercised over both Roman citizens and Britons. If, as Bede suggested at the end of his *Historia*, many Britons were subject to the English and enslaved, then the English (or Jutish) Æthelberht could be portrayed as quite as legitimate an 'emperor' in Britain as any Roman king of old.

Bede now took the opportunity to restate that Æthelberht had ruled (*imperavit*) a territory equivalent to that of the Mercian king Æthelbald of his own day.[9] This oft-repeated claim presumably did much to establish the breadth of Æthelberht's power in the minds of an eighth-century Northumbrian audience who must, however grudgingly, have recognised the Mercian kings at that date as wielding an authority which was more powerful and more widespread than their own. Æthelberht was thereby invested by Bede with a supremacy equivalent to the greatest contemporary king in England: indeed, such was surely his intention in this thrice repeated claim. At the same time, that supremacy was recognisably exclusive of his own Northumbria – a fact which may also have been important to the perspective and political prejudices of his audience, as well as his own vision of the development of English rule over Britain which was at this stage far short of its triumphant climax under Northumbrian leadership. If any of Æthelberht's contemporaries suffered in consequence of Bede's claim, it was surely the Mercian, King Cearl, whose demotion to the status of a client king would certainly have caused Bede no concern. Indeed, such a prospect may even have encouraged his version of Æthelberht's *imperium.*[10] It would be rash to suppose that Bede's portrayal of Æthelberht's 'overkingship' implied that he was unaware of his apparent exaggeration of it.

In offering his list of 'overkings' there are no indications that Bede was quoting from some pre-existing (but now lost) text which had been written for some very different purpose. It is not, therefore, a satisfactory interpretation of it merely to assume that the group has no coherence and was not contrived by Bede himself but came from some pre-existing legend which he only half understood.[11] Without far clearer evidence to the contrary we should assume that Bede compiled this list and that he did so with the same clear intelligence which is discernible elsewhere in his work. There must, in other words, be a logic to this list: it is our task to identify that logic as the first stage in interpreting its contents in an appropriate context.

The key to Bede's choices herein must lie in the purpose he intended his grouping to perform. The subject of the chapter is King Æthelberht's death. Already in his first chapter of book two Bede had applied himself to elegy to mark the death of his especial hero, 'the blessed Pope Gregory', the 'apostle of the English', whose role as initiator of the mission and patron and mentor of Augustine Bede considered crucial to the conversion of his own people. Æthelberht's role was very different but likewise of fundamental importance to this same conversion. Bede therefore apparently felt impelled to portray Æthelberht, like Gregory, as both supremely virtuous and (up to the date of his death) uniquely successful in his own particular role. Unlike St. Gregory, his exceptional attainments and his unique moral status had necessarily to be identified through his exceptional achievements as a king.

Bede had little room for manoeuvre here. He had already informed his own audience that Pope Gregory had promised Æthelberht that he would surpass his predecessors in fame as much as in good works, and be received into the kingdom of heaven.[12] He had previously shown himself determined to bring the promises, prophecies or even curses of Archbishop Augustine to fulfilment, however circuitous the causation that he was forced to invoke in so doing: his treatment of Æthelfrith's victory at Chester was appended to the Augustine's Oak conferences for precisely this purpose.[13] In this context, he could hardly treat Pope Gregory's promises to King Æthelberht with less respect than those of his agent, Archbishop Augustine, since to do so would be to belittle Pope Gregory himself. Bede was constrained by his own rhetorical context to do his utmost to enhance and sustain the reputation of King Æthelberht.

Bede therefore introduced his elegiac treatment of Æthelberht in terms which recalled both his own comments on Gregory and Gregory's letter to the Kentish king. His temporal reign was *gloriosissimus* and he had, at his death, 'entered upon the eternal joys of the heavenly kingdom.' References to his *imperium* were similarly gauged to impress Bede's readers and so enhance his reputation by association: it was on his behalf that Bede first deployed the analogy of the Roman emperors of yore whose virtuous governance of Britain had featured so prominently in his first book; furthermore, Æthelberht, he once more claimed, had ruled the same group of 'Southumbrian' peoples as were under the control of the Mercian king of his own day. The comparison was apparently to Æthelberht's advantage and over-estimated his power.[14]

It may be possible to reconstruct Æthelberht's *imperium* from the Tribal Hidage, which I suggest (below) was the tribute-list of King Edwin, drawn up in its final form in the 620s.[15] If so, Æthelberht's tributaries were probably the peoples of the secondary list, with the addition of the last three peoples of the primary list (Figure 1).[16] Between Æthelberht's *imperium* and the Humber lay a Mercian 'overkingship' which is barely recognisable in literary sources and which was apparently dismantled by Æthelfrith after his victory at Chester, probably not before the last months of Æthelberht's life.[17]

Whether or not Bede knew he was exaggerating the extent of Æthelberht's *imperium*, it seems that he had some difficulty in finding evidence to deploy in support of his purpose, to accord Æthelberht greater 'praise and merit than the ancient kings of his race'.[18] When dealing with Rædwald, Edwin, Oswald or Oswiu, Bede shared with his audience some knowledge of their several military reputations: each had gained some great victory of a kind guaranteed to be remembered by, and still impress, the kings and lay aristocracy of his own generation, let alone their own.[19] Bede had already, when treating of the Roman period, made it quite clear

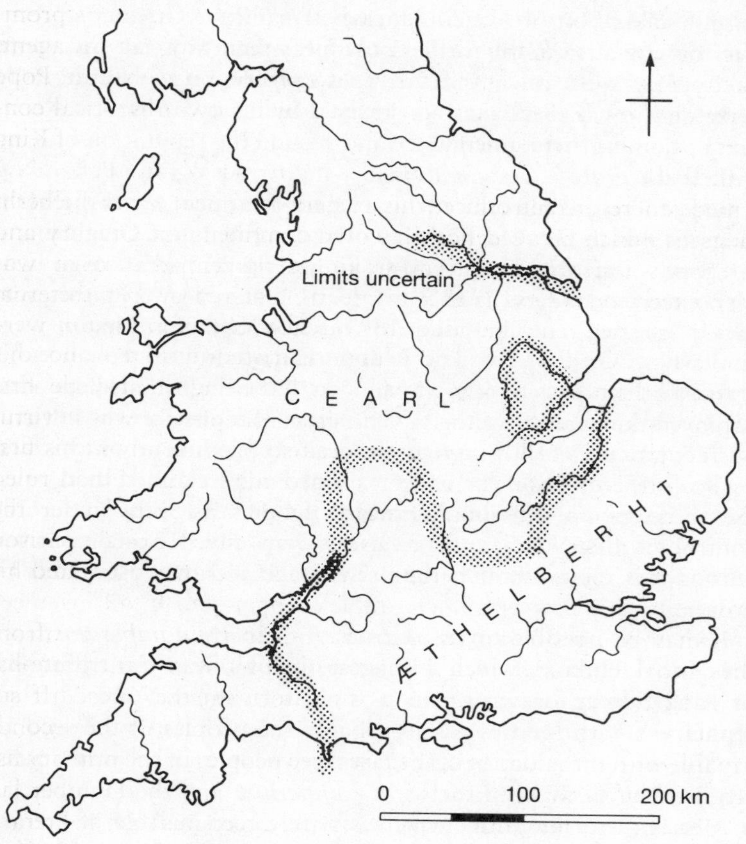

Figure 1 The 'overkingships' of kings Æthelberht of Kent and Cearl of the Mercians prior to the battle of Chester, as based on interpretation of the Tribal Hidage.

that a victory was a normal prerequisite of *imperium* and the ultimate source of the military prestige by which that *imperium* was sustained,[20] but when writing of Æthelberht Bede made reference to no such triumphs. Either he had no military successes of note to his credit or Bede knew nothing of them. Given that the Christian historiographical tradition which Bede had inherited can be almost guaranteed to have fastened eagerly on such proofs of God's interest in and support of Æthelberht, whether they occurred before or after his conversion, the former possibility seems by far the more likely, if not quite certain. Æthelberht's position was exceptionally dependent on diplomatic and dynastic links, and this was something of an embarrassment.

Bede therefore had some difficulty in attributing an outstanding reputation to Æthelberht compared to other *imperium*-wielding kings known to his audience. He could describe his reign in general in the superlatives appropriate to an 'overking' and account it of very exceptional (and highly improbable) length,[21] but this was hardly an adequate reputation for the first Christian king in England whom Gregory had laid it upon Christian writers to honour above all the previous, renowned kings of the English race. Famous barbarian kings were victorious in battle: Æthelberht was not and his reputation can only have been weakened by this apparent fact.

Faced by this difficulty, it seems that Bede lent Æthelberht further distinction by the simple process of comparing him favourably with other great kings and in various ways interlocking his reputation with theirs, in the hope that his standing would gain by proximity as much as by favourable comparison. In all instances known to us, those chosen were victors in memorable battles.[22] Bede provided, therefore, a selected group of kings for the purposes of analogy, organised in such a way as to provide Æthelberht's reputation with the greatest boost possible. That they should be capable of representation as *imperium*-wielding rulers was a basic requirement of this context.

Amongst them, Æthelberht was distinguished as the third English king to rule (*imperavit*) over all the *provinciae* south of the Humber but the first to ascend to heaven. His one great claim to unique status compared to the great kings of English antiquity was, therefore, stated at the outset. In this respect, if in no other, he had surpassed the achievements of the two earlier pagan kings, Ælle and Ceawlin, whom Bede offered here in fulfilment of Gregory's promise.

Ælle and Ceawlin

That Bede chose to write nothing further concerning Ælle of the South Saxons or Ceawlin of the West Saxons is irrelevant to the use to which he put them here.[23] With the sole exception of the Bernician, King Æthelfrith,[24] he was shy of recognising the achievements or virtues of kings who died pagans. Their role here was simply to provide examples of ancient English kings whose fame Æthelberht's could be said to have surpassed. That function did not require that their achievements be further elaborated. Indeed, that might have proved an embarrassment.

That Bede chose these particular kings does not require that they had successively enjoyed a southern *imperium* in the years immediately preceding Æthelberht's – although the analogy with the sequence of Æthelberht, Rædwald, Edwin and Oswald might support that interpretation. Provided only that each still enjoyed a formidable reputation, other figures, or even periods without any clear *imperium*, could have intervened. The reconstruction of their respective exploits in the *Anglo-Saxon Chronicle* appears to be based on nothing more concrete than Bede's slender references to them and whatever legends had reached its authors from the eighth century – when they were still apparently remembered, perhaps as the heroes of epic poems. The historicity of this late ninth-century account is so doubtful that it is best set aside as a source for the sixth century.[25] Ælle and Ceawlin necessarily preceded Æthelberht and post-dated the *adventus*. Concerning their dates and their deeds, no more can now be known. That Bede had recourse to these particular figures in this context does, however, suggest that their reputations were still high as late as the eighth century, since his purpose of lauding Æthelberht would have been but poorly served had he invoked the memory of kings who were considered undistinguished or of whom few of his audience had heard. They were, therefore, kings of high repute, so had probably been, like the later figures named in this list, victors in famous battles. However, Bede's knowledge of them may have been no more detailed than that which we have of the great 'overking', Scyld Sceffing, whose achievements provide a preface to *Beowulf*.[26]

This tells us next to nothing about the *imperium* which either Ælle or Ceawlin had wielded and it seems most unlikely that either Bede or his audience had any detailed knowledge of the territories over which they had exercised hegemonal influence, although their association with the South Saxons and West Saxons, respectively, must imply that their *imperia* were focused in the south. That Bede portrayed Æthelberht as interfering on Augustine's behalf on the border between the West Saxons and Hwicce does at least indicate that the *imperia* of Ceawlin and Æthelberht overlapped,[27] and it is difficult to conceive of an extensive and meaningful *imperium* centred in either Kent or Sussex which was without influence in the other. Bede's reasoning was, therefore, probably accurate, at least in general terms, albeit his basic model of a southern *imperium* was so strongly influenced by the Mercian supremacy of his own day as to render the putative geography of these earlier *imperia* quite apocryphal.

In his positioning of Æthelberht within this list, Bede was invoking a powerful analogy between the life of Christ and the reign of Æthelberht, so of their respective deaths and ascents to heaven. The interface between the Old and New Testaments provided an obvious parallel for the passage of England from paganism to Christianity, so from the *imperium* of pagan, to Christian, kings. Just as the Emperor Augustus's reign provided a context for the arrival of Christ, the salvation of the world which distinguished a Jewish past from a Christian future, so did Æthelberht's reign enable Gregory, the 'apostle of the English',[28] to bring salvation among the English – that 'people whom God foreknew'.[29]

A second analogy is between this list of English 'emperors' and the Roman emperors already discussed, of whom seven were named by Bede as relevant to Britain (if Julius Caesar and Constantine be included and all those whom he treated more pejoratively than Constantine be excluded). The strong sense of momentum from a militarily virtuous, but pagan, Roman Empire, through conversion to a triumphant Christian Empire both replicates and offers a fundamental precedent for Bede's vision of the English as a God-chosen people whose rule over other nations was rendered just by divine approval, even when their kings were still heathen.[30] Pagan kings were, therefore, even without Gregory's letter, a necessary starting point in Bede's list, without whom Æthelberht's role would have seemed far less significant to the Christian audience whom Bede was addressing.

In addition, Bede cannot have been unmindful of Gregory's characterisation of Constantine the Great as *piissimus imperator* ('most pious emperor').[31] Despite his own caustic treatment of the first Christian emperor earlier in his work,[32] parallels between Æthelberht and Constantine may have been obvious to the more literate of his own readership and would have served to enhance Æthelberht's reputation, just as Gregory had intended.

Æthelberht was named as the third king. Bede presumably had considerable leeway in his choice of starting point. To have dispensed with one or other of Ælle or Ceawlin would have conflicted with Gregory's reference in the plural to English kings of antiquity but he could have included others had he so wished, such as Hengist (or Hengest).[33] He must therefore have made a conscious selection of third place for Æthelberht. A contemporary audience would have been aware of the importance of the number three to the Christian faith and Bede may have calculated that portraying Æthelberht as the third king to wield *imperium* would associate his rule with the coming of the third member of the trilogy, that is the Holy Ghost – an apt analogy given his sponsorship of the English conversion and the numerous miracles which Bede ascribed to Augustine's mission. The role of Gregory as a latter day apostle again seems of relevance. Alternatively this may be associated with the use of the same number in less clearly Christian contexts, such as the Tribal Hidage,[34] Gildas's numbering of the first group of ships which carried the Saxons to Britain,[35] or even Bede's own claim that three savage tribes had migrated from Germany.[36] It is possible that the standard warrior band of the early English was based on a boat which held around thirty men – hence the thirty war bands by which Bede emphasised the magnitude of Penda's army defeated by Oswiu's small (but Christian) force beside the *Winwæd*.[37] Whatever reasoning is preferred, this numbering – like much of Bede's numeracy regarding the seventh century – is likely to have been more a literary device than a matter of historical fact.

Bede was probably also attracted for religious reasons by the number seven, a number of very special significance in the early Church, for the creation of the world was complete on the seventh day which God blessed.[38] To this analogy we shall return when discussing the role of King Oswiu in this list. Bede preferred to avoid unnecessarily favourable comments on the successful careers of pagans like Penda and his sensitivity to Northumbrian perceptions of the Mercian–Northumbrian struggles contemporary with his own childhood probably encouraged him to exclude them and so limit the number of kings named here to seven.[39] Familiarity with a British view that seven Roman emperors had been active in Britain might be relevant, if it could be demonstrated: but despite similarities between Bede's treatment and that of the *Historia Brittonum*, the individuals differed.[40] It may be significant that Bede had already used the same number for the British bishops attending the Synod of Chester,[41] details of which presumably reached him ultimately from a British source, if they were not in this respect (at least) his own invention.

Having compared Æthelberht favourably with two legendary but famous English kings of antiquity, Bede had fulfilled the promise of Pope Gregory. He had, however, achieved little in his self-appointed task of convincing an eighth-century, primarily Northumbrian audience that Æthelberht had achieved truly exceptional status. He therefore proceeded to do what else he could to bolster Æthelberht's reputation by carrying his comparisons forward in time. Beyond Æthelberht's reign, Bede had far less room for exercising his own discretion. The reputations of Rædwald, Edwin, Oswald and Oswiu were presumably all well-known at the time of writing and both he and his audience arguably knew more about the extent of their power and influence than that of Æthelberht.

The great Rædwald's *imperium* was also portrayed as no more than *huiusmodi* – 'of like kind' – with that of Æthelberht. In Bede's view, therefore, each of Ælle, Ceawlin, Æthelberht and Rædwald had exercised *imperium* of a kind familiar to his own audience from Æthelbald's present Mercian hegemony. That this now seems improbable is irrelevant to Bede's dialectic.[42] In contrast, Edwin's power was greater and the difference between his *imperium* and that of the first four names was explained both in terms of greater power and the wider extent of its efficacy: he ruled 'almost all the inhabitants of Britain'.

To Edwin we must return but up to this point Bede seems to be collecting up the reputations of the greatest of the English kings whose powers he could portray as broadly analogous with those of Æthelberht and using those reputations as a means of enhancing contemporary opinion of the first Christian king. From a modern viewpoint, the obvious omission is that of Æthelfrith, a king to whom Bede similarly referred in superlatives but who exercised his authority, unlike Ælle and Ceawlin, at the same time as Æthelberht and in a different part of Britain.[43] There does, therefore, seem to be a geographical factor influencing Bede's choice of kings. To this point at least, all exercised *imperium* over the deep south and none was obviously Æthelberht's rival for power. Just as Northumbria was a political system separate from the southern hegemony in the eighth century, so did Bede portray it as separate at the turn of the sixth–seventh centuries – and he was arguably correct in so doing. To have included the great warrior king Æthelfrith as a successful and pagan contemporary would have undermined the stature both of Æthelberht himself and of the Christian God whom he espoused. Additionally, it would have conflicted with Bede's development of the theme of a divinely sanctioned Bernician supremacy, which finds its starting point in the appearance of Æthelfrith, in the guise of an English Augustus, in the very last chapter of book one. In this passage Bede implied that the Bernicians had already played a significant role in the preparation of Britain for Augustine's coming, and so began the process of associating this dynasty with the Canterbury mission which he brought to fruition at Whitby in 664. The appearance of Æthelfrith at this stage was important, therefore, to Bede's rhetoric on behalf of Northumbrian hegemony in Britain but it would have seriously detracted from his efforts to enhance Æthelberht's reputation. Hence he retained a diplomatic silence on this point: he generally kept his references to these two kings sufficiently distant from one another within his narrative as to discourage comparisons between them, comparisons which could only have benefited the pagan at the expense of the Christian.

Rædwald

Rædwald's inclusion in Bede's list has proved by far the most difficult to interpret. Bede wrote that:

> *quartus Reduald rex Orientalium Anglorum, qui etiam uiuente Aedilbercto eidem suae genti ducatum praebebat, obtenuit;*

The standard translation reads:

> the fourth was Rædwald, king of the East Angles, who even during the lifetime of Æthelberht was gaining the leadership for his own race.[44]

Problems centre on Bede's use of *praebere*, a word meaning to 'offer', 'present' or 'hold out'. It is difficult, therefore, to justify the conventional translation, even though that still commands widespread respect.[45] There have been several alternative interpretations of this passage in recent times,[46] among which are two which require comment. Nicholas Brooks and Patrick Wormald preferred the meaning 'Rædwald was conceding leadership in war of his own people even during the lifetime of Æthelberht.'[47] The second stays far closer to the traditional interpretation, if with a very different result, namely that Bede was noting that Æthelberht's supremacy had begun to dissipate before his death since Rædwald managed to obtain control of the East Angles even while he was still alive.[48]

Since the Latin is a little ambiguous, it is to the context that we should turn for assistance. Bede was, as already noted, here attempting to write up Æthelberht's reputation. He did this by favourable comparison of this ruler with others whose warlike reputations were greater. Neither the traditional interpretation nor the last offer any support to Æthelberht in this respect – indeed, both detract significantly from that reputation. This leaves Rædwald conceding the war-leadership of his own people even during the lifetime of Æthelberht as the only plausible option that could be expected to have enhanced his reputation. That this also seems preferable on semantic grounds is all to the good.

Bede's purpose here can be identified. Rædwald was apparently still too famous, or infamous, a king at the time of writing to be omitted from his list of analogues. The great East Anglian king was remembered in the early eighth century as the protector of Edwin in exile and the victor in the great battle by the River Idle against King Æthelfrith,[49] and this triumph over a fearsome enemy was presumably – on the analogy of Bede's preceding discussion of Roman *imperium* – the basis of his 'overkingship'.[50] His reputation as a warrior-king was therefore still high in the early eighth century. Bede took advantage of this by seeking to enhance Æthelberht's reputation by reminding his audience that even the mighty Rædwald had been subject to Æthelberht's *imperium* right up to the latter's death. His use of *etiam* ('even') serves to emphasise the point he is making here, that Rædwald's rise only occurred after the death of Æthelberht, who was, therefore, implicitly even mightier than Rædwald, having kept him tributary throughout his own lifetime.[51] At the same time, he was doing what little he could without gross distortion to minimise the credit here accorded the apostate Rædwald, whose reputation he was elsewhere determined to minimise.[52]

Edwin

Bede's subtlety is further illustrated by his next entry in the list. Edwin's power, he stated, was greater than that of Æthelberht, if otherwise of like kind. He therefore ruled more extensive provinces than had the latter but Bede made one exception to the universality of Edwin's *imperium*: it was *praeter Cantuariis tantum* – 'except only for the Kentings'. This exception is particularly significant in being totally unhistorical. When treating more specifically of Edwin's *imperium*, Bede described it as extending to the limits of Britain, and even beyond to Anglesey and Man, without exception.[53] This was no accident: he quoted in full the letter from Pope Honorius to Edwin in which the former described the Archbishops Honorius and Paulinus as *uestri sacerdotes* – 'your bishops'.[54] Honorius travelled northwards for consecration as archbishop at Lincoln, a centre of Edwin's own royal power,[55] rather than Paulinus travelling to Canterbury. This level of involvement in the affairs of the Canterbury mission must imply that Edwin's protection and *imperium* encompassed Kent. Even if his relationship with Eadbald was something of a partnership, it was certainly an unequal one.[56]

This interpretation is not upset by later correspondence between the papacy, Archbishop Justus and King Eadbald,[57] which refers variously to 'peoples placed under him' (i.e. King Eadbald) and the 'peoples subject to him'. Æthelberht's establishment of two dioceses for Kent implies that the West and East Kentings were, at this date, recognisably two peoples and administered as such. The letter to Justus recognised that spreading the Word to the neighbours of Eadbald's subjects would be a key part of the role of the mission, so Pope Honorius was aware that Eadbald's power was constrained within comparatively narrow bounds. No such inhibitions affected Gregory's correspondence with Æthelberht, the *gloriosissimus atque praecellentissimus rex Anglorum*.[58] Honorius was, then, out of politeness, pushing to the limit the honours which he could legitimately credit to King Eadbald – whose newfound enthusiasm for Christianity he wished to encourage – but never exceeded thereby the reality of his powers.

Kent's relationship with Edwin's otherwise universal *imperium* was presumably that of a highly favoured, if technically subordinate, ally. Eadbald had been Edwin's earliest known associate in southern Britain after the death of Rædwald and the two kings were uniquely co-religionists and brothers-in-law.[59] Before his northern ministry, the Italian priest Paulinus had presumably been under the protection and patronage of Eadbald.[60]

A desire to remark on this special relationship is unlikely to have been Bede's motive for his comment on Edwin's *imperium* in book two, chapter five, even if it may have encouraged him to venture therein an entirely spurious comment concerning the limits of Edwin's power, which he would later contradict. If the primary purpose of his list of *imperium*-wielding kings was to enhance Æthelberht's reputation, then mention of Edwin posed problems: Edwin's *potentia* ('power') had been greater and his *imperium* far more extensive than those of Æthelberht and were probably widely known so to have been in Northumbria at the time of writing, when Edwin was still venerated in at least two key locations as a saint, and where his daughter and great-nieces had achieved high rank within living memory.

The comparison with Edwin was therefore potentially damaging to Æthelberht's reputation. In order to protect that reputation and, indeed, convert this potential weakness into a source of strength, Bede compensated for the inequality of their respective powers by claiming that, even after the Kentish king's death, his own people were immune from the demands of a far greater king. Bede's account therefore represented Æthelberht's protection of his people as operative even *post mortem*. It was just such future protection that early medieval heroes, such as Beowulf and Vortimer, were so often unable to provide, their own deaths heralding ruin to those whom they had protected in life.[61] This heroic endeavour had, by Bede's lifetime, been translated into a Christian idiom with the advent of royal martyrs and saints of the stamp of Edwin and Oswald, whose powers continued to offer protection to their followers long after their own deaths.[62] Bede was perhaps thereby making an implicit claim that Æthelberht likewise should be venerated as a saint.

The exemption of Kent from Edwin's *imperium* is therefore quite unhistorical. It was a strategem adopted by Bede to circumvent the danger which Edwin's greater power posed to Æthelberht's reputation. Although it may have been suggested to him by the special relationship between Edwin and Eadbald between *c.* 625–33, it is a piece of sophistry which offers yet one more instance of Bede's careful and subtle dialectic on behalf of Bernician claims.[63]

Oswald and Oswiu

Oswald and Oswiu follow Edwin without further apology to Æthelberht, whose reputation can only have suffered by comparison. To an extent, Bede had no option but to include these later kings if he were to reach the count of seven Anglo-Saxon wielders of *imperium* which he apparently had in mind. Additionally, for a Northumbrian audience many of whom would have been able to recall the reigns of Oswiu and his sons, or whose recent forebears will have served them, it would have been difficult to omit the brethren who had been the greatest of Bernicia's kings. Nor is there any sign that Bede would have preferred to have remained silent on the matter. He was profoundly Northumbrian in his prejudices throughout this work and he seems to have positively courted Northumbrian opinion in his reference to the Bernician kings. He broke away, therefore, from the static picture of a southern *imperium* common to Ælle, Ceawlin, Æthelberht and Rædwald – and to which his own contemporaries had reverted under Æthelbald of Mercia – only when a greater *imperium* was wielded by a Northumbrian king. The impact of this on Æthelberht's reputation had been ameliorated by the claim that Kent was exempt from Edwin's supremacy and this was sustained thereafter by Bede's insistence that Oswald's rule was 'within the same boundaries' – so putatively still exclusive of Kent.

However, the protection which this device provided to Æthelberht's reputation seems alarmingly thin once Bede focused on Oswiu:

> The seventh was his brother Oswiu, who held a similar realm for some time, and even overcame and made tributary to a great extent the peoples of the Picts and Scots who hold the north of Britain.

In his use of *septentrionales* – literally 'the seven stars' – to refer to the north, Bede, not normally one to use a flowery style, was perhaps using a pun to draw attention to, and glorify, Oswiu's status as the *septimus* (seventh) *imperium*-wielding king of his list. This literary device linking his achievements with the heavens would have been relished by the more literate of his Northumbrian audience. This last *imperium* was, therefore, served up by Bede resplendent in a metaphor peculiarly appropriate to Northumbrian supremacy over Britain. It was necessarily the greatest of his

English *imperia*, encompassing all that each of the other kings named had ruled and more besides, particularly in the far north. It was surely in support of this vision of a great Bernician *imperium* that Bede had developed his vision of legitimate Roman *imperium* even beyond the northern walls.[64]

Oswiu's *imperium* is portrayed as the climax and end point of the development of the entire notion of English *imperium* in Britain. After Oswiu, no English king had achieved such an *imperium*. His was, therefore, the greatest political achievement in English history and this sense of the ultimate *imperium* – that which most fully paralleled Roman rule over Britain – offers perhaps the most cogent justification of Bede's decision not to go on to include the later kings whose rule extended to only parts of it.[65] Just as God had rested on the seventh day and blessed it, having completed creation,[66] so did Oswiu's *imperium* symbolise the completion of the divinely ordained process by which English rule became established throughout Britain as the true successor of Rome. The biblical allegory was the most powerful that Bede could devise. In its final extent, therefore, Oswiu's rule approximated at last to the Roman *iure dominatio* which Bede supposed had collapsed in the year of Rome's fall.[67] It was via this 'lawful' Roman rule that he constructed a precedent appropriate to his own perceptions of English kings – and particularly Bernician kings – and the justice of their rule over the other peoples of Britain. The parallel had profound implications for Northumbrian claims to erstwhile British territory and to supremacy throughout Britain, as well as to the general supremacy of English kings and the English people over other inhabitants of Britain.

Bede's lionisation of Oswiu may additionally owe much to his responsibility for the unification of the Northumbrian Church with that of Canterbury, under ultimate papal authority.[68] This was a fundamental *sine qua non* of Bede's own dialectic, without which his analogy of English and Roman *imperium* would have been unsustainable.

Bede's rhetoric and *imperium*

It may be appropriate at this point to bring together the various themes which have been explored in the last two chapters: these are primarily Bede's use of *imperium* in the context of Roman

Britain and secondly his formulation of the famous list of *imperium*-wielding English kings in the context of King Æthelberht's death. With these uses in mind, it may be possible to come to certain conclusions concerning his use of *imperium* in a secular, English context:

1 By analogy with his retrospective view of Roman rule in Britain, Bede expected *imperium*-wielding English kings to enjoy extensive powers over numerous tribes and peoples, or *provinciae*;
2 Peoples and their kings were at least as likely to acknowledge the superior power of another without fighting as in consequence of military defeat. Indeed, this process was a central characteristic of the way Bede expected an *imperium* to come into existence. Bede's use of *imperium* in treating of Roman Britain offers a close analogy with, and a justification for, the very extensive *imperia* which Bede claimed for kings like Edwin, whose sole victory recorded in this text was over only a single one of his subsequent subordinates. As the case studies of Claudius and Nero demonstrate, *imperium* in Bede's perception ultimately rested on a military reputation and that could be consequent upon a single, and signal, victory. *Imperium* was only so good as the last decisive engagement, as was long ago realised.[69] The *imperia* of such kings as Æthelberht, Rædwald and Edwin were fundamentally personal in character and not institutionalised, despite Bede's belief that *imperium* was properly to be exercised by Bernician kings. There was no office of Bretwalda;
3 If the condition of Britain under Roman rule was an analogy which was in any respect appropriate to Bede's usage, then most seventh-century kings were subordinate to some more powerful king most of the time and the protection they gained thereby was the principal guarantee of their own security. That such was true of England in the 730s is not in doubt;
4 Given the deployment of Roman rule as an effective analogy for Anglo-Saxon domination, Bede necessarily envisaged universal control by the English over the Britons. This applied not only to subservient Britons within and beneath Anglo-Saxon society, who were subject to the *gens Anglorum*, but also to British kings who might be subject to the *imperium* of particular early

> English kings.[70] Indeed, reference to the British king Lucius suggests that Bede expected many of the various British kings of his own day to recognise the superior authority of one of their own number, and the ultimate authority of an English 'overking' only through him.[71] Whatever the ethnicity or culture of the individuals concerned, such relationships were presumably regulated by oaths of the sort which Magnus Maximus was supposed to have broken.[72]

Bede's analysis suggests that there was a need for protection which was so pressing that the collapse of the *imperium* of one king created a situation of great danger to his tributaries. Although the greater among them might aspire to *imperium* in their own right, for most this was a time of great peril until the next protector should emerge. For the numerous kings of local dynasties, a personal ambition to become an 'overking' cannot have been a serious proposition. Adherence too early to a candidate who subsequently failed posed risks potentially as great for the king of a minor people as might isolation outside the protection of a greater king. A single battle could resolve the issue, convincing large numbers of nervous, lesser kings of the effectiveness of the protection which the victor could provide and so bring widespread *imperium* to the victor when numerous kings who were not party to the actual conflict sought his protection. The domino theory is perhaps the best model for this phenomenon, with the most advantageous terms available to those who were already in some way associates of the victor or who first recognised and sought the protection of the new *imperium*-wielding king.

It was in such a context that Adamnan named Oswald *imperator* of all Britain.[73] In the light of Bede's comments on his widespread *imperium*, there is a strong case for his protection reaching even to the limits of what had been Roman Britain and beyond.[74] His ability to participate in the baptism of Cynigils in Wessex certainly implies that his *imperium* reached deep into the south, so it necessarily encompassed Mercia. That the West Saxon king recognised him as a superior and protector is a fair interpretation of his role as god-father.[75] During Edwin's later years (*c.* 626–33), kings throughout Britain became used to a near universal *imperium.* Edwin was killed by Cadwallon of Gwynedd,[76] who may well have taken tribute very widely among Edwin's erstwhile tributaries, albeit without Bede recognising the fact for reasons which are transparently ideological. It is unsurprising that, a year or two later, those same tributaries should have sought the protection, and recognised the *imperium*, of Oswald, the king whose military reputation rested on his destruction of that same British warrior king who had slain the great Edwin. With Edwin's own heir already destroyed and no other royal general of renown then living (with the dubious exception of Penda), there was no other candidate, so no obvious alternative focus capable of protecting a group of insular kings from Oswald's wrath. This was to be the case at least until Penda succeeded in mobilising the military resources of Mercia and its satellites against him, in 642.

To an extent, the list of *imperium*-wielding kings in book two, chapter five of the *Historia Ecclesiastica*, is a distraction from our understanding of English *imperium*. It is a selection from the more numerous ranks of 'overkings' known to Bede, albeit one which reveals a clear sense of purpose. It was conceived primarily in order to bring Pope Gregory's promise to Æthelberht to a posthumous but triumphant fulfilment. Bede attempted this by calling upon what he and his contemporaries knew of the powers of other kings, both before and after Æthelberht, to add an appearance of distinction to what seems to have been a somewhat lacklustre royal reputation. He was depicted, therefore, as greater than the legendary Kings Ælle and Ceawlin; he had even been overlord of the mighty Rædwald right up to his death; despite the greater power and *imperium* of Edwin, Æthelberht's people were (quite spuriously) depicted as free of Edwin's 'overkingship' even after his death. He therefore fulfilled, even *post mortem*, the hero's role of protecting his people and so was deserving of the highest praise.

It was a subtle performance but one which ultimately gave way to Bede's own Bernician prejudices. Only the *imperia* of Oswald and Oswiu were described without overt reference to Æthelberht and Bede left his audience with a vision of the triumphant *imperia* of the most powerful Bernician kings, which he wrapped around with Christian allegory and sustained through his previous development of the analogy of Roman rule in Britain – particularly as regards his own special pleading as regards Roman authority over the far north. At this point his purposes transcended those which had led him to start the list, reverting to those of a Bernician jingoist. It was, therefore, with Oswiu that Bede portrayed the rule of the *gens Anglorum* in Britain as equal at last, both qualitatively and quantitively, to the *imperium Romanum* and *dicio Romanorum*, so bringing to fruition God's long-conceived plan for the English.[77] Examination of Bede's discussion of Roman Britain is in many respects more informative about his perception of English *imperium* than is his treatment of Æthelberht, and the list of *imperium*-wielding kings contained therein, despite the greater attention which that has received. It is, however, the combination of the two which offers the best opportunity to explore the greater kingships of the seventh century.

Throughout, it was the moral status of the Britons which suffered most from the attention of Bede's quill but he also had other victims in mind: among the English, the ultimate victim of his dialectic was Æthelbald of Mercia, whose own contemporary *imperium* was depicted as no greater than Æthelberht's, so, by definition, much less than those of the greatest of Northumbria's kings. Within Bede's scheme of historical development, the Mercian supremacy of the present was a throwback to an earlier and lesser stage of the development of English *imperium*. It was, therefore, a regressive step which was implicitly undesirable and ought to be reversed. Æthelbald's reputation can only have been damaged by the comparison. Additionally, Bede's repeated assertion that Æthelberht's *imperium* had stretched to the Humber implied that Æthelbald's predecessors as kings of Mercia had been tributary to the king of Kent. Again, the status of the Mercian kingship was a victim of Bede's dialectic. In respect of these imputations, at least, Bede's comments were highly contemporary and designed to serve current political and ideological purposes.

Oswiu's kingship

Bede's claims in favour of Oswiu were comparatively accurate as regards the few years after *Winwæd* (655–8), when Oswiu did indeed stand head and shoulders above all the other kings of the English. Between 642 and *c.* 652, however, his power was clearly less, although it may not have been as minimal as some commentators have supposed outside the glory years.[78] That southern kings should have been present at the Bernician court before 655 implies that Oswiu was even then free of the hegemony of Penda – or at least attempting so to be – and that his hostility to Mercia was shared by some at least of the kings of the south-east. Poorly understood wars between Penda and both the West Saxons and East Angles suggest that the Mercian 'overking' experienced considerable resistance to his attempts to expand his hegemony over Æthelberht's old 'overkingship'. Oswiu's marriage to Eanflæd can certainly be interpreted as an attempt to revive the Northumbria–Kent axis against Mercia which had sustained King Edwin's *imperium* until his death. Once Deira was reunited with Bernicia under one king (in 651), Oswiu may have been an effective counterweight to Penda. That Peada, Penda's own son and his appointment to the new-fangled and highly artificial Middle Anglian sub-kingdom, saw fit to marry into Oswiu's family and accept baptism under Oswiu's patronage implies that he thought to mobilise Northumbrian support in the event of a succession struggle with his brothers over the inheritance of the by-now (presumably) ageing Penda. Again, Peada's actions seem ill-judged unless Oswiu exercised considerable influence.

The eventual crisis of 655 was apparently precipitated by some shift in the balance of power between Penda and Oswiu, which may hitherto have been poised. Bede described Æthelhere of the East Angles as *auctor* – 'originator' – of the campaign which ended at *Winwæd* with Penda's destruction in battle. It may be that the transfer of East Anglian support from Oswiu to Penda was sufficient to encourage the Mercian king to undertake his invasion of Northumbria. Whether or not (and the meaning is necessarily obscure), Bede's comment does imply antagonism between Æthelhere and Oswiu and so contact of some sort in the immediate past.

Oswiu's standing in 642 was obviously far less, however, and Bede was clearly guilty of over-generalisation in his treatment of Oswiu in book two, chapter five. Northumbria had been partitioned in consequence of the Mercian victory over Oswald in 642: although Bede portrayed this process and its consequences solely in terms of a dynastic struggle which was internal to Northumbria and exclusive of outside influences, it seems almost certain that Penda had exercised considerable influence therein and particularly on Oswine's behalf. The Mercian king clearly opposed the revival of Bernician power which Oswiu sought to effect, and seems to have enjoyed the best of the various wars which occurred between them, despite being unable to bring his opponent permanently to heel.

After 658, a Mercian rebellion destroyed Oswiu's attempt to impose his own direct kingship on the Mercians. It may not, however, have brought his hegemony of the Midlands to an end, although it was clearly thereafter fragile. Bede provides no mention of a battle between Oswiu and Wulfhere so a political solution seems possible, in which case the recognition of Northumbrian 'overkingship' and adherence to Northumbria's Christianity by a native Mercian king of Penda's lineage seems a practical solution to the political impasse. It was only when Oswiu had died that a Mercian king sought to shake off Bernician hegemony.[79]

If Oswiu actually died with his status as a universal 'overking' intact, Bede had every reason to offer him up as the apogee of English *imperium*-wielding kings. Such would surely have been received enthusiastically by King Ceolwulf, his brother bishop Ecgbert and the Northumbrian thegns and religious assembled at a court which still recalled the past greatness of the northerners. It was this parochial, Northumbrian audience which Bede was addressing as he brought his list to a close, and it was Northumbrian claims to *de iure imperium* in Britain that his work sought to develop and sustain. The Mercians had no intellectual of Bede's standing capable of responding. That their kings began to use titles such as *rex Brittaniae* during this very period does suggest, however, that they were conscious of the need to support their own supremacy with a more compelling ideology than the simple military protection and personal oaths between kings which had sustained *imperium* of old.[80]

It may be possible to extract from the *Historia Ecclesiastica* a valid reflection of the political world in which King Æthelberht ruled but that is best approached in conjunction with a re-examination of the Tribal Hidage – the sole written source which is entirely independent of Bede yet arguably relevant to the period. Only once the context, authorship and purpose of that source have been explored shall we return to the problems of identifying and interpreting the several, rival *imperia* inside England during the last years of the sixth and the first few decades of the seventh century.

Notes

1 *HE*, I, 25.
2 *Ibid*. See also I, 26 and II, 3. The term was used by Bede exclusively

of Canterbury and London, which was also subject to Æthelberht's influence at this date, and elsewhere only of King David's capital at Hebron: *HE*, V, 17.

3 *HE*, I, 32: *Dominio gloriosissimo atque praecellentissimo filio Aedilbercto regi Anglorum* . . . Use of *filius* does, of course, reserve a higher authority to Gregory, himself. See also *gloriosus filius*.

4 *HE*, I, 32.

5 *HE*, II, 2. For discussion, see N. K. Chadwick, *The Age of the Saints in the Early Celtic Church*, Oxford, 1961, p. 122; P. Wormald, 'Bede, the *Bretwaldas* and the origins of the *Gens Anglorum*', in *Ideal and Reality in Frankish and Anglo-Saxon Society*, ed. P. Wormald, Oxford, 1983, p. 114.

6 *HE*, I, 25; II, 3; II, 5.

7 *HE*, II, 5; II, 15.

8 *HE*, II, 5.

9 *HE*, II, 5; V, 23.

10 See below, pp. 143–6.

11 As postulated by S. Fanning, 'Bede, *Imperium* and the Bretwaldas', *Speculum*, 66, 1991, p. 25.

12 *HE*, I, 32.

13 *HE*, II, 2. This is supposing that this passage was also his rather than deriving from some otherwise unknown source, as argued by Chadwick, *Age of the Saints*, p. 122. For discussion, see N. J. Higham, 'King Cearl, the battle of Chester and the origins of the Mercian "Overkingship" ', *Midland History*, 17, 1992, pp. 6–7; *ibid*, *The origins of Cheshire*, Manchester, 1993, pp. 87–8.

14 See my arguments for a separate *imperium* in the Midlands at this date: 'King Cearl', pp. 1–15. Bede and his northern audience were perhaps more confident of the fact that Æthelberht did not rule north of the Humber than of the proposition that he ruled up to it.

15 N. J. Higham, *Rome, Britain and the Anglo-Saxons*, London, 1992, p. 148; *The kingdom of Northumbria: 350–1100*, Gloucester, 1993, pp. 115–18.

16 See discussion below, p. 87ff.

17 The date is unknown. The battle was entered in the *Annales Cambriae* under the year 613 but, since the conversion of the English by Augustine (arrived 597) and Mellitus (arrived 601) was dated therein to 595, this is generally corrected forwards by two years for this period. For discussion of the sequence, see D. P. Kirby, *The Earliest English Kings*, London, 1991, pp. 63, 72; Higham, 'King Cearl', pp. 5–6. See also figure xx.

18 *HE*, I, 32.

19 *HE*, II, 12; II, 9; III, 1; III, 24.

20 See above, pp. 27–30.

21 *HE*, II, 5, so much confusing the history of England in the late sixth century. See Kirby, *Earliest Kings*, pp. 31–3; N. Brooks, 'The creation and early structure of the kingdom of Kent', in *The Origins of Anglo-Saxon Kingdoms*, ed. S. Bassett, Leicester, 1989, pp. 65–7. Bede's preference for a reign of 56 years *might* stem from a desire on his part to enhance the reputation of Æthelberht by comparison, for example, with Augustus, who reigned for forty-one years and who was responsible for the peace during which Christ's ministry occurred. Alternatively, the several improbably long-lived figures of the Old Testament may have inspired Bede to make this claim. For comparable manipulation of numbers, see Bede's treatment of St. Hild: *HE*, IV, 23, on which see comment in Higham, 'King Cearl', p. 3.

22 Despite the *Anglo-Saxon Chronicle*, we have no reliable information concerning the prowess of Ælle or Ceawlin; otherwise, see note 19.

23 *Contra* Fanning, 'Bede', p. 16.

24 *HE*, I, 34; II, 2.

25 P. Sims-Williams, 'The settlement of England in Bede and the *Chronicle*', *ASC* 12 (1983), 1–41. For Ceawlin, see also B. York, 'The Jutes of Hampshire and Wight and the origins of Wessex', in *Origins*, ed. Bassett, p. 64.

26 *Beowulf*, lines 1–52.

27 *HE*, II, 2.

28 *HE*, II, 1, but recall that Æthelfrith offered an alternative, and in many respects preferable, political and ideological focus for Bede's audience, because of his Northumbrian credentials.

29 *HE*, I, 22, last sentence.

30 *Ibid*, and I, 34.

31 *HE*, I, 32.

32 *HE*, I, 8.

33 *HE*, I, 15: Bede termed both Hengist and Horsa *duces*, so he recognised their military credentials for kingship. That they shared descent from Woden with so many other English royals suggests that their regality was in little doubt.

34 See discussion below, p. 95. See also *HB*, XX.

35 *DEB*, XXIII, 3, using the OE *keeils* for ships.

36 *HE*, I, 15.

37 *HE*, III, 24.

38 *Genesis*, II, 1. See also frequent reference to the number seven in *Revelations* and indeed throughout the Bible.

39 See also above, pp. 10–13.

40 *HB*, XXVII but this was, of course, written after *HE*. Bede's seven emperors were Julius Caesar, Claudius, Vespasian, Severus, Diocletian, Constantine and Honorius, if Nero be omitted as an antithesis of imperial behaviour. *HB* added Severus and Constantius to a slightly different list, the criterion being that they had been active inside Britain.

41 *HE*, II, 2.

42 See below, pp. 199–200.

43 *HE*, I, 34; II, 2. His conquests in the Midlands may well have threatened Æthelberht's *imperium* in the last months of his life (his death is conventionally dated to 616), when the territories he controlled probably bordered Æthelberht's hegemony.

44 B. Colgrave and R. A. B. Mynors, *Bede's Ecclesiastical History*, Oxford, 1969, p. 149.

45 F. M. Stenton, *Anglo-Saxon England*, Oxford, 3rd ed. 1971, p. 60; Kirby, *Earliest Kings*, p. 17; Fanning, 'Bede', p. 3; H. Mayr-Harting, *The Coming of Christianity to Anglo-Saxon England*, London, 3rd ed. 1991, p. 65.

46 The options are usefully summarised by S. Keynes, 'Rædwald the Bretwalda', in *Voyage to the other world: the legacy of Sutton Hoo*, edd. C. B. Kendall and P. S. Wells, Minneapolis, 1992, pp. 106–7 and his rebuttal of the earliest of these alternative interpretations seems convincing but see H. Vollrath-Reichelt, *Königsgedanke und Königtum bei den Angelsachsen bis zur Mitte des 9. Jahrhunderts*, Cologne and Vienna, 1971, p. 83.

47 Wormald, 'Bede', p. 106, footnote 30; N. Brooks, *The Early History of the Church of Canterbury: Christ Church from 597 to 1066*, Leicester, 1984, p. 63. My thanks to Professor Brooks for bringing this point to my attention.

48 T. Charles-Edwards *Addenda*, in J. M. Wallace-Hadrill, *Bede's Ecclesiastical History of the English People: A Historical Commentary*, Oxford, 1988, pp. 220–22.

49 *HE*, II, 12.

50 Rædwald appears in four separate passages of the *HE*, II, 5; II, 12; II, 15; III, 18, as well as in *The Earliest Life of Gregory the Great by an Anonymous Monk of Whitby* ed. B. Colgrave, Cambridge, 1985, XVI, which was the earlier reference by about a generation. His opponent was the best-remembered military leader of the age (at least among Northumbrians), with unnamed successes against the northern Britons, *Degsastan* against the Scots and Chester against the Welsh (at least), to his credit: *HE*, I, 34; II, 12.

51 This does not, to my mind, invalidate Professor Brooks's interpretation of the Latin, as argued by Keynes, 'Rædwald', p. 106.

52 As in *HE*, II, 15.

53 *HE*, II, 9. See also the opening line of II, 20, wherein he ruled over the English and Britons and Cadwallon *rebellavit* against him. For the subordination of the Welsh to him, see N. J. Higham, 'Medieval "Overkingship" in Wales: the earliest evidence', *Welsh History Review*, 16, 1992, pp. 149–53.

54 *HE*, II, 17.

55 *HE*, II, 16, 18.

56 As implied by Pope Honorius's letter to Archbishop Honorius referring to *filiorum nostrorum regum* in terms which imply that he was in receipt of correspondence jointly from Edwin and Eadbald: *HE*, II, 18 and Colgrave and Mynors, *Bede's Ecclesiastical History*, p. 198, footnote 1. It is unfortunate that it is the restricted view of Edwin's authority which was later incorporated into the *ASC* against the year 617. *HE*, II, 5 is surely the source used here by a West Saxon annalist who might be forgiven for accepting any of Bede's comments which seemed to detract from the status of Edwin, who had been the nemesis of Wessex.

57 *HE*, II, 8, 10.

58 *HE*, I, 32.

59 *HE*, II, 9, 14. If some peoples had literally been 'placed' under Eadbald, only Edwin can have so placed them.

60 *HE*, II, 9.

61 *Beowulf*, l.3150–5; *HB*, XLIV.

62 The removal of remains claimed to be those of Edwin to Whitby was presumably intended to serve this function: *Life of Gregory the Great*, XVIII–XIX. The portents and vision associated with him at Rædwald's court smack of hagiography: *ibid*, XVI; *HE*, II, 12; for miracles associated with Oswald, see *HE*, III, 9–13.

63 For an analogy, compare the virtuous characterisation of Æthelfrith in *HE*, I, 34 and II, 2, with his murderous qualities in II, 12. Æthelfrith's moral status is clearly a product of Bede's dialectic and changes with the context in which he appears. See J. McClure, 'Bede's Old Testament kings', in *Ideal and Reality*, pp. 90–1, for Samuel's treatment of Saul, with whom Bede compared Æthelfrith. See also Bede's treatment of Constantine the Great.

64 See above, p. 31ff.

65 Such as Aldfrith, whom Bede described as *rex Anglorum* (*HE*, V, 15) as well as *rex Nordanhymbrorum* (*ibid*, V, 18), Osred, his son, whom he depicted as succeeding to his father's *imperium* (*ibid*), or Æthelbald of the Mercians, to whom the 'Southumbrian' kings were subject in 731 (*ibid*, V, 23). This sense of anti-climax was recognised by Stenton, *Anglo-Saxon England*, p. 34.

66 *Genesis*, II, 1.

67 An *imperium* which Bede had already been careful to define, probably for this very purpose, in *HE*, I, 12.

68 *HE*, III, 25.

69 J. M. Kemble, *The Saxons in England*, II, London, 1849, pp. 8–22.

70 As is implied in *HE*, II, 2 and in the Tribal Hidage, at least in the case of Elmet. British Strathclyde was clearly subject to Northumbria's English kings throughout much of the seventh century. For speculation concerning further British kingships, see N. J. Higham, 'King Cearl', pp. 11–12; '"Overkingship" in Wales', *passim*; *contra* Stenton, *Anglo-Saxon England*, p. 35, whose insistence on entirely separate political structures for the English and British has dominated most modern thought on the subject.

71 Higham, '"Overkingship" in Wales'.

72 See above, p. 30.

73 Bede's comment in *HE*, II, 5, is entirely consistent with his treatment of Oswald elsewhere; in II, 3, he is credited, like Æthelberht before him, with the rule of the *gens Anglorum*. *Angli* was the term Bede preferred to describe the entire Anglo-Saxon nation, despite the consistent *Saxones* which he found in Orosius and *DEB*.

74 Although such widespread English *imperia* have been the subject of much recent cynicism: e.g. Fanning, 'Bede', p. 17; Keynes, 'Rædwald', p. 108 but see Campbell, 'Age of Bede', pp. 53–4 and Kirby, *Earliest Kings*, pp. 18–20.

75 *HE*, III, 7, wherein Oswald was appropriately described as *sanctissimus ac victoriosissimus*. Æthelberht's role in Rædwald's baptism and Oswiu's in those of Peada (in 653) and Sigeberht are comparable examples of 'overkings' acting as god-fathers of lesser kings, although all these, unlike Oswald's, occurred in the heartland of an *imperium*-wielding kingship: *HE*, II, 15; III, 21, 22.

76 *HE*, II, 20.

77 *HE*, I, 22, quoting *Romans*, XI, 2.

78 E.g. Wormald, 'Bede', pp. 111–12.

79 *Life of Wilfrid*, XX.

80 E.g. P. H. Sawyer, *Anglo-Saxon Charters: An Annotated List and Bibliography*, London, 1968, nos. 89, 155.

3

The Tribal Hidage: its context and purpose

> There can be no doubt that Tribal Hidage *is* problematic, and will remain so unless some new evidence appears: the text is late and corrupt, and the name forms ungrammatical, the original is very uncertainly reconstructed, and there is no evidence pertaining to the circumstances in which it was produced.[1]

Although a new facsimile and transcript of this document was published in 1989,[2] no new evidence has so far appeared. Consequently there is little consensus concerning either its date[3] or its precise function. Although there has been substantial support for a Mercian origin,[4] this view has never been quite universal.[5]

Despite problems of interpretation, most are agreed that the Tribal Hidage is by far the earliest 'fiscal' document from the medieval period in England. As such, it has been pressed into service by those seeking to interpret the nature and geography of kingships and of 'peoples' in pre-Viking England.[6] The context of this document is, therefore, a matter of some importance.

Since the Tribal Hidage exists only in the form of late transcripts or translations, is undated, and contains no explicit reference to its authorship or place of composition, investigation is necessarily a matter of testing the considerable detail within it against what is known of the tribal politics of the pre-Viking Age.

The Mercian candidature

The near consensus in favour of a Mercian origin is based on three factors: Mercian rulers were the most powerful kings in England from *c.* 685 until the rise of Wessex in the early ninth century and exercised extensive 'overkingship' over variable proportions of southern England; the Tribal Hidage consists almost exclusively of peoples located south of what became Northumbria; the Mercians head the list. It is Mercian, because it looks Mercian.[7]

A Mercian solution suffers, however, from a chronic failure to agree even an approximate date of composition. Given the large amount of information contained within the document, this failure concerning the date-range or even the reign in which it was composed weakens each and every Mercian candidature.

Two further criticisms have recently been voiced concerning its putative Mercian origins:

> it seems unlikely to have been Mercian, for the first people whose hidage assessment is listed are the Mercians themselves – '30,000 hides'. An early medieval king did not impose tribute upon his own kingdom. A Northumbrian origin for the Tribal Hidage deserves consideration since it would explain both the document's overall form and the fact that the Elmetsæte are included while both the Deirans and the Bernicians are omitted.[8]

The Tribal Hidage lists thirty-five peoples (against only thirty-four hidations since Lindsey and Hatfield share one), the majority in the Old English genitive plural. The word *land* occurs, also in the genitive singular (*landes*), in the first entry (and is reintroduced in the dative singular (after *mid*) in the sixth entry. The syntax requires there to be understood a word in the nominative in each instance, meaning 'the tribute (*feorm*) of (people name)', which has been omitted for the sake of brevity and to avoid repetition. It is, therefore, almost certainly a tribute list, the tribute owed being assessed uniformly in hides. In practice, tribute payment was presumably the responsibility of the various kings fronting each tributary people and a component of the personal relationship between the 'overking' and each of his tributaries.[9] The Tribal Hidage is technically, therefore, a list of the payments or obligations owed to an 'overking' by his tributary kings.

While the list may conceal a multitude of different relationships, it is an essential of any interpretation that the interface between the unnamed tribute-receiving king and each of the kings listed be capable of expression in identical terms. Were the 'overking' the king of Mercia, this document would require that he collected tribute from his own people then ceremoniously handed it over to himself as superior king. As Professor Brooks recognised, such an interpretation is entirely implausible.

The presence of the *Elmedsæte* in the Tribal Hidage is equally pertinent. Elmet was attached to the Deiran kingship by King Edwin and was never thereafter, to our knowledge, separated from it.[10] The argument for an otherwise unknown but later period of Mercian overlordship of Elmet without Deira depends exclusively on interpretation of the Tribal Hidage and is, therefore, in this context entirely circular. That Elmet was separately listed in the Tribal Hidage, without Deira, makes a Mercian origin improbable. Equally pertinent is the association of Hatfield with Lindsey. While Lindsey was detached from Northumbria by Mercian kings in the late seventh century and eventually became part of Mercia, part at least of Hatfield was retained by the northern kings and ultimately became a part of Yorkshire. To postulate a Mercian-sponsored dual kingship in Lindsey amd Hatfield at any stage after Edwin's death is, likewise, to argue for the improbable, *ex silentio*.

With such substantial objections outstanding, a Mercian origin is unsustainable. Since the list had an English origin which was exclusive of every people named on it, it must, as Professor Brooks opined, have derived from Northumbria.

The Northumbrian candidature

No Northumbrian king after 685 had the power to levy tribute on southern England. Realistic candidates are limited to the kings who were listed by Bede as exercising an *imperium* greater than that of Æthelberht,[11] with the possible addition of Ecgfrith between *c.* 674 and 679. These were: Edwin (killed 633); Oswald (634/5–42); and Oswiu (642–70). The candidature of Oswald, Oswiu and Ecgfrith each suffers from at least one of the weaknesses of the case for the Mercian kings: the inclusion of Elmet in the Tribal Hidage. This effectively excludes them from consideration, since they were themselves apparently kings in Elmet, as well as of Bernicia and Deira, at any time when they may have been in a position of superiority over the south. All three were probably also kings of Lindsey whenever they were in a position to levy tribute on the south, so compounding the difficulty. Even if not, they were arguably kings of Hatfield. Attention must, therefore, focus on Edwin.

The Tribal Hidage: chronological parameters

The author of the *HB* noted that Edwin expelled Ceretic, the (British) king of Elmet.[12] That Edwin was, by the end of his life, the direct ruler of Elmet is confirmed by Bede's observation that he constructed a church at his palace at *Campodonum*.[13] Palace and church were, thereafter, burnt by the pagans – presumably the Mercians – and the palace was replaced by another near Leeds by Oswald or one of his successors.[14]

Bede was, therefore, quite clear that Edwin was king in Elmet by about 630 – long enough before his death to commission and have erected a basilican church. He also portrayed Edwin in his last years as exercising control of Lincoln through a *praefectus*, so he was presumably by this stage exercising tighter control than was usual in the exercise of *imperium* over the *Lindesfaran* who derived their name from the site.[15] Since this people also occurs in the Tribal Hidage and was then, with Hatfield, apparently ruled by kings of a status equivalent in this respect at least to other *subreguli* such as the *W(r)ocensæte*, this usurpation (if that is what it was) was likewise an event which postdates the Tribal Hidage. Whichever of these kingships Edwin first appropriated provides a *terminus ante quem* for the Tribal Hidage.

Two events provide a *terminus post quem* for the document: Edwin's staged rise to supremacy is one; the second (assuming that the pagan king and his equally pagan advisors were illiterate) is the availability of a priest capable of writing it on his behalf. An investigation of these several events is a necessary prerequisite of establishing the political context of the Tribal Hidage, if that was written for this King of Deira.

The career of Edwin

Edwin fled from Deira when Æthelfrith of Bernicia displaced his dynasty from the kingship of that people in the early years of the century.[16] Æthelfrith was described by Bede as a conqueror and tribute-taker among the Britons and was clearly an 'overking' of some importance in the north.[17] The attack from Dal Riata that he defeated at *Degsastan* implies that his 'protection' was active as far north as Strathclyde. If that victory was on a scale to match Bede's description of it, his superiority was presumably thereafter recognised by the Scots in Britain.

It was arguably British territory close to Bernicia within which he displaced one or more British kings and assumed direct control of patronage.[18] It was as the direct ruler of Bernicia and of this unnamed but erstwhile British territory, and as the 'overking' of all Britain between the Clyde (perhaps Argyll) and Lancashire, that Æthelfrith attacked Deira, expelled the male representatives of the local dynasty and seized the kingship, reinforcing his usurpation by marriage to a princess of that house.[19] Whether or not Deira had until then been tributary to Æthelfrith is unclear but it is more than a possibility, particularly given that Ida, his grandfather, was credited with the rule of both kingdoms.[20]

Edwin fled south and ultimately found refuge and succour amongst the Mercians of the Trent valley, where his cause gained the committed support of King Cearl, who allowed this penniless *ætheling* to marry his own daughter, presumably in the expectation of extending his own influence into Northumbria.[21] A decade later, Æthelfrith struck southwards and gained a notable victory over the Britons at Chester, killing at least two prominent leaders. The battle was inserted in the *Annales Cambriae* against the year 613 (corrected 615) and this date is probably approximately correct.[22] Bede's account of this battle, as of *Degsastan*, probably derived from a Bernician epic story celebrating the deeds of their 'Saul-like' warrior king.[23]

This campaign seems to have been a disaster for Edwin and his Mercian patron. It presumably left the north-east Welsh incapable of resisting Æthelfrith's superiority, which now breached the line of the Mersey. That they had not been under the protection of Æthelberht of Kent is clear from Bede's description of the Synod of Chester,[24] but it seems unlikely that they were entirely isolated from the 'overkingships' around them. Their defeat coincided with far-reaching dynastic changes in Mercia. If King Cearl had been their protector, the battle of Chester was a severe blow to his prestige. Since it was 'the Britons' who were defeated at Chester, it is quite likely that Æthelfrith disrupted whatever political accord may have existed between the Welsh kings and Mercia. It seems likely that the Mercians were also defeated.

The facts are beyond reconstruction, but Edwin's father-in-law and his dynasty disappear from history at this stage, to be replaced ultimately by what seems to have been an alternative Mercian dynasty headed by Penda. Mercia's dependence on the

Northumbrians prior to Penda's kingship was noted in the *Historia Brittonum*.[25] His dynasty was to be exclusively associated (during the eighth century) with palace and minster sites in Mercia south of the Trent and particularly with Tamworth.[26] If Mercia shared the division into two which was common among the Anglo-Saxon peoples during this period,[27] Edwin's protector may have been king of the north Mercians, while Penda's kin represented a rival, south Mercian dynasty which was prepared to acknowledge the superiority of Æthelfrith in return for the kingship, or a part thereof. Alternatively Eowa (Eobba), Penda and Pybba may have derived from a rival line of the same royal kin as Cearl himself, pursuing contrary policies as part of their competition for power, much as did Oswald's son, Œthelwald, against King Oswiu.

Driven out of Mercia and its protectorate, Edwin took refuge at the court of Rædwald of the East Angles but was followed there by a succession of messengers from Æthelfrith armed with promises and, latterly, threats designed to secure his murder.[28] That Rædwald took these threats with the utmost seriousness demonstrates that Æthelfrith was capable of launching an attack against the East Angles. This implies that his *imperium*, at least, now extended across the core of Mercia in the east Midlands. Rædwald had long been tributary to Æthelberht of Kent and had been baptised there at his behest.[29] With the old 'overking' of the south either dead or dying, Rædwald was now sufficiently free of his oversight to entertain his own foreign policy but had no protection to fall back on in the event of an attack from the north. Æthelberht died at an advanced age, probably in February 616.[30]

Rædwald ultimately decided to honour his obligation to protect Edwin, his guest, and marched against Æthelfrith. The battle is undated but probably occurred in the spring, summer or autumn of 616, shortly after Æthelberht's death (on 24 February) liberated him from any remaining constraint upon his freedom of military action. The *Historia Brittonum* noted Edwin's reign lasted seventeen years.[31] If it ended in October 633, his first full calendar year as king was 617.

Immediately after the departure from his court of the third set of Æthelfrith's messengers, Rædwald raised his army and followed them northwards, attacking before his enemy became aware of him or could assemble a credible army. Æthelfrith reputedly fought at a numerical disadvantage,[32] and perhaps at a tactical one. That this attack found Æthelfrith unprepared but on the east bank of the River Idle, inside Mercian territory,[33] confirms that he was then exercising *imperium* over the Mercians. He may even have made himself king of the northern Mercians, as Oswiu, his son, would later do. Whether political considerations or necessity forced Æthelfrith to fight south of his core Northumbrian provinces is unknowable but he died fighting, perhaps at the ruinous Roman fortlet beside the crossings of the Idle, opposite Bawtry.[34]

Rædwald thereafter installed his guest and protégé, Edwin, in Æthelfrith's place. That he took over both Deira and Bernicia is certain from the flight of Æthelfrith's sons.[35] There can be little doubt that he also took over other attributes of Æthelfrith's kingship – the direct rule of British territory as recently conquered and supremacy over the surviving northern British kingdoms, those Welsh kings defeated at Chester, perhaps the Scots[36] and almost certainly the Mercians and their neighbours.[37]

Rædwald could safely place so much power in Edwin's hands because his resounding victory over Æthelfrith had impressed other erstwhile tributaries of King Æthelberht to the extent that they sought his protection, thus catapulting him into the role of 'overking' in the south.[38] If a grateful Edwin should be added to the ranks of his tributaries then his supremacy was acknowledged, by proxy, as far north as lowland Scotland. The consequence was a complex hierarchy of 'overkingship' within Britain, centred for the first time in recorded history (but not necessarily for the first time) on a single English king.

Rædwald's death brought his *imperium* to an end. The date is not recorded but subsequent events make it unlikely to have occurred before 624. The demise of his protector left Edwin supreme in the north, the west and the northern and central Midlands, but without influence in southern Britain, where he was vulnerable to the rise of a less sympathetic 'overking' from among Rædwald's more powerful and ambitious tributaries.

In an entirely different context, Bede recorded a defeat of the East Saxons by the West Saxons, placing it after the crisis at Canterbury occasioned by the deaths (*c.* 616) of Kings Æthelberht of Kent and Sæberht of the East Saxons.[39] Open conflict between them was unlikely to have occurred while both were tributary to Rædwald. Unless this struggle occurred between Æthelberht's death and Rædwald's victory – which seems too short a timescale for Bede's reference – it was fought after Rædwald's death, *c.* 624–5. The victory won by the West Saxons presumably threatened to carry their superiority across the entirety of the south.[40]

Edwin was distant from these events but threatened by them. He may already have been married to the sister of King Eadbald of Kent, Æthelberht's daughter, Æthelburh. If not, he married her now.[41] Whichever, the death of Rædwald presumably enabled these two kings to develop a joint policy for their mutual protection in 624/5. If Bede's version of the terms of the marriage be accepted, it was probably envisaged that Eadbald, the son of a recent 'overking' and sole sponsor of Christianity in England, should exercise *imperium* over the south, with Edwin supreme in the Midlands and the North and tied to him by marriage. The marriage was negotiated in Kent, at Edwin's instigation but largely on Eadbald's terms, implying that he may have been the senior partner. He and his sister were Christian by *c.* 624, at latest, and they imposed conditions on the marriage, dispatching Paulinus to Deira and extracting a series of half-promises from Edwin concerning his own conversion. That Paulinus was consecrated bishop on 21 July 625 signals that the alliance was then active.[42] Their plans were presumably intended to contain the threat posed by the West Saxon defeat of Eadbald's cousins, the kings of the East Saxons, whether this occurred immediately prior to, or even marginally after, the marriage.

During the great pagan feast of Eostre, 626, an attempt was made by King Cuichelm of the West Saxons to destabilise their alliance by assassinating King Edwin,[43] the militarily more powerful of the two, when he was holding public court at his palace near the Derwent.[44] The attempt was foiled but not before the king was wounded and two of his retainers slain.[45] As Edwin contemplated revenge, he was persuaded by Paulinus that the Christian God had taken a hand in events within his household during this critical time, and allowed the daughter opportunely born to his new wife on Easter Day to be baptised.[46] If Paulinus's God should give him victory over his enemies in the hazardous campaign he now proposed to launch, the king promised to 'convert'. On his recovery from his wound:[47]

> having collected his army the king came against the people of the West Saxons, and war having been launched against the whole people, he either killed or enslaved those who had conspired his death.

We can confidently assign his campaign to the summer of 626. His army was raised at leisure and will have been as large as possible. The result was an overwhelming victory.

This, his first and only clear-cut military victory over a powerful king who had a military reputation, catapulted Edwin, in turn, into the role of 'overking'. He was able to dictate terms to the West Saxons. The other kings of the south sought his protection and recognised his supremacy by the offer of tribute. As Bede noted in book two, chapter nine, his *imperium* grew even before he converted (in 627):

> The king's power of earthly *imperium* increased as an omen that he would adopt the faith and the *regnum* of heaven. So, like no Englishman before him, he received under his *dicio* the entire island [literally 'the entire bounds'] of Britain, not only kingdoms [*provinciae*] inhabited by the English but also by the Britons.

By this stage even Man and Anglesey lay within his power and Edwin's protection extended to the entirety of what had been Antonine Britain. His authority was, over the next few years, to be significant even in distant Canterbury.[48]

The two preconditions for the composition of the Tribal Hidage had, therefore, been fulfilled by the late summer/early autumn of 626: Edwin was 'overking' of Britain, and he had at his court a bishop only too keen to involve himself in royal government.

The eviction of Ceretic

To a king as powerful as Edwin – even prior to 625 – Elmet posed no threat. One can surmise that Ceretic would have been only too willing to buy the protection of his powerful neighbour by the recognition of his *imperium*, of his *ducatus* in war and by payment of tribute. After the English takeover, the political and ecclesiastical geography of Elmet was left largely intact.[49] Edwin apparently did little more than substitute himself for a petty Welsh king as the ruler of this comparatively poor kingdom. Why did he bother?

Ceretic's eviction may have been at the prompting of Paulinus. The controversy between Augustine and the British clergy at Augustine's Oak highlighted the problem of authority among the Christians in Britain and Paulinus necessarily shared Augustine's frustration at his inability to chastise the Welsh.[50] Once Edwin had been convinced of the efficacy of Christianity in the summer of 626, his universal supremacy enabled him to throw his weight far more wholeheartedly than had Æthelberht behind the Roman mission.[51] Much of the summer of 627 was probably taken up with the mass baptisms organised by Edwin and carried out in his presence in Deira and Bernicia,[52] but it is quite possible that Paulinus had already obtained access to Elmet by this stage. At the Deiran court from 625, Paulinus had presumably met Edwin's British clients when they attended upon him for the purpose of delivering their tribute. With Edwin fervently committed to Roman Christianity, Paulinus might be expected to have pressed for the immediate expulsion of those British kings who continued to sustain the British Church. His endeavours probably spread far beyond Elmet. When listing the vast estates granted to Ripon by the Northumbrian kings, Wilfrid's Romanist biographer was later to boast of the flight of the British clergy for fear of 'our sword' from the minor British kingdoms of the Pennines. This, too, may have been a consequence of takeover by Edwin at the instance of Paulinus. Cadwallon of Gwynedd may have been a further casualty.[53]

To this point, Celtic kings had been able to protect the British Church within their own territories even while recognising the superiority of pagan English 'overkings'.[54] If Paulinus launched such a crusade it may have precipitated the largest flood of British clerical refugees since the initial Saxon conquests of the fifth century. When, after Hatfield, Cadwallon of Gwynedd set about the systematic destruction of Anglian Northumbria, his war aims apparently went far beyond the conventional collection of booty or raising of tribute.[55] Both he and Penda seem to have hated both the Bernician and Deiran royal families with unusual intensity, perhaps because of blood feuds dating to Æthelfrith's victory at Chester. It seems likely, therefore, that his was a serious attempt to destroy English lordship and revive British kingship in the north and so reinstate and protect the British Church.[56] Throughout the following generation, Penda was to rely on the sustained hostility of Welsh kings to the Northumbrians and their willingness to follow a pagan king in pursuit of their objectives. The wounds inflicted by Æthelfrith, and then perhaps also by Paulinus, went deep.

Edwin and the Tribal Hidage

The Tribal Hidage consists of a list of nineteen kingships (one of which is referred to by the names of two peoples) followed by a (correct) total of the number of hides allocated to them, appended to which is a further list of fifteen peoples followed by a grand total (which is incorrect) of the hides allocated to the full list. It has been stressed that the full document must be meaningful in its entirety,[57] but it is equally important both that the primary list be meaningful in its own right,[58] and that the sequential combination of the two groups be explicable in whatever political context they belong.[59]

The primary list

The primary list opens with the 'original lands of the Mercians'. This elaboration exceeds the terse descriptions accorded the other peoples and must be both intentional and meaningful. The phrasing implies that at least one other people had recently been extracted from the kingship of Mercia, or its *imperium*, perhaps to appear elsewhere on the list. Such a recent reduction of the stature of the Mercian kingship makes a Mercian candidature entirely implausible.

Given that a Mercian *ætheling* was to share responsibility for Edwin's death, the latter probably had good cause to limit Mercian power. It may be, however, that the removal of one or more peoples from the Mercian kingship coincided with the dynastic *volte face* in Mercia which preceded Edwin's reign, in which case it should be associated with Æthelfrith's Chester campaign and brief 'overkingship' over the Midlands before the battle by the River Idle.[60]

The Mercians are followed by a series of peoples in an order which implies a clockwise, south-west – west – north – east – south circuit around Mercia. The *W(r)ocensæte* of the central and northern marches are followed by the *Westerne*, the *Pecsæte* of the Peak, then Elmet and Lindsey with Hatfield. Only if the *Westerne* are placed in the central or southern Welsh marches,[61] is this circuit broken. This is not a typical tribal name but a generic term. From Deira, the literal meaning of 'the westerners' would have been the peoples west of the *W(r)ocensæte* who precede them on the list – that is the Britons of Wales. Since Bede specifically stated that Edwin exercised *imperium* over all the Britons, including Man and Anglesey,[62] this entry would seem to accord well with what is otherwise known of Edwin's reign.

It may be that Man, Strathclyde, and even Dal Riata should be included under this heading but the general omission of the northern Britons implies a different explanation. The most plausible might be that they were accorded separate treatment by Edwin as king of Bernicia and paid their tribute at a ceremony further north, perhaps at the unique theatre or auditorium at Yeavering.[63] That all the Welsh kings were intended is confirmed by the high assessment of 7,000 hides, which, by comparison with Elmet, would have been a level of tribute payment entirely inappropriate to petty and otherwise undocumented kingships in southern Lancashire or Cheshire. Given Elmet's presence on the list and Bede's testimony on the matter, there can be no objection to such identification of British kings, disguised under an Old English nomenclature. One king was presumably responsible for this tribute payment and, given the role of Cadwallon in bringing Edwin's career to an end, this can only have been the King of Gwynedd who was, therefore, exercising a subordinate 'overkingship' in large parts of Celtic Britain, comparable to that exercised by Edwin under Rædwald.

Given this configuration, the king of the *W(r)ocensæte* was the most westerly of those kings who paid tribute direct to the English 'overking', rather than via the intermediacy of Gwynedd. Ever since the Iron Age, the tribal people focused within the plain of Shropshire extended into Cheshire and it was only during the Roman period that the *territorium* of a legionary fortress created an artificial frontier to their territory to the north-west. With that removed, there is every reason to suppose that the Cornovii re-established their territorial and political interests in the eastern Dee valley and as far north as the Mersey. The *W(r)ocensæte* were a continuation of this same people with the tribal name substituted by the name of the Roman *civitas* capital. Their kings were probably at this stage still British.[64]

There follows a series of eleven minor peoples, many of whom were denoted by names otherwise barely known, assessed at 300 hides or multiples thereof. Valiant attempts have been made to locate them and, although several identifications are contentious, most belong to the people later known as the Middle Angles. This was, significantly, an area in which Penda was to undertake wholesale political engineering under Mercian authority a generation later.[65] Within the structure of the Tribal Hidage, they continue the clockwise sweep around 'the original lands of the Mercians' (Figure 2).

Figure 2 The primary list of the Tribal Hidage. The southern enclave as represented by 9, 10, 18, 19, is highly problematic and several other identifications are comparatively insecure. The primary list reads (with slight emendation in favour of correct syntax, conventional spellings or modern names, as appropriate):

		Hundreds of hides
[1]	Original lands of the Mercians	300
[2]	W(r)ocen sæte	70
[3]	Westerne	70
[4]	Pecsæte	12
[5]	Elmetsæte	6
[6]	Lindsey with Hatfield	70
[7]	South Gyrwa	6
[8]	North Gyrwa	6
[9]	East Wixna	3
[10]	West Wixna	6
[11]	Spalda	6
[12]	Wigesta [unlocated]	9
[13]	Herefinna	12
[14]	Sweordora	3
[15]	Gifla	3
[16]	Hicca	3
[17]	Wight	6
[18]	Noxgaga	50
[19]	Ohtgaga	20
		That is 66,100

The ordering of the list to this point is in deference to Mercia and implies that all these peoples had been only recently detached from a dismantled Mercian 'overkingship'. That 'overkingship' must necessarily have been that exercised by Cearl, Edwin's sometime protector and father-in-law, so its dismantling had apparently been undertaken by Æthelfrith *c.* 615/16. To this point, therefore, the list corresponds to what one might expect of Cearl's, then Æthelfrith's, south-Humbrian tributaries, thereafter forcibly transferred *en bloc* by Rædwald to Edwin. A possible exception is Lindsey, which – if Æthelberht's superiority ever reached the Humber – may have been an addition, but this is more likely to have been a misunderstanding on the part of Bede, whose notions

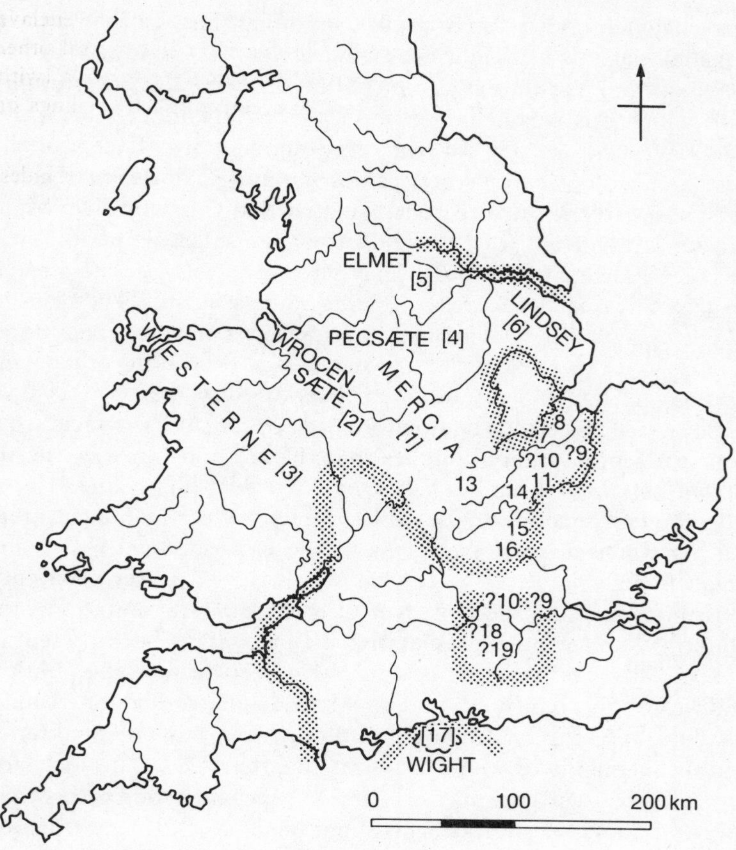

of the geography of the south-Humbrian 'overkingship' were dominated by the Mercian supremacy of his own day.[66]

There follow, however, three peoples who do not fall within this system. The location of the *Noxgaga* and *Ohtgaga* in the Thames valley is little more than inspired guesswork,[67] but *Wihtgara* (seventeenth on the list and assessed at 600 hides) certainly refers to the inhabitants of the Isle of Wight.[68] If this primary list should be interpreted as Edwin's tributaries before his abrupt rise to a general 'overkingship' in the summer of 626, the presence amongst them of a king of Wight is a matter which requires explanation.

That seventh-century Wight was dependent on outside protection is a matter of record.[69] Bereft of protection through the killing of Æthelwalh and isolated by its continuing (and by then anachronistic) paganism, Wight was conquered by Cædwalla of the Gewissae and its ruling house proscribed.[70] The excessive brutality with which this was achieved implies that the conquest of Wight was a West Saxon objective of very long standing. Exceptionally clear archaeological links between Wight and Kent during the late sixth and early seventh centuries suggest that the people of Wight had looked to Kent for protection for a considerable period even before Augustine's arrival.[71] It may have been this by then ancient association which led Bede to describe both as Jutish.[72] The kings of Wight presumably provided valuable services in return, acting as the eyes and ears of Kentish kings in the west, where an earlier West Saxon king had already attained 'overkingship' beyond his own agglomerate 'people'. The flow of costly and exotic artefacts from Kent to Wight certainly implies that the relationship was one on which the kings of the Kentish people placed a high value.

In the early to mid-620s, Edwin's agents were in Kent arranging his marriage with a princess of the Kentish royal house and organising a joint reaction to Cuichelm's rise to power. As Kent's most loyal ally and the most fearful of West Saxon ambitions, the king of Wight or his representative may well have been present at the betrothal and it would be entirely in keeping with the political realities of the day if he had sought Edwin's protection. Unlike Eadbald, the king of Wight could not achieve this on equal terms and the inequality of the relationship apparently led to his inclusion on a list of Edwin's tributaries. These events are beyond reconstruction but they are at least consistent with the little information which is available. Wight's presence on the primary list is not, therefore, an impediment to Edwin's responsibility for it. If they too belonged to the deep south, the rulers of the *Noxgaga* and *Ohtgaga* may have taken the same opportunity for the same reasons with the same result. If this interpretation is correct, when Edwin's representatives returned home with his bride and her Italian bishop, they also carried with them responsibility for the protection of several southern kings threatened by the West Saxons. If any one event could be guaranteed to have precipitated Cuichelm's attempt on Edwin's life, it was the establishment of the latter's protection over the island *provincia* off his own coast. Edwin's interference in his own backyard was impossible for him to ignore.

It may be that it was the addition of these kings of distant and little-known peoples to those already owing him tribute that led Edwin to seek the advice of Paulinus. The primary list of the Tribal Hidage was the result, drawn up before the actual ceremony at which the kings presented him with their gifts, at latest in the autumn of 625.[73]

The appended names

To the primary list were later added the names of a further fifteen peoples, followed by a total for the entire list of thirty-four. This total demonstrates that the primary list was at this stage subsumed within the full list, reflecting an abrupt expansion of the *imperium* of the recipient. The order was again clockwise, beginning with the Hwicce, the first people outside his own pre-existing 'overkingship' whom Edwin would have encountered in the course of his war against the West Saxons, then running eastwards along the southern borders of that 'overkingship' to the Wash and returning along the Channel (Figure 3).

It is the additional group which includes the names of those peoples likely to have held aloof, but been sympathetic to Edwin, in the campaign of 626. The appending of their names reflects his heightened prestige as the principal leader of the successful army. In the aftermath of his victory, all the kings of southern Britain sought his protection and recognised his superiority. It is this process which is enshrined in the second list.

That his allies or sympathisers were accorded high levels of hidation – 7,000 hides for the East Saxons and 15,000 for Kent, for example – need not detract from this interpretation of the list. Kings of the Cantware had long benefited from inflows of tribute and were presumably at this time exceptionally well-endowed with the types of goods normally used in this type of transaction. If the kings of the East Saxons had been contenders for *imperium* (as their struggle with the West Saxons implies) they were presumably also rich and powerful. The close relationship between Æthelberht and Sæberht had probably worked to their mutual advantage over many years. In any case, the Tribal Hidage records only one side of these relationships. An early medieval king advertised his prestige and power by the quality and quantity of the gifts he bestowed on those he favoured, but such gifts were necessarily a

Figure 3 The secondary list of the Tribal Hidage. Several identifications are insecure. The secondary list reads (with slight emendations for syntactical reasons and in favour of modern spellings where appropriate):

		Hundreds of hides
[20]	Hwinca [Hwicce]	70
[21]	Ciltern sæte	40
[22]	Hendrica [unlocated]	35
[23]	Unecu'n'g[a]ga [unlocated]	12
[24]	Arosæte	6
[25]	Faerpinga	3
[26]	Bilmiga	6
[27]	Widerigga	6
[28]	East Willa	6
[29]	West Willa	6
[30]	East Angles	300
[31]	East Saxons	70
[32]	Cantwarene [Kent]	150
[33]	South Saxons	70
[34]	West Saxons	1000
		This all 242,700 [incorrect]

matter of his discretion and variable, so no list of them would have been made.[74]

Bede recorded both Edwin's *dicio* – 'rule' – of all the English and Britons, and the fiction that his 'overkingship' was exclusive of the people of Kent.[75] Although Bede had his own reasons for the latter assertion, it may have suggested itself to him in consequence of the special relationship between the two dynasties, based on their kinship by marriage and their joint sponsorship of the Roman Church. Put simply, Bede probably had good reason to imagine that Kent had been free of tribute: Eadbald may well have received from Edwin at least as much as he gave and his tribute payments could even have been entirely waived as an especial mark of favour. That

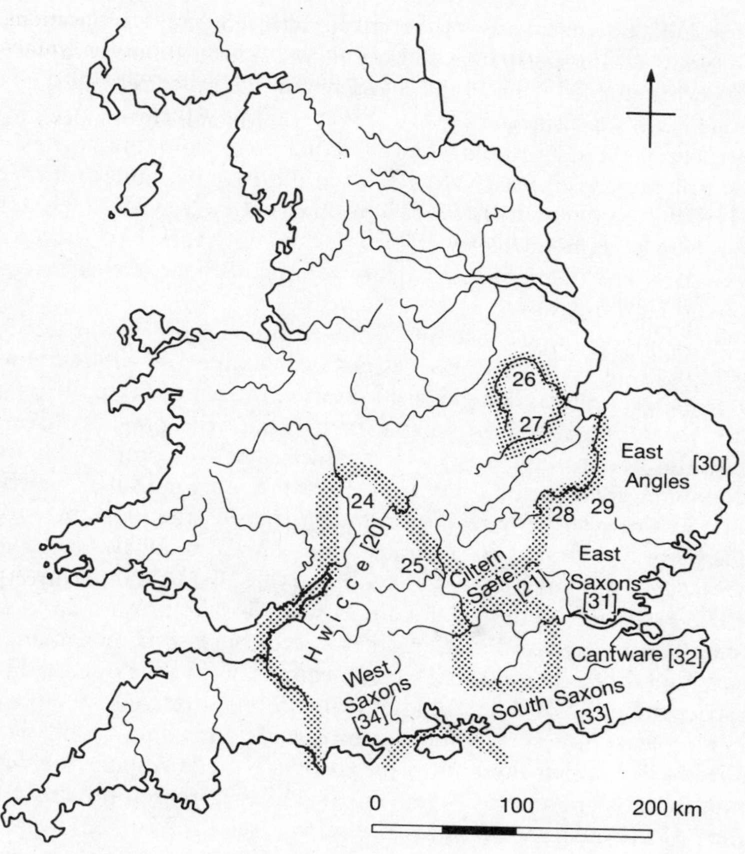

Kent was outside Edwin's protection is implausible. Indeed, his superiority there is demonstrated by his responsibility for dealings with the papacy concerning the southern archbishopric.[76]

At 30,000 hides, the hidation of the East Angles was equal to that of the Mercians and second only to that of the West Saxons. This unfavourable treatment of Rædwald's successor may reflect the unusual tribute-derived wealth of the dynasty as much as the new 'overking's' fear of the power and ambitions of this recently dominant people. That, of all his tributary kings, Edwin uniquely persuaded Eorpwald to convert is consistent with a special interest in the attitudes of this kingship as regards Eorpwald's capacity to generate divine support in favour of his own political ambitions. By so doing, Edwin seems to have destabilised the East Angles. Eorpwald was assassinated and a pagan reaction followed before Sigeberht returned from Frankia and restored Christianity, perhaps with Edwin's assistance.[77] Edwin, Eorpwald and the East Anglian aristocracy were presumably well-acquainted from the former's stay as a fugitive at Rædwald's court and it may be significant that it was Æthelric, not Eorpwald, who married Hereswith, daughter of Edwin's nephew, Hereric, but the circumstances are beyond reconstruction. There was probably a penal element in this exceptionally high hidation.

The southern kings severally came to terms with Edwin which recognised the realities of the resources available and the relationships between them. For the vast majority, the tribute actually paid may have been based on what they had paid the previous 'overking'. In most instances it was substantial but was presumably an acceptable alternative to ravaging by a far more powerful neighbour. It was also perhaps important in bringing the kings face-to-face, even in years when tributary kings did no military service in the army of the 'overking'.[78]

The exception to these generalities was clearly the West Saxons. That, despite a vast hidation, they were the last people named may imply that the ordering of the secondary list was intended to restrict the new West Saxon king or his representative to the position of least honour in the ceremony of tribute payment. The hidation for which these unfortunates were made responsible was transparently punitive.[79] The Tribal Hidage, therefore, records some of the means devised by Edwin to place the West Saxons on the rack, both psychologically and financially. This vicious treatment can be accounted for by Edwin's vengeance on Cuichelm and his people, fuelled by his own treacherous wounding and the murder of his thegns at Easter, 626. This important detail is entirely consistent with Edwin's responsibility for the Tribal Hidage. Indeed, it requires circumstances of this kind to render it comprehensible.

The additions therefore seem to belong to the late summer or autumn of 626. Edwin returned triumphant to Deira and had Paulinus bring up to date the tribute list which he had made the previous year. The full list was most probably used as a check on the actual exchanges between Edwin and the various kings at his palace that same autumn (Figure 4).

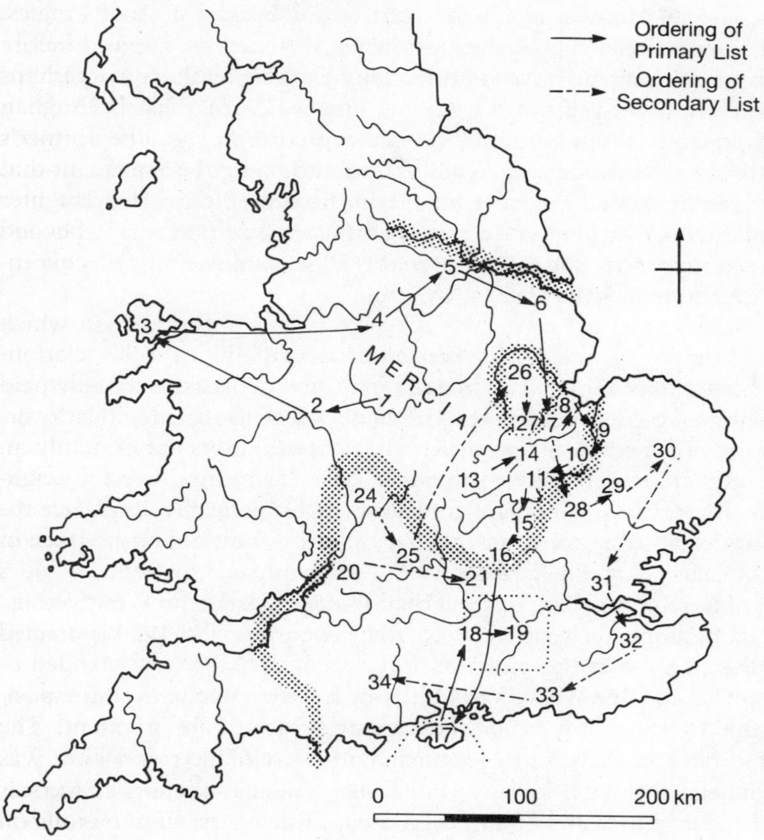

Figure 4 The full Tribal Hidage, juxtaposing the primary and secondary lists and with indications of the ordering of each list. Entries 12, 22 and 23 are omitted owing to difficulties of location.

By that date, Edwin may have already moved against Elmet. If not, he was soon to do so. By *c.* 630, he had extended his direct rule into the rich provinces of Lindsey and Hatfield, outflanking his dangerously powerful and untrustworthy clients in Mercia and obtaining a measure of direct control over the crucial roads south of Doncaster, where a high proportion of the major battles of the century already had occurred, or would occur.[80] The primary list may therefore have already been outdated when the second group of names was appended. If not, it became so soon after in consequence of political adjustments instituted by Edwin himself. Even so, it would have continued to be usable by those aware of its shortcomings right up to Edwin's sudden death. That both totals would have been outmoded seems unimportant. It is difficult to see that the totals were of much value to the king, except for him to boast about, compared with the individual entries. That the ultimate total was uncorrected implies that the addition was Paulinus's own initiative and of little practical importance in the coinless 'exchequer' of the Deiran 'overking'.

Hides and tribute

The hides of the Tribal Hidage were units of account by which the value of tribute was first established and then audited. As such, the term was necessarily consistent in meaning across the entire document and understood by all parties to it. The actual value attached to the term is unknown but most entries probably respected the ability of a regime to pay – excepting the West Saxons, Mercians and East Angles. That this value was expressed in terms of hides implies that the hide of the Tribal Hidage was identical in meaning to that applied elsewhere to specific peoples or individual estates, as discussed below (pp. 240–50).

The massive West Saxon hidation demonstrates beyond reasonable doubt that political considerations could be paramount in establishing the scale of payment, and it would be presumptuous to imagine that such considerations were absent in any single instance. To treat the Tribal Hidage as a census list,[81] a list of households,[82] or a detailed measure of actual cultivation or productivity,[83] is to entirely misrepresent the very limited purpose which it performed, as a record of the value of the tribute promised, then delivered, to King Edwin.

That the figures on this list differ from other figures derived from other sources is a matter of no concern.[84] If these figures represent a series of contracts between unequal kings arrived at in the specific circumstances of the years 625–6, then they were never likely to be replicated *in toto*. The figures of the Tribal Hidage have no universal application but should be seen as specific to the particular circumstances in which they were agreed and written down.

The hidations arrived at were clearly artificial and the very rounded numbers adopted may derive in part from the need for simple numbers: without Paulinus they would presumably have been committed to memory. The largest – the 100,000 hides allotted to the West Saxons – was probably the largest figure that Edwin could articulate.[85] Otherwise, the figures adopted betray several discrete patterns:

1 Most numbers were written in hundreds. This term had a special meaning in the Germanic languages as early as the first century AD.[86] While this meaning apparently changed over the millennium, it had a fundamental if poorly understood relevance to both Anglo-Saxon and British societies throughout the period.
2 The numbers adopted betray a tendency to count in threes – three hundred or multiples thereof occur in twenty-three instances out of thirty-four. This appears to be a feature of pre-Christian as well as Christian numeracy – that Gildas's Saxons arrived in three ships[87] probably derived from a pagan Saxon source. Bede's description of the battle of Chester, perhaps from a similar source, had the British monks numbered in communities no less than 300 strong and fasting for three days.[88] The prevalence of three, 300, etc. in early medieval Celtic literature may reflect some linkage between these two systems of composition.[89]
3 Less pervasive but still significant was the repetition of 7,000 hides (eight instances including the *Noxgaga* and *Ohtgaga* combined, and the *Hendrica* listed at 3,500) but the distribution is probably instructive. Seven is a peculiarly Christian number,[90] and it is perhaps significant that two of the kingships which were, on other grounds, probably or certainly British and therefore Christian, were allotted 7,000 hides (*W(r)ocensæte*, *Westerne*, but not the far more lightly hidated *Elmed sæte*). It is possible that other kings and peoples assessed at this level were likewise British, or had at least been under British rule until very recently – the *Hwicce* and *Hendrica* seem plausible candidates and the late survival of Christianity at Lincoln may imply that Lindsey's rulers were at this date at least ambiguous concerning their ethnic and cultural origins.[91]

Little of Edwin's tribute will have reached him in the form of livestock or food. His own renders from Deira, Bernicia and his other territories presumably sufficed to feed his household as it proceeded on circuit within his core kingships. Tribute from outside was more likely to be in artefacts appropriate to the rank of those giving and receiving them. This was an area in which subordinate kings may well have competed amongst themselves for the favour of the 'overking', and the medium of their competition is likely to have been in objects old and new, wrought of precious metals by craftsmen of the highest calibre, working both inside and outside Britain.[92] Tribute payments enabled Edwin to augment his treasure and advertise his own exceptional status by the dispersal of items from it to those who had his favour.

Although it was only one such mechanism for the movement of goods, tribute collection on a large scale and over wide distances, and its subsequent dispersal by gift giving, is likely to have been a major factor in the re-distribution of artefacts of high status, such as accompanied a minority of pagan Anglo-Saxon burials. Such is the likeliest explanation of, for example, the numerous southern English artefacts – some bearing Christian motifs – discovered in the apparently pagan inhumations deposited in the seventh century in the barrows of the *Pecsæte* in the White Peak,[93] or the widely scattered artefacts of Celtic origin found in Anglo-Saxon graves.[94]

Authorship and descent of the original

The Italian missionary, Paulinus, was a permanent member of Edwin's household from *c.* 624/5 until the king's death. Although he eventually trained up other, presumably local,[95] men, in 625–6 he and whatever staff had accompanied him (if any) were the only ones present with the skill to commit Edwin's tribute list to writing, and likely to have had a store of papyrus at their disposal. His years in Italy and Kent may have familiarised Paulinus with fiscal documentation – Æthelberht might have commissioned something broadly similar earlier in the century and Paulinus may even have seen or used such a document. He was clearly believed by Bede to have been responsible for the introduction of various exotic Roman practices in support of Edwin's kingship.[96] Paulinus's responsibility for the original seems, therefore, entirely in character.

The numerous lapses of syntax and spelling (e.g. *Hwinca* for *Hwicca* [*Hwicce*], *Elmed* for *Elmet*) in the late Old English copy may reflect not copyists' errors so much as errors already incorporated into the original. Paulinus was probably an accomplished writer of Latin but unused to writing in Old English, particularly under dictation. Edwin perhaps spoke in a northern dialect not at this stage yet fully familiar to his bishop and was listing names many of which were unknown to Paulinus, for the spellings of which no conventions as yet existed.[97] There are few difficulties concerning the peoples in the south and east with whose names Paulinus was presumably already familiar. For the remainder, bearing in mind that this list was written for his sole readership, the extent of its comprehensibility is a testimony to the effort which Paulinus made on Edwin's account.

Paulinus's involvement also helps to explain the descent of this document. On the death of his patron and protector, the bishop abandoned his northern ministry and shepherded the dowager queen and her children by sea to Kent, where he ultimately became bishop of Rochester.[98] As principal counsellor and secretary to the illiterate Edwin, Paulinus presumably had all royal documents in his charge. That these should have been among the effects he shipped south is unsurprising, although his first concern would have been to salvage the books and muniments of his ministry from the pagan and Celtic Christian backlash. His *pallium* as Archbishop of York was amongst his possessions at Rochester at his death in 644,[99] and the original of the Tribal Hidage may also have been stored in his archive there, or at Canterbury where Bede noted the presence of other relics of Edwin's Christianity.[100]

Conclusions

The internal organisation of the Tribal Hidage is incompatible with each and any Mercian candidature. Of the several potential Northumbrian candidates, only Edwin can have been responsible for it. The full list divides into primary and secondary groups which were necessarily written at different times and in different political circumstances, the primary list being subsumed into the full one. Circumstantial evidence suggests that these two stages can be equated with specific and dateable stages in the development of Edwin's *imperium*.

The primary list is dominated numerically by those peoples who had, until *c.* 615, been under the protection of Cearl of Mercia. Following his poorly understood downfall, they came under the control of Æthelfrith of Bernicia and were then transferred *in toto* by Rædwald to Edwin. The ordering of entries two to sixteen implies that a pre-existing, but unwritten, Mercian list formed the basis of Edwin's sequence. The Mercians had presumably then been placed at their head by the triumphant Æthelfrith.

To these western and Midland peoples Edwin added three southern kingships including Wight. These additions imply that the primary list was compiled only after Edwin came into contact with the allies and dependants of King Eadbald of Kent through his marriage, when, in any case, he first obtained the service of a literate cleric. Although the relationship between Edwin and the king of Wight is not otherwise documented, the reliance of the kings of Wight on outside protection against the West Saxons is a matter of record, and a close but unequal alliance between the kings of Wight and King Æthelberht is a plausible interpretation of the archaeological evidence. The primary list was, therefore, arguably written late in 625 by Paulinus to audit the arrival of tribute from Edwin's dependencies at a highly public ceremony, perhaps in November of the same year.

To this list were later appended a further fifteen peoples (or kings) and a grand total. These additions necessarily post-date the campaign of the summer of 626 in which Edwin destroyed King Cuichelm of the West Saxons. In the aftermath of that victory he imposed a punitive tribute on his defeated enemies and his superiority was recognised by every other king in southern England. That the West Saxons were the subject of savage discriminatory treatment is a clear feature of the Tribal Hidage which can only be adequately explained by such a confrontation as occurred in 625–6. Edwin's grievance against, and victory over, the West Saxons, and his universal 'overkingship' prior to his baptism in 627, are all matters of record. These additions to the Tribal Hidage were probably made in the late summer upon Edwin's triumphant return from war, and the full list was first used at the tribute ceremony in the autumn of 626.

Thereafter, political realities eroded the situation as enshrined in the list, as Edwin followed the familiar policy of ejecting, or reducing in status, the kings of neighbouring peoples and extending his own direct control of local renders.[101] The kings of Elmet and of Lindsey with Hatfield were victims of this process. The events of 625 and 626 therefore provide a context which is uniquely appropriate to the two-part composition of the Tribal Hidage and the dispositions within it.

The collapse of Edwin's regime in 633 led to Paulinus's departure to Kent and his appointment as bishop of Rochester. It was probably in Kent that this document survived up to the eleventh century. A copy was then made (in a still unidentified scriptorium) and appended to a version of Ælfric's Grammar, perhaps because of the dilapidation of the original,[102] or perhaps because of the interest in matters fiscal then current among the episcopal counsellors of Æthelred II and Cnut. The Tribal Hidage was still, at this stage, self-evidently a fiscal document, but it is difficult to imagine that eleventh-century clerks learnt anything from it of benefit to the kings they served, even supposing that they were attracted to it by the very large hidations recorded therein.

Given that the evidence is largely circumstantial, it is not possible to prove beyond any shadow of doubt that responsibility for the Tribal Hidage should rest with Edwin of Deira. This document must, however, derive from the court of a king known to history. Even discounting the presence of the Mercian territories on the primary list, its internal organisation is uniquely reconcilable with Edwin's career and his rise to power. The fit with the shadowy 'overkingships' of Wulfhere or his successors in Mercia is far less satisfactory, not only because of problems concerning Elmet and Hatfield but also because of the staged composition of the two lists and the evolving organisation of the various Middle Anglian peoples by that date. Souvenirs of their reigns were also less likely to have survived the Viking Age than was a document lodged in a diocesan archive in Kent by that stormy petrel of the early church, Paulinus, Archbishop of York then Bishop of Rochester.

Notes

1 W. Davies and H. Vierck, 'The contexts of the Tribal Hidage: social aggregates and settlement patterns', *Frühmittelalterliche Studien*, VIII,

1974, p. 223.

2 Dumville, 'Tribal Hidage', in *The Origins of Anglo-Saxon Kingdoms*, ed. S. Bassett, Leicester, 1989, unpaginated but by computation p. 227. Note that the subordinate total which follows the hides of the second group of names is an editorial addition (and marked as such) which is absent from the MS. The earliest and only Old English text of which this is a copy and transcript is BL MS Harley 3271.

3 C. R. Hart, 'The Tribal Hidage', *Trans. of the Royal Historical Soc.*, 5th series, XXI, 1971, pp. 138–57, preferred the eighth century; J. Morris, *The Age of Arthur*, London, 1974, p. 492, opted for '661 or immediately after . . .'; Davies and Vierck, 'Tribal Hidage', pp. 226–7, preferred 670–90; P. H. Sawyer, *From Roman Britain to Norman England*, London, 1978, p. 111, considered the surviving text to be a late recension '. . . compiled in the ninth or tenth century by a West Saxon'. For further comments, see the annotated bibliography in *The Defence of Wessex*, edd. D. H. Hill and A. R. Rumble, Appendix III.

4 F. M. Stenton, *Anglo-Saxon England*, 3rd edn, Oxford, 1971, pp. 43, 296–7; Hart, 'Tribal Hidage', p. 133; Davies and Vierck, 'Tribal Hidage', p. 225; D. H. Hill, *Atlas of Anglo-Saxon England*, Oxford, 1982, p. 77; P. Sims-Williams, *Religion and Literature in Western England*, Cambridge, 1990, p. 17; although unwilling to commit himself, D. P. Kirby, *The Earliest English Kings*, London, 1991, p. 11, inclines to this view but is sympathetic also to Sawyer's preference for West Saxon authorship (see above, n. 3).

5 W. J. Corbett, 'Tribal Hidage', *Trans. of the Royal Historical Soc.*, XIV, 1900, p. 207 proposed that it was 'Edwin's tribute-roll or a modification of it evolved by succeeding Bretwaldas' but not for reasons which his contemporaries (or later commentators) found convincing. See also J. C. Russell, 'The Tribal Hidage', *Traditio*, V, 1947, pp. 192–209; N. Brooks, 'The formation of the Mercian kingdom', in Bassett, *Origins*, p. 159.

6 Most recently by Kirby, *Earliest Kings*, p. 10 and *passim*, and Yorke, *Kings and Kingdoms of Early Anglo-Saxon England*, London, 1990, pp. 9–15, but see also Bassett, *Origins*, *passim*.

7 P. Wormald, 'Bede, the *Bretwaldas* and the origins of the *Gens Anglorum*', *Ideal and Reality in Frankish and Anglo-Saxon Society: Studies Presented to J. M. Wallace-Hadrill*, ed. P. Wormald, Oxford, 1983, p. 114, whose reasoning is echoed by D. N. Dumville, 'Essex, Middle Anglia, and the expansion of Mercia in the south-east Midlands', in Bassett, *Origins*, p. 129.

8 Brooks, 'Formation', p. 159.

9 J. Campbell, 'Bede's *Reges* and *Principes*', Jarrow Lecture, 1979, pp. 5–8.

10 The damage done at *Campodonum* in 633 was repaired and a Northumbrian monastery established in the 'wood of Elmet'. Despite the power of successive Mercian kings in the eighth century, Ecgbert's meeting at Dore with Eanred of Northumbria in 829 (*ASC*), implies that Northumbria then still retained the small British kingdoms of the West Riding, and that Dore, Whitwell Gate and the Humber were still the southern frontier in 944. Assuming the Roman Ridge dykes to have been Northumbrian, there is evidence of a defensive barrier which defends Elmet, but not Hatfield, from Mercia: C. R. Hart, 'The Kingdom of Mercia', *Mercian Studies*, ed. A. Dornier, Leicester, 1977, p. 53. Excepting only the undocumented possibility that Penda laid tribute on Oswine of Deira (642–51), there is no evidence that Mercian superiority was ever recognised in Elmet after the fall of King Cearl. For the geography of Elmet and Hatfield, see N. J. Higham, *The Kingdom of Northumbria, AD 350–1100*, Gloucester, 1993, pp. 84–9.

11 *HE*, II, 5, *contra* S. Fanning, 'Bede, Imperium and the Bretwaldas', *Speculum*, LXVI, 1991, pp. 16–17. Bede's understanding of *imperium* was overshadowed by the realities of his own lifetime. For the earlier *imperium*-wielding kings, see above, pp. 47–73. Limitation of the kings in this list to seven betrays Bede's providential view of history, wherein the Northumbrian supremacy of Oswiu was the climax of the historical development of the English. Adamnan's description of Oswald as '*imperator* of the whole of Britain' (*Adamnan's Life of St. Columba*, ed. and trans. A. O. and M. O. Anderson, Edinburgh and London, 1961, pp. 200–1), reflects his general superiority following his victory over Cadwallon, but he had considerable difficulty in maintaining this position without the Kentish support which had sustained Edwin. His attempt to substitute an alliance with Wessex fell foul of Penda and his Welsh allies. More powerful was Oswiu after the killing of Penda in 655 (*HE*, V, 24). He extended his direct kingship and his superiority among the Scots and Picts (*HE*, II, 5) but his direct rule of the northern (and eventually of the southern) Mercians (*HE*, III, 24) rules out his candidature. Oswiu's supremacy was under threat at his death but Ecgfrith put down rebellion among the Picts and laid tribute on the Mercians *c.* 674–6 and perhaps even up to his defeat at the battle of the Trent (679): *HE*, IV, 21. He was styled *rex Humbronensium* in the preamble of the Council of Hatfield, implying that he was still, in 679, king on both sides of the Humber, so of Lindsey; *Life of Wilfrid*, ed. B. Colgrave, Cambridge, 1927, caps. XIX-XX; *HE*, IV, 17.

12 *HB*, LXIII. The few references to 'Ceredig' in the *Annales Cambriae*, *HE* and *HB* are not entirely consistent. Bede referred to him solely in the context of Hereric's death, probably in or shortly after 604: *HE*, IV, 23; The *Annales Cambriae* dated his death to 616 but Edwin's succession to 617; *HB*, LXIII, states that Edwin '*occupavit*' Elmet and expelled Ceretic. Assuming these all to refer to the same individual, 616 seems too early for Ceretic's death seeing that that necessarily followed his expulsion. This date is independent of both *HE* and *HB*. If the error was solely due to the omission of a Roman '*x*' from the text from which it derived, the expulsion of Ceretic may have occurred in 626, in which case Paulinus's influence was considerable even before the formal baptism of Edwin. There is a hint of this in *HE*, II, 9. Stenton (*Anglo-Saxon England*, p. 80) suggested that Ceretic's murder of Hereric provided Edwin's motive but Bede neither states nor implies that the British king was responsible for this breach of the peace of his own court. That was far more likely to have originated with Æthelfrith, the persecutor of Edwin in exile.

13 *HE*, II, 14. *Campodonum* has been too confidently assigned to Leeds: M. Faull and S. Moorhouse, edd., *West Yorkshire: An Archaeological Survey*, Wakefield, 1981, pp. 157–63; A. L. F. Rivet and R. Smith, *The Place-Names of Roman Britain*, London, 1979, p. 293, acknowledging the work of Margaret Faull prior to publication. For a note of caution, J.M. Wallace-Hadrill, *Bede's Ecclesiastical History of the English People: A Historical Commentary*, Oxford, 1988, p. 75. For the alternative of a *feld* name associated with Doncaster (*Campus Danum*), see *Bede: A History of the English Church and People*, translated L. Sherley-Price, revised by R. E. Latham, London, 1968, p. 130, fn. 1; Higham, *Northumbria*, pp. 85–6. If at Doncaster, this palace would have been on the southern borders of Elmet, on the main Roman road system and a convenient centre for oversight of (and collection of renders from) Elmet, *Loidis* and Hatfield. The *Cambodunum* of iter xvii of the Antonine Itinerary is corrupt and should probably not be confused with Bede's *Campodonum*. The basilican church would presumably have been stone like those at York and Lincoln: *HE*, II, 14, 16; *Life of Wilfrid*, XVI.

14 *HE*, II, 14: the replacement may have been at any stage between 635 and 731 but Doncaster remained an important royal palace site: M. S. Parker, 'Some notes on the pre-Norman history of Doncaster', *Yorkshire Archaeological Journal*, LIX, 1987, pp. 29–44.

15 *HE*, II, 16; the expulsion of local dynasties by more powerful neighbours was common practice in the seventh century and later, as evidenced by Bede's comments on Æthelfrith, Oswiu and Cædwalla: *HE*, I, 34; III, 14; IV, 16. The term 'usurping kingship' might be appropriate in this context. It is, however, possible that the *praefectus* was a member of the native dynasty. For recent discussion, see S. Bassett, 'Lincoln and the Anglo-Saxon see of Lindsey', *Anglo-Saxon England*, XVIII, 1989, pp. 1–32.

16 Æthelfrith was said to have reigned twelve years in Deira: *HB*, LXIII. If he was killed in 616 he expelled Edwin as a teenager in 603 or 604, depending whether or not only years in which he was reigning at the year's start be counted. However, the recurrence of the apostolic number in early Bernician history is too common to pass unchallenged and this should be taken as no more than an approximation.

17 *HE*, I, 34. Bede did not use the term *imperium* in respect of Æthelfrith. The reason is unclear. Æthelfrith's paganism is unlikely to have been the problem since Bede referred to Ælle and Ceawlin as exercising *imperium*. That several *imperia* could have existed in parallel is a point made by Fanning, 'Bede', p. 20.

18 *HE*, I, 34. For recent reviews of *imperium*, see Kirby, *Earliest Kings*, p. 17; Fanning, 'Bede', pp. 7–14.

19 Edwin's dates have been a matter of debate. P. H. Blair, 'The Moore Memoranda on Northumbrian History', in *Early Cultures of North-West Europe*, edd. C. Fox and B. Dickins, Cambridge, 1950, pp. 243–59 demonstrated that Bede's dates were based on royal genealogies; D. P. Kirby, 'Bede and Northumbrian Chronology', *English Historical Review*, LXXVIII, 1963, pp. 514–27 argued for the addition of one year but this is probably unnecessary: see discussion by M. Miller, 'The Dates of Deira', *Anglo-Saxon England*, VIII, 1979, p. 42 and S. Wood, 'Bede's Northumbrian Dates Again', *English Historical Review*, XCVIII, 1983, pp. 280–96. It is Bede's dates which are here used throughout. A very similar tactic to Æthelfrith's was used by his son, Oswiu, in establishing himself as king in Deira: he married Edwin's daughter and subsequently murdered her cousin, King Oswine; *HE*, III, 14; V, 24.

20 *HB*, LXI; as were the Deiran kings down to Soemil, *ibid*.

21 *HE*, II, 14. Children of this marriage were of weapon-bearing age by 633 and one was then married and a parent. Unless Edwin's second marriage was (by Christian standards) bigamous, the marriage was over by 625. The sources used by Bede for his treatment of Edwin are unknown but the extent and detail of his account implies at least one well-informed Christian source sympathetic to the Deiran dynasty. Hild, Edwin's great-niece, did not die until 680 (*HE*, V, 24) and stories concerning the heroic era of Northumbrian Christianity were probably preserved at Whitby, York (where Edwin's head was deposited as a relic) and at Gilling, as well, perhaps, as in Kent. There is a distinctly hagiographical side to Bede's comments in II, 12 and the dialogue at the conference (II, 13) was presumably reconstructed, either by Bede himself or by his informant. By contrast, the detailed description of Paulinus given Bede by Abbot Deda from an eye-witness, and the survival of James the Deacon to the 680s (II, 16) both demonstrate the existence of oral sources of good quality.

22 *AC*, 613: Selyf son of Cynan (of Powys) was a casualty and the death of Iago son of Beli (of Gwynedd) was noted in the same year. Bede recorded the name of another senior Briton present: *HE*, II, 2.

23 *HE*, II, 2; compare Tacitus, *Germania*, edd. T. E. Page and W. H. D. Rouse, London, 1914, cap. 2, who noted that 'ancient songs (or poems)' were the only form of 'history and annals' known to the Germans. Gildas appears to have used a similar source for his description of the departure of the Saxons from their homeland: *DEB*, XXIII, 3. For a recent review, J. M. Wallace-Hadrill, *Bede*, pp. 47–8, 54 and see references, but note the caution of R. Frank, 'The search for the Anglo-Saxon oral poet', *Bulletin of the John Rylands University Library*, LXXV (1993), pp. 11–36.

24 *HE*, II, 2; provided that interpretation of Bede's text and sources avoids the levels of nihilism reached by N. K. Chadwick, *The Age of the Saints in the Early Celtic Church*, Oxford, 1961, p. 122, followed by Sims-Williams, *Religion and Literature*, pp. 9–10; for alternative views, see Wallace-Hadrill, *Bede's Ecclesiastical History*, p. 52, H. Mayr-Harting, *The Coming of Christianity to Anglo-Saxon England*, London, 1991, pp. 71–2.

25 *HB*, LXV: 'He [Penda] first separated the kingship of the Mercians from the kingship of the Northerners . . .'. For a discussion, see N. J. Higham, 'King Cearl and the origins of the Mercian "Overkingship"', *Midland History*, XVII (1992), pp. 1–15.

26 Hill, *Atlas*, map 145, p. 83.

27 The Mercians were divided into two in 655: *HE*, III, 24. That this may have renewed an ancient division finds support in the widespread occurrence of comparable duality within early peoples: hence the 'north folk' and 'south folk' of the East Angles (although that is not evidenced until the late Saxon period), West and East Kent and the numerous paired peoples of the Tribal Hidage itself, each of which presumably had a separate kingship.

28 *HE*, II, 12.

29 *HE*, II, 5, 15.

30 *HE*, II, 5; V, 24.

31 *HB*, LXIII.

32 *HE*, II, 12, but see below, p. 197.

33 If Æthelfrith was now 'protector' of the Mercians and of even more southerly erstwhile dependencies of the Mercians, his authority necessarily marched with the *regnum* of Rædwald in the Fens. However, Bede could have been recognising only that the spot was, in 731, actually inside Mercia: his language is ambiguous.

34 The battle site is unknowable but Rædwald probably proceeded via the Roman road system to the River Idle opposite Bawtry (where it left Mercian territory). Bede's comments imply that he supposed this geographical detail to be contemporary with the events he described but he may have been wrong, particularly if Hatfield had been divided between Northumbria and Mercia after the battle, by a boundary along the River

Trent, under the peace treaty sponsored by Archbishop Theodore. Thereafter, this stretch of the river was a long-standing boundary between Mercian and Northumbrian territory, ultimately between Yorkshire, Nottinghamshire and Lincolnshire. The several seventh-century battles named by Bede imply that armies regularly travelled via the Roman roads: e.g. Hatfield, II, 20; *Hevenfelth*, III, 2; *Maserfelth*, III, 9; *Winwæd*, III, 24.

35 *HE*, III, 1.

36 Bede considered Iona to be in Pictish territory when Columba founded the monastery (*HE*, III, 4), and there were probably Scottish monasteries among the Picts where Æthelfrith's sons could have found refuge beyond Dal Riata. That, after *Degsastan*, the Scots never again dared attack the English (*HE*, I, 34) implies that they generally recognised the 'overkingship' of Northumbrian kings (including Edwin), at least until 685, although Northumbrian superiority was clearly weakened by Penda's attacks on the Bernicians and then much extended when Penda was destroyed by Oswiu: *HE*, III, 25.

37 Higham, 'King Cearl'.

38 He was the fourth *imperium*-wielding king named by Bede (*HE*, II, 5), and no other is likely to have obtained extensive recognition in the south since Æthelberht's death. Note the incredulity of Fanning, 'Bede', pp. 15–16, but Rædwald's inclusion in Bede's list is alone sufficient to justify this interpretation and Bede in no way contradicts it.

39 *HE*, II, 5. The juxtaposition by Bede of the apostasy of the East Saxons and the battle *non multo tempore* later is directly comparable with that of the 'Augustine's Oak' conference (*c.* 601/2) and the battle of Chester (*c.* 615/16) *siquidem post* . . . (*HE*, II, 2). Both are literary devices designed to convey an impression of causation and divine intervention which conform to general chronological succession without giving precise indications of date.

40 That a West Saxon king had earlier achieved 'overkingship' was noted by Bede: *HE*, II, 5. There was, therefore, a precedent for Cuichelm's ambitions and good cause for his neighbours to treat his activities with the utmost gravity. Given his military success over the East Saxons, some may already, by 625–6, have obtained his protection and become tributary.

41 *HE*, II, 9; Kirby, 'Bede and Northumbrian Chronology', p. 522, argued for a date for the marriage as early as 618/19 but broadened the period to 'by 624' in *Earliest English Kings*, pp. 39–42. Bede's account is most easily reconciled with a date for the marriage immediately following Rædwald's (undated) death, when the two kings drew together to combat rival challenges for *imperium*-wielding status.

42 *HE*, II, 9; this is Bede's date. 21 July fell on a Sunday in 626, but not in 625. Only if it is assumed that his consecration *must* have occurred on a Sunday is there a case for amending the date. See n. 19, particularly

Wood, 'Bede's Northumbrian Dates', p. 289. Bede clearly believed that Paulinus was a bishop from before their departure from Kent, and so head of a mission. Perhaps the appropriate precedent should be Bishop Liudhard who came to Kent with Bertha: *HE*, I, 25. His status is confirmed by the *Leudardus Ep(iscopu)s* of the 'medalet' from St. Martin's Canterbury now in Liverpool Museum (catalogue no. 7018), for which see M. Werner, 'The Liudhard Medalet', *Anglo-Saxon England*, XX, 1991, pp. 27–41.

43 *HE*, II, 9; the dagger used in this attempt was poisoned. Note that Edwin's nephew, Hereric, had died of poison in a similar assassination attempt at a royal court a decade or more before (*HE*, IV, 23).

44 The palace site has never been identified but should probably be sought in the general vicinity of Goodmanham, perhaps near the large cemetery of Sancton I. The traditional association with Malton is implausible. It was probably here, too, that the putative conference occurred: *HE*, II, 13.

45 Bede's description implies that the men within Edwin's hall were unarmed (*HE*, II, 9). It is circumstantial detail of this kind which confirms that Bede's description at least conformed with standard practice in the early English period. For a parallel, see *Beowulf*, lines 325–30.

46 *HE*, II, 9; her name (Eanflæd) derived from her membership of the Kentish, rather than the Deiran dynasty. The number of her household baptised with her was the apostolic number, twelve, again implying substantial Christian influence, either in the historiography or the decision-making. The date of her birth confirms that the marriage occurred no later than mid-summer, 625. For a further collection of Christian numbers associated with the event, *HB*, LXIII.

47 *HE*, II, 9.

48 *HE*, II, 9. It was from Edwin's court that negotiations were conducted with the papacy for the *pallia* for both Archbishop Honorius of Canterbury and Paulinus at York: *HE*, II, 17, 18.

49 M. Faull, 'Place-Names and the Kingdom of Elmet', *Nomina*, IV, 1980, pp. 21–3.

50 The letter written by Gregory to Æthelberht of Kent (*HE*, I, 32), presumably at Augustine's request, stressed the orthodoxy of Augustine's Christianity and exhorted the king to follow his advice. There can be little doubt that that included the proscription of the rebellious British clergy. Augustine may well have complained to Gregory of Æthelberht's failure to act against the kings of the Britons (*HE*, II, 2), once their clergy had defied Augustine; C. Plummer, ed., *Venerabilis Baedae Opera Historica*, Oxford, 1896, II, p. 73; see also Wallace-Hadrill, *Bede's Ecclesiastical History*, p. 52.

51 *HE*, II, 14. Contrast with the letter to Æthelberht the benevolent approval exhibited by the letter from Pope Honorius to Edwin, whose

support of Paulinus seems to have been considered beyond reproach: *HE*, II, 17.

52 *HE*, II, 14.

53 *Life of Wilfrid*, XVII; for Cadwallon, see R. Geraint Gruffydd, 'Canu Cadwallon ap Cadfan', *Studies in Old Welsh Poetry*, edd. R. Bromwich and R. Brinley Jones, Cardiff, 1978, pp. 25–43.

54 As in Elmet. Æthelfrith similarly had British kings as his tributaries.

55 *HE*, III, 2, but beware of Bede's vituperative rhetoric on the subject.

56 N. J. Higham, 'Medieval "Overkingship" in Wales: the earliest evidence', *Welsh History Review*, 1992, pp. 149–53.

57 Davies, 'Tribal Hidage', p. 226.

58 E.g. Stenton, *Anglo-Saxon England*, p. 296.

59 That the entire document should belong to a specific political context was stressed by Wormald, 'Bede, the *Bretwaldas* and the origins of the *Gens Anglorum*', p. 114.

60 Penda had nothing but antipathy for Æthelfrith's son Oswald whom he killed at the battle of *Maserfelth* (perhaps Makerfield in Lancashire: D. Kenyon, *The Origins of Lancashire*, Manchester, 1991, p. 27), so it seems unlikely that he or his kin had been recognised as kings in Mercia, which may suggest that both Æthelfrith and then Edwin had usurped that kingship to themselves.

61 As by Davies, 'Tribal Hidage', p. 231, followed by Hill, *Atlas*, map 136, p. 76 and Yorke, *Kings and Kingdoms*, p. 13; Stenton, *Anglo-Saxon England*, p. 296, preferred Cheshire with north Staffordshire and is followed by Sims-Williams, *Religion and Literature*, p. 18; see also M. Gelling, 'The early history of western Mercia', in Bassett, *Origins*, p. 192 and *The West Midlands in the early Middle Ages*, Leicester, 1992, pp. 83–5.

62 *HE*, II, 5; II, 9.

63 B. Hope-Taylor, *Yeavering: An Anglo-British Centre of Early Northumbria*, London, 1977, p. 121.

64 *W(r)ocen* is a version of *Wr(e)ocen* – the Wrekin hillfort in Shropshire. The name had been associated with this people and a territory which encompasses the entirety of the northern marches since the pre-Roman Iron Age: Rivet and Smith, *The Place-Names of Roman Britain*, London, 1979, pp. 505–6. Ptolemy referred to Chester as a *polis* of the Cornovii in the second century: *Geography*, book II, cap. 3, 11. That this kingship was still British in the early seventh century may be implicit in the presence of a bishop and monks at *Letocetum* (Wall, Staffs.) which has caused so many difficulties of interpretation: e.g. Brooks, 'Formation', p. 169. The total absence of pagan Anglo-Saxon burials must also be an important factor. Higham, *The origins of Cheshire*, Manchester, 1993, pp. 68–77.

65 Davies, 'Tribal Hidage', pp. 231–2. For close links between the

Mercians and Middle Angles, *HE*, III, 21, 24; IV, 3, 12. The marginalia in Recension A of Tribal Hidage concerning *Færpinga* apparently derived from *HE*, III, 21.

66 The language is reminiscent of Bede's notice of the 'overkingship' of Æthelbald of Mercia in 731: *HE*, V, 23, and this was probably what was in his mind.

67 Davies, 'Tribal Hidage', pp. 232, 236.

68 *Ibid*, pp. 232, 234.

69 Wight was granted by Wulfhere to Æthelwalh of the South Saxons, a favoured client king, along with the Meonware, hitherto under West Saxon rule: *HE*, IV, 13. This does not imply that Wulfhere had campaigned on Wight, merely that, as the 'overking' of all concerned, he could dispose as he saw fit of *imperium* over its native dynasty, for whom see *HE*, IV, 15. He was, effectively, delegating *regnum* over two minor peoples to a loyal *regulus*.

70 *HE*, IV, 13.

71 C. J. Arnold, *The Anglo-Saxon Cemeteries of the Isle of Wight*, London, 1982, pp. 102–9.

72 *HE*, I, 15, which also included among the Jutish peoples in England those on the mainland opposite Wight, presumably the Meonware, who were, by the mid-seventh century, already within the West Saxon kingship: *HE*, IV, 13, but who were extracted therefrom by Wulfhere. The absence of the Meonware from the Tribal Hidage may imply that they were already under West Saxon control at this stage. In general, see B. Yorke, 'The Jutes of Hampshire and Wight and the origins of Wessex', *Origins*, ed. Bassett, pp. 84–96.

73 If the great sacrifice of animals to the gods in 'Blodmonath' be considered the religious parallel to tribute payments to kings, then the latter may have occurred in November: Bede, *De Temporum Ratione*, cap. 15, *Bedae Opera*, VI, 2, *Corpus Christianorum*, *Series Latina*, CXXIIIB, Brepols, 1977, pp. 329–32. That kings are likely to have attended in person is a fair inference from the frequency with which the baptism of subordinate kings occurred at the court of their superiors, the earliest documented being that of Rædwald in Kent: *HE*, II, 15. They, or close family members, also led their troops in the army of the 'overking': e.g. *HE*, III, 24. Edwin's death at Hatfield on 12 October 633 suggests that he was returning from Lindsey to his principal palace in Deira in time for the annual ceremony of tribute-taking. If so, his passage could have been predicted by the returned renegade, his erstwhile tributary the *rex Brettonum*, Cadwallon, and his ally, Penda.

74 For parallel gifts passing between the rulers of nations, see *Beowulf*, lines 1173–4; for promise thereof, *HE*, II, 12.

75 *HE*, II, 5, 9.

76 *HE*, II, 17.
77 *HE*, II, 15.
78 *HE*, III, 24.
79 Hart, 'Tribal Hidage', p. 157.
80 See n. 34. Edwin's occupation of Lincoln could alternatively be seen as another move against the British Church since there is new archaeological evidence from the work of the Lincoln Archaeological Unit of continuing Christian activity in that city as late as the early seventh century. For a summary, P. Stafford, *The East Midlands in the Early Middle Ages*, Leicester, 1985, pp. 87–8; my thanks to Michael Jones, Director of the Unit, for his advice on this subject.
81 Russell, 'Tribal Hidage', p. 201; Davies, 'Tribal Hidage', p. 225.
82 Davies, 'Tribal Hidage', p. 225.
83 Kirby, *Earliest English Kings*, p. 11.
84 Davies, 'Tribal Hidage', p. 229. Contrast Hart, 'Tribal Hidage', pp. 147, 156.
85 Similarly, Procopius's Frankish informants used the figure of 100,000 to describe the very large army with which what can only have been an 'overking' of the Angles attacked the continental Varni: *History of the Wars*, ed. and trans. H. B. Dewing, London and New York, 1928, book VIII, cap. 20, 26.
86 Tacitus, *Germania*, cap. II.
87 See above, n. 23. See discussion in P. Sims-Williams, 'Gildas and the Anglo-Saxons', *Cambridge Medieval Celtic Studies*, VI, 1983, pp. 22–3.
88 *HE*, II, 2; K. Harrison, *The Framework of Anglo-Saxon History to AD 900*, Cambridge, 1976, p. 132. The status groups identified in the laws of Æthelberht are similarly in three categories: F.L. Attenborough, ed., *The Laws of the Earliest English Kings*, Cambridge, 1922, pp. 2–17, and see above, nn. 23 and 86.
89 E.g. *Trioedd Ynys Prydein*, ed. R. Bromwich, Cardiff, 1961, *passim*; the *Gododdin*, *passim*. P. Lambert, '"Thirty" and "sixty" in Brittonic', *Cambridge Medieval Celtic Studies*, VIII, 1984, pp. 29–43.
90 E.g. *Genesis*, II, 2–3, and *Revelation*, *passim*, and almost every book in between. 7,000 hides recurs in *Beowulf*, line 2195 and in *HE*, IV, 13.
91 P. Stafford, *East Midlands*, p. 87.
92 This view differs from that of T. Charles-Edwards, 'Early medieval kingships in the British Isles', in *Origins*, p. 30 and owes much to consideration of the problems of scale involved. Livestock may have been part of Edwin's tribute, particularly from poorer kings with little access to precious objects, but it is difficult to see that the arrival of one beast per hide (for example), so most of a quarter of a million beasts, would have been considered desirable. Compare the grave goods from Sutton Hoo:

R. L. S. Bruce-Mitford, *The Sutton Hoo Ship Burial*, London, 1975–83, *passim*; compare also the view of the writer of the *HB*, XXX, looking back to the protection of Britain by the Romans which it was envisaged would have been paid for in 'gold and silver and bronze, and all her precious raiment and honey'. This probably reflects customs of tribute paid in Wales *c.* 800 but it could derive from Gildas's reference to the imposition of imperial images on (so coining of) Britain's bronze, silver and gold: *DEB*, VII; seventh-century instances of diplomatic payment include *HB*, LXV and Æthelfrith's offer to Rædwald of *pecunia multa* for Edwin's head (*HE*, II, 12). A second reference to Æthelfrith's offer merely specified *aurum*, 'gold'. Merovingian coins may be implied, as occurred in the Sutton Hoo ship burial. Alternatively reference to 'money' merely mirrors Bede's retrospective assumption, made in ignorance of the fact that this was a coinless era, that such payments would have been made in coin. The earliest implicit reference to tribute payments to Saxon kings occurs in *DEB*, I, 5, discussed in Higham, *The English Conquest*, Manchester, 1994, pp. 75–8. For Frankish parallels see T. Reuter, 'Plunder and tribute in the Carolingian Empire', *Transactions of the Royal Historical Society*, 5th series, XXXV (1985), pp. 75–94, who records 'a rich diversity of payments from livestock to corn and treasure'.

93 A. Ozanne, 'The Peak Dwellers', *Medieval Archaeology*, VI–VII, 1962–3, pp. 15–52.

94 R. H. White, *Roman and Celtic Objects from Anglo-Saxon Graves*, Oxford, 1988, *passim*.

95 *HE*, II, 16. That James the Deacon resided after 633 in the vicinity of Catterick and that the actual settlement reputedly bore his name in the eighth century implies that he was a landholding nobleman of local extraction with family holdings, but his by-name suggests that his education for the priesthood had reached only an elementary stage at Edwin's death.

96 So, for example, his use of the *tufa*: *HE*, II, 16.

97 It might be worthwhile to examine the Tribal Hidage for evidence of northern pronunciation as conveyed through an Italian ear with considerable experience only of southern Old English.

98 *HE*, II, 20.

99 *HE*, V, 24, although it need not have reached Paulinus before his departure from the north.

100 *HE*, II, 20. The earliest Recension surviving (A) is attached to a copy of Abbot Ælfric's Grammar which dates to the first half of the eleventh century, but it is unclear where either this copy was made or the attachment occurred, albeit a southern context seems most likely, if not almost obligatory. The later Latin text (Recension C) is based on a lost OE original which was superior to Recension A as regards some name forms. See discussion and references in Dumville, 'Tribal Hidage'.

101 Compare Æthelfrith and his British neighbours, *HE*, I, 34.
102 For a discussion of late copies of putative early Kentish documents, see M. Deanesley, 'The court of King Æthelbert of Kent', *Cambridge Historical Journal*, VII, 1942, pp. 101–14.

4
Regional governance and *imperium*

That communities exhibited a strong sense of regionalism in their social identity and governance throughout the mid- to late Anglo-Saxon period is a view with which few would now disagree. The subdivision of England into earldoms and shires, dioceses and parishes, is plainly discernible from the tenth century and becomes ever more visible as the Norman Conquest (and Domesday Book) approaches. While these subdivisions were bonded together to form a composite English state by the omnipresent mechanisms of royal and ecclesiastical governance (viz taxation, shire and hundred courts, royal councils, synods, etc.) they retained considerable relevance for regional communities. Indeed, although theoretically dependent on the crown, provincial systems of patronage, under earldormen and then earls, retained the capacity to pursue political objectives which might be at variance not only with neighbouring systems but even with those of the current incumbent of the throne.

An important characteristic of this phenomenon was the integration of patronage, and therefore governance, at the very local level with the structure of regional and national government. This enmeshing of local society with larger and more potent systems of patronage and control can be seen to have been operative in both the secular and ecclesiastical spheres, and does much to explain the durability and considerable strength of the late Anglo-Saxon state.

If, on the other hand, we direct our attention back beyond the Viking Age, the general picture changes in important ways. Most importantly, no single dynasty had then established itself as the sole legitimate kingship among the English. Instead, several regionalised political systems existed in tandem, in conditions which hovered between active hostility, at one extreme, and a dynamic harmony, at the other.

Despite this fundamental difference, several of the conditions met with in late Anglo-Saxon England were already in place. For example, the bifocal system of archdioceses was instituted (or more accurately re-instituted) in the 730s, when the archdiocese of York was re-established. Indeed, this event brought to an end a period of some seventy years during which all the English Church had answered to a single head. In this respect, if in no other, it could be argued that England was more centralised between the 660s and 730s than would ever be the case thereafter. Additionally, several dynasties (of East Anglia, Deira, Mercia and Bernicia) had each pursued, with more or less success, the chimera of universal hegemony or *imperium*. None had of course succeeded – and it was to take the Viking onslaught on England's dynasties to smooth the way for Alfred's heirs – but there can be little serious doubt that each in turn made the attempt.

The more successful of these dynasties were likewise successful in suppressing, or at least demoting, the kingships of lesser and perennially dependent kings. What Edward the Elder achieved in Mercia in the early tenth century had already been achieved centuries earlier by Mercian kings, for example, in Lindsey and among the *Wrocensæte*, as these were converted from tributary kingships to Mercian provinces (see below).

Even so, despite considerable interest in, for example, the Mercian hegemony of the eighth century,[1] most attention in recent years has focused on the individual kingships and kingdoms of the pre-Viking Age, and primarily (but not exclusively) on those which long went under the misnomer of the 'Heptarchy',[2] or small parts thereof.[3] This may be because they offer what is for long periods the most consistent unit of investigation. Moreover, most apparently sought to emphasise their own unique group identity and sense of separateness by the concoction of an individualised origins myth, several of which were recorded apocryphally, albeit only in outline, in the *Anglo-Saxon Chronicle*. It is most disturbing how often such myths resurface even today in the guise of history.[4]

Such kingships served important functions within local society: they acted as the foci of localised systems of patronage in both the secular and religious spheres, resourcing their activities perhaps from taxes in kind and certainly from renders drawn from a network of estates within the territory of the people over whom they exercised kingship; they acted too as representatives of that people in dealings with other peoples and their kings, with whom there might be contacts of many different kinds; each king was, therefore, the protector of his own people, and retained soldiers in part for that purpose; additionally he was the patron of the regional Church, which was headed by a bishop who either administered exclusively to his people (or a discrete part thereof) or to his folk alongside several others. Whichever was the case, the frontier of the kingship was the most important single factor in determining the boundaries of the diocese and royal patronage dominated the pattern of church foundation and the transfer of renders to support clerical communities and minsters. The sacral functions of pre-Christian kingship evolved into the fundamentally proto-Erastian role of the greater kings in the early Christian period.

Although many such kingships, or kingdoms, were incorporated into the larger, agglomerate Anglo-Saxon states which characterised the eighth and ninth centuries, many (particularly of the larger examples) exhibited considerable resistance both to change (in terms of boundaries, etc.) and to the loss of all regional identity. Even some comparatively small kingdoms successfully retained their own kingships and native dynasties into the ninth century (as did the East Angles). Others let go the more prominent features of separateness in return for what were presumably significant benefits, in a mutually advantageous 'trade' with politically (and militarily) dominant neighbours. For the *Wrocensæte*, for example, abandonment of their own tribal kingship, seemingly in the mid-seventh century, in favour of provincial status within the Mercian state arguably brought substantial advantages, in access to patronage as well as security from aggression and from tribute payment, for example. The name survived, however, at least into the second half of the tenth century (so even beyond the shiring of Mercia), as did the diocese of Lichfield, which was apparently focused on that ancient people (with additions), at least once the initial, single Mercian diocese had been subdivided by Archbishop Theodore. As this region belatedly emerges into history in the eleventh century, it becomes clear that the tribal and provincial system of governance and patronage had survived virtually intact (to the extent that we are qualified to comment) from the seventh century, to re-emerge as the late pre-Conquest earldom of Edwin.[5] If, as I have suggested elsewhere, the *Wrocensæte* were the Cornovii of the Iron Age and Roman period, renamed but otherwise largely unchanged, then the period over which this region exhibits a fundamental continuity in regional and tribal governance and group identity is stretched beyond a millennium.[6]

To the best of our knowledge, throughout the Anglo-Saxon period the *Wrocensæte* were embedded in a supra-tribal system of patronage and obligation – an 'overkingship' or *imperium* – the focus of which consistently lay outside their own territory (at least until the Viking Age). Again, to the best of our knowledge, this people never challenged their neighbours in the expectation that their own leader might become an 'overking'. In brief, the regional community which found expression as the *Wrocensæte* and which was itself an agglomeration of patronage systems, estates and minster parishes, existed over a long time period within a cluster of similar tribes or kingships. Although these varied enormously in size (and probably therefore also status), the pattern of clustering itself appears to have been relatively durable, focusing as it did throughout the entirety of pre-Viking history on the Mercian kings. The earliest date at which this pattern becomes visible depends on the dating of the Tribal Hidage – which I have herein already suggested belongs to the 620s.[7] Whenever it was, the cluster of kingships which characterise the primary list within that document already extends across the vast bulk of the territory of the later Mercian state which emerged from it and we are entitled to question just how well-established that pattern of clustering already was.

Nor was there anything unusual about the historical development of the *Wrocensæte*. The evolution from dependent kingship to Mercian province can be deciphered in many areas of the Midlands under a variety of centralising pressures which are but poorly understood. Similar developments can likewise be found within the mid- to late Anglo-Saxon kingdoms of Wessex and Northumbria. Regional *imperia* or 'overkingships' were in each instance the starting point from which the larger, mid- to late Anglo-Saxon kingdoms evolved. These clusterings of dependencies under the leadership of an 'overking' exhibit more signs of flux than do the local kingships themselves, as regards both boundaries and foci. Even so, their patterning is far from random. On the contrary, comparatively few of the thirty to forty kingships known to us seem ever to have sought *imperium*, and recurring clusters of kingships exhibit a strong tendency to act in consort when either rejecting or affirming the hegemony either of one of themselves or of an outsider. Regional *imperia* were, therefore, an important part of the political and psychological fabric of early England. They conditioned the advance of Christianity. They conditioned too the development of certain kingships and the extinction of others, as the total numbers declined.

This chapter will, therefore, open by attempting to establish as a sort of benchmark the extent, objectives and mutual interactions of the several regional *imperia* as these existed immediately after the battle by the River Trent in *c.* 679, which brought to an end (if arguably by inadvertence) a duel for universal *imperium* in erstwhile Roman Britain between the two greatest Anglian dynasts of the day, Oswiu's heir, Ecgfrith of Northumbria, and Æthelred of Mercia, Penda's son and Ecgfrith's own brother-in-law. Thereafter will follow a brief examination of each of the historic subdivisions of Britain, focusing on their constituencies and, once again, on their mutual interaction prior to *c.* 680. Particular attention will be attached to evidence for the very early history of these same regional groupings of peoples in the early seventh century, and even before, and the tendency for such clusters of kingships to behave in ways which interlock one with another over very long periods.

Archbishop Theodore's peace

It is a matter of fact that two great *imperia* or 'overkingships' dominated Britain in the late seventh and eighth centuries – those headed by the kings of Mercia and Northumbria. The land frontier of their respective areas of influence apparently changed little, if at all, during this period. The eastern third of this boundary was probably a compromise which may actually have been hammered out as part of the settlement negotiated between the two warring dynasties with Archbishop Theodore as umpire, following the battle by the River Trent. It is likely that this agreement finally conceded the long-disputed province of Lindsey to Mercia; Elmet was presumably secured to Deira and Northumbria;[8] Hatfield was either to be Northumbrian in its entirety or divided between the two.[9]

Theodore held a synod at the 'plain of Hatfield', within twelve months of the treaty. Given that Bede had only hitherto referred to the northern Hatfield in his *Historia*, there is a strong *prima facie* case for supposing this synod to have occurred at Hatfield in Yorkshire rather than Hertfordshire,[10] in which case it should arguably be associated with Theodore's role in separating the two warring dynasties. King Ecgfrith's name occurs at the head of the list of kings whose authority and protection (*imperium*) were invoked in the subsequent account of proceedings (which Bede is generally believed to have quoted from, practically verbatim). Ecgfrith's name occurs quite alone, even before notice of the relevant indiction, and so is carefully segregated from mention of the other three rulers named. The four are grouped as if paired equals (which, in terms of raw power, they were certainly not). The special treatment accorded Ecgfrith looks intentional and suggests favoured treatment as regards his dignity by the churchmen responsible.

If the territory of Hatfield had indeed been divided, or if it had been just separated *de novo* from Lindsey, then this was probably the most sensitive point along what had for generations been a much-disputed boundary between the spheres of influence of Bernician and Mercian kings. The siting of the synod here within a year or so of the great battle by the River Trent and certainly within a twelvemonth of the subsequent, church-negotiated peace agreement was clearly no accident: it was presumably designed to reinforce that peace and the role of the archbishop himself in its formulation. More particularly, its occurrence within the frontier of Ecgfrith's much reduced territory, and under his much-publicised protection and patronage, emphasised and was surely intended to emphasise the mutual interests of the archbishop and the northern 'overking'.

To that issue we will return. In the Pennines and to the west, the Northumbrian/Mercian frontier was probably less a matter of conflict: the very name of the Mersey (*(ge)mære-ea*: 'boundary-river') recalls its frontier role; although armies did on occasion breach this boundary (as *c.* 615 for the battle of Chester and perhaps in 642 for the battle of *Maserfelth*, but see p. 221 below), there is no evidence that kings on either side attempted to take direct control of territory beyond the river until the putative seizure of Lancashire as far as the Ribble by West Saxon kings in the tenth century.[11]

The resolution of disputes over marginal provinces was an important and long-lasting feature of this peace treaty, although there is no reason to imagine that Ecgfrith – who was the loser – was in the long term reconciled to a solution which was clearly contrary to his own interests. This was not, however, the sole area of negotiation: Bede remarked on the agreement reached between the two principals to offer and accept *wergild* for the death of Ecgfrith's brother (and Æthelred of Mercia's brother-in-law), the prince Ælfwine.[12] More to the point, reference to kings other than Ecgfrith and Æthelred, and use of their regnal years as dating mechanisms, implies that other parts of Anglo-Saxon England were then recognised by both parties as lying outside the hegemony of either of the great 'overkings'. Given that both Ecgfrith and Wulfhere (Æthelred's brother and predecessor), had earlier competed for, and exercised hegemony over, the bulk of England,[13] universal recognition as 'overking' must have been a legitimate aspiration of both principals at the battle by the Trent. The battle was clearly sufficient in scale to attach substantial kudos to the victor – such as we have already established was a normal precondition of widespread *imperium* in England. This was a battle between two kings each of whom already enjoyed regional *imperium* and a military reputation,[14] so effectively a battle of the Titans. Ecgfrith obviously survived the battle and retained the ability to defend himself and even to attack his neighbours,[15] so the conflict was clearly not a total disaster for him. He retained in addition considerable influence at the Mercian court, in part through his sister, King Æthelred's queen.[16] His subsequent autonomy from Mercian supremacy may, therefore, be comprehensible. It is, however, a legitimate question why Mercian *imperium* remained so tightly circumscribed, despite Æthelred's victory, when it might have been expected to have thereafter immediately encompassed all England below the Humber. Lindsey, even if it came with the larger and more profitable part of Hatfield, seems a poor reward for such a victory, when one considers that Æthelred's brother and predecessor had sought only a few years before to levy soldiers from the southern kingdoms, so presumably to establish hegemony thereover, and might have succeeded more completely had he not been worsted in battle by Ecgfrith. Æthelred's devastation of Kent in 676, his own first regnal year, confirms his interest in the south.[17] If Archbishop Theodore's peace successfully contained Mercian ambitions to universal hegemony in the south, then it was necessarily more subtle than has generally been credited.[18]

The two kings who were additionally named in the record of the synod of Hatfield were Eadwulf, King of the East Angles, and Hlothhere, King of Kent, both of whom held powerful kingships which lay within what had once been the *imperium* of King Æthelberht of Kent (Hlothhere's great-grandfather). Definition of the influence of the principal parties to Theodore's treaty over southern England was an issue which necessarily interested Archbishop Theodore and his immediate patron, Hlothhere of Kent, at least as much as it did either Ecgfrith or Æthelred. Indeed, it was as much in Theodore's interest as King Ecgfrith's to exclude Mercian domination from the (presumably) rich and well-populated south: Ecgfrith had as good and very obvious reasons to fear the political, economic and military effects of Mercian domination as Æthelred had to pursue it, while Theodore could expect a resurgence of Mercian influence in the south to stifle his own independence of action as supreme head of the insular Church and to weigh heavily on Hlothhere himself, whose alliances had long been with the northern enemies of Mercia (see below). The Mercian acquisition of archdiocesan status for Lichfield in the next century was the natural consequence of Kentish resistance to just such Mercian political supremacy two generations later.

In 664 King Oswiu had delivered the Anglo-Irish Church – which his dynasty had created and patronised in the north for three decades – into the arms of Canterbury. His reward was a major share in royal patronage over the archdiocese and influence over preferment to what was then an empty throne. He probably anticipated close co-operation with a new English primate, who could not have been unmindful of the vast debt he owed the Bernician king, only to be baulked by the unexpected death of his preferred candidate on arrival at Rome. Notwithstanding this, his eventual successor, Archbishop Theodore, though a foreigner who owed nothing to Oswiu as regards the appointment itself, seems to have been sensitive to the obligations owed by his office to the Bernician dynasty and consistently lent his support to Northumbria in its struggle with the Mercians.

That the leading kings of the south should, in 679–80, have remained free of Mercian control – even despite the Mercian victory over Ecgfrith – was therefore fundamental to Theodore's interests as archbishop. The naming of Eadwulf and Hlothhere in the official record of the Council of Hatfield both confirms and even advertises their freedom from Mercian domination. Such suggests that the policies of Theodore and his political allies triumphed in the peace accord, despite their failure on the field of battle: Ecgfrith lost to his rival the very minimum of territories and influence that was appropriate in the circumstances and he could even claim a moral victory in the payment of wergild for his brother, so could salvage much of his own pride. His attacks on Ireland and the far north in subsequent years suggest that the Bernician king was busy extending his own list of tributaries and accruing new treasure, so increasing his capacity to reward service. These wars additionally provided his army with experience and morale-boosting victories and (until his own sudden, unexpected and disastrous death) enveloped himself with a successful, martial reputation. These several factors will have encouraged young noblemen from diverse backgrounds to offer themselves for service in his court in expectation of quick rewards from the hand of a generous, successful and wealthy patron.[19] The entire exercise is best understood as a rebuilding process preparatory to a renewed assault on Mercia in pursuit of universal *imperium*.

Reference to kings of Kent and East Anglia in the record of Hatfield cannot be due solely to the (anonymous) author's desire to record all those 'kings to whose realms the attending bishops belonged',[20] since this was apparently a synod of the entire Roman Church in Britain to which the bishop of the East Saxons,[21] for example, was presumably also summoned. On the contrary, it seems likely that those named were either themselves *imperium*-wielding kings or, at the least, kings who were not subject to the *imperium* of another – so kings whose protection was of equal status, one with another. The recognition of kings of Kent and of the East Angles alongside Northumbria and Mercia therefore reflects a peace accord negotiated with numerous political interests and pressure groups in mind, among whom the Mercians – despite their success in battle – had been unable to secure what they might legitimately have considered to have been the full fruits of their victory.

Hlothhere, at least, has some claim to regional 'overkingship' at about this date: a law code issued jointly by himself and his nephew Eadric is most unlikely to have been the product of a court which recognised the hegemony of some outsider;[22] indeed, the precedent offered by King Æthelberht's laws would imply that *imperium*-wielding status was a normal prerequisite of the formulation and publication of a law code. Æthelberht had been the last king of the Kentings to exercise *imperium* over his neighbours and he was similarly the last Kentish king who is previously known to have produced a set of laws. When Hlothhere and his nephew fell out, Eadric led a South Saxon army against his uncle – implying that he was a member of a royal dynasty of status enough to attract a significant subking to his interest.[23] He may well have been the king of western Kent or some other lesser part of the total Kentish kingship, but subordinate to Hlothhere at Canterbury, since the latter was the first named in the preface to the law code and was the elder, so probably senior in rank. That Eadric had some such stake in the Kentish kingship is implicit in their joint sponsorship of laws, since the circumstances of Hlothhere's death (on 6th February 685), while wounds received in battle against his nephew were being dressed, imply that joint rule after their conflict is most improbable.[24] The joint, but probably unequal, rule of Hlothhere and Eadric can be compared to the association of various Bernician 'overkings' and subkings of Deira,[25] Penda's construction of a Middle Anglian subkingship for his son Peada,[26] and (in the ninth century) subkings of Kent and its near neighbours drawn from the immediate family of the West Saxon kings.[27]

The native dynasty in Sussex was headed by Æthelwealh, who had been a close political ally of Wulfhere of Mercia (died 675): indeed, Æthelwealh had received baptism at Wulfhere's court and been rewarded for his co-operation with the provinces of Wight and *Meonwara* so the Mercian king may well have attempted to rule the south-east via a client king of the South Saxons. Friction between Mercia and Kent is certainly evidenced by King Æthelred's ravaging of the latter in 676, which was the first full year of his reign: given that Ecgfrith was at this stage in the ascendant, it may be that the new Mercian king was attacking the weaker of his two principal enemies – Kent and Northumbria – in the opening engagement of his reign, with the intention of reasserting his brother's erstwhile influence in the deep south preparatory to challenging Ecgfrith himself for universal *imperium*.

Æthelwealh's chequered career as a subking came to a violent end, probably in 686, when he was killed by Cædwalla,[28] king of the Gewisse, or West Saxons, and the man responsible for uniting the Isle of Wight with Wessex.[29] His own earlier tenure of the 'Jutish' territories of *Meonwara* and Wight under Mercian 'overkingship' may have played some part in stimulating this West Saxon attack. It is, however, surely relevant that this event occurred in the year of King Eadric's death in Kent, after which Bede noted that 'usurping or foreign kings plundered the kingdom' (of Kent), until King Wihtred (son of Ecgbert, so Eadric's brother) succeeded in establishing himself (about 690).[30]

Hlothhere's death in civil war had already coincided with Cædwalla's seizure of the West Saxon kingship from a far less warlike predecessor and may have been a significant factor affecting that event; Eadric's death led to a crisis in Kent which lasted several years and which coincided with Cædwalla's intervention among the South Saxons (*c.* 686) and conquest of Wight (*c.* 687/8). It seems unlikely that this Kentish crisis can have been exclusive of Cædwalla's activities (rather it is generally supposed that he was responsible for it) and it probably reflects the savage transfer of *imperium* over the south from the Kentish kings to Cædwalla,[31] resistance to which was exploited by the Mercians who then took over control of the south-east as far as the Thames (so including Essex).

In 675, Abbot Eorcenwald of Chertsey, who was perhaps a relative of Hlothhere, was consecrated Bishop of London by Archbishop Theodore. If his origins were royal as well as Kentish, this appointment may indicate that London – so the East Saxons, Surrey and Middlesex – then lay under Kentish control. He was, however, named in the preamble to the law code issued by Cædwalla's successor, Ine of Wessex (688–726), as 'my bishop', suggesting that tutelage over these peoples had fallen to the West Saxon kings at latest by 693 (the year of Eorcenwald's death). This factor, as much as Ine's responsibility for a law code, supports the view that he was by then an *imperium*-wielding king in the deep south. Kent, however, ultimately lay beyond his reach, having its own native king in Wihtred, who was to be the last of the Kentish kings whose law code has survived.

Consideration of Hlothhere's position therefore suggests he was 'overking' over parts at least of southern England in 679–80. The interlocking histories of Kent, the East Saxons, the South Saxons and the West Saxons during the 670s, 680s and 690s suggests that this 'overkingship' extended at times across all these peoples and their lesser neighbours (such as Wight). Kentish influence had been contested by the South Saxons, who fronted Mercian interests; it eventually gave way to West Saxon hegemony in *c.* 685/6, but none of these initiatives appears to have been securely founded or beyond challenge from other quarters. Kent, at least, resisted West Saxon control in the late 680s and 690s, only to fall under the domination of Mercia during the eighth century, even to the extent of being forced to accept Mercian princes as subkings.

A characteristic of this period in the south was, therefore, the absence of consistent leadership from any one kingship – the persistent domination of the Midlands and North by the Mercian and Bernician kingships, respectively, offers a clear contrast. Its great size always rendered Wessex the likeliest kingdom to establish a more permanent southern *imperium* – as it eventually did – but its kings enjoyed comparatively little success outside their own immediate vicinity during the seventh century.

A significant factor in the struggle for control of the south was intervention from outside. The 670s had opened with the Mercian king, Wulfhere, apparently favouring the South Saxon king over against his neighbours. His purpose was possibly to dominate the region through a loyal and self-interested satellite but one whose own resources alone would have been inadequate as a basis for controlling England south of the Thames; the Kentish kings owed the longevity and sustained robustness of their challenge in part to the presence of the archbishop – whose jurisdiction over other bishops and influence with kings gave their immediate patrons an extraordinary advantage in the struggle for power – but additionally to their long-running co-operation with the Northumbrians.

To illustrate this last point, Hlothhere was the son of King Eorcenberht (died 664) and his East Anglian bride, Queen Seaxburh (died *c.* 700), so the nephew by marriage of King Ecgfrith of Northumbria, via his marriage (by 666) to Æthelthryth, daughter of King Anna. His brother, King Egberht, had been a close political associate and satellite of King Oswiu. In the very year in which he succeeded to the throne (673), King Ecgfrith acted in person as the protector of Archbishop Theodore's synod at Hertford, so advertising his own interest and influence in the sensitive, erstwhile Mercian dependency of Middle Anglia and his own claim to *imperium* throughout southern Britain.

Ecgfrith's marriage to Æthelthryth arguably reflected an attempt by King Oswiu, his father, to provide his dynasty with a power base in the Fenland from which to oppose the revival of Mercian influence there: Æthelthryth was the widow of *princeps* Tondberht of the South Gyrwe so presumably well-provided with dower in the region,[32] as well as being a princess of the East Anglian royal house. Her failure to produce him heirs, allied perhaps to the collapse of Northumbrian territorial ambitions in the southern Fenland during the 670s, led ultimately to Ecgfrith's agreement to Æthelthryth's withdrawal from the Northumbrian court to Coldingham Abbey. She, however, apparently still retained an interest in her first husband's land and was appointed abbess of Ely only a year later. Her presence in the region as the ruler of a rich house cannot have done Ecgfrith any harm: indeed, she may have provided him with an effective viceregent for his own interests there. That it was her sister Seaxburh, Hlothhere's mother, who succeeded to her abbacy at her death reinforces these connections between the several dynasties of Northumbria, East Anglia and Kent and the extent to which the political ambitions of their several kings had become interdependent.

It may have been this connection which led Hlothhere to ransom Imma, a thegn of the Northumbrian prince Ælfwine's following but formally of the household of Æthelthryth herself, following his capture by the Mercians at the battle of Trent (679) and subsequent sale into the slave market at London.[33] The deed certainly displays his political preference for, and support of, the Northumbrian cause. Whether or not, Ecgfrith's 'divorce' of his overly saintly queen does not seem to have disturbed the general accord between Kent and Northumbria – indeed, it may have provided both dynasties with an opportunity to strengthen it. Ecgfrith subsequently married one Iurminburh (in or before 678): her ancestry is unknown but it has been suggested that her name implies a royal Kentish origin,[34] in which case she was probably close kin to Hlothhere himself. If King Centwine of the West Saxons (676–85) married her sister, Hlothhere may have been using marriage as a means both of cementing the crucial but unequal relationship between himself and his powerful political ally, Ecgfrith of Northumbria, and of his potentially dangerous (and possibly tributary) neighbour, the king of Wessex. His relationship with Ecgfrith was clearly both cordial and mutually supportive. Such a conclusion leaves us with little option but to assume that he and his dynasty were far less favoured by the Mercians and had good reason to oppose any extension of Mercian power in consequence of their victory in battle *c.* 679. While marriages between the royal families of Northumbria and Mercia certainly limit the extent to which marital links can be assumed to reflect political accord during this period, these associations do appear both consistent and to mutual advantage.

Ecgfrith's eclipse by the Mercians in *c.* 679 may have been as much a threat to Eadwulf, Hlothhere and Centwine as it was to himself but Theodore's negotiation of a settlement preserved their interests as well as his own and rendered Æthelred's victory comparatively hollow. Both Hlothhere and Centwine, however, lost their kingdoms in or about 685 (Centwine through retirement into a monastery), which was the year in which Ecgfrith was himself killed invading Pictland. Hlothhere had already died before Ecgfrith marched to his doom but the synchronism of their respective fates is unlikely to have been entirely coincidental. Centwine, in particular, had been an undistinguished king of the West Saxons who had apparently already lost control of the episcopal seat at Dorchester to the Mercians.[35] Dynastic and political crises in Northumbria and Kent now exposed him to a serious challenge to his own throne from the royal West Saxon émigré, Cædwalla, an ambitious war leader who presumably represented the more aggressive and expansionist aspirations of the West Saxons. In the new circumstances heralded by Northumbria's disarray and the collapse of her influence in the south, it was apparently Cædwalla's policies which attracted the wider support among the West Saxons. The fates of Ecgfrith, Hlothhere, Eadric and Centwine may, therefore, have been closely linked.

Eadwulf of East Anglia was similarly associated with the Northumbrian dynasty: he was the son of Hereswith, King Edwin's great-niece and sister of St. Hild (abbess of the royal abbey and sepulchre at Whitby which was the scene of King Oswiu's famous synod).[36] Through this connection he was closely related to Ecgfrith, who was Edwin's grandson on his mother's side. Eadwulf's family had resisted Mercian domination with some consistency (if less success) during the mid-seventh century,[37] and were obviously threatened by any expansion of Mercian interests into the Fenland or its borders. The marriage of Æthelthryth to a prince of the South Gyrwe may reflect East Anglian attempts to secure control of territory which appears in the primary list of the Tribal Hidage – so was perhaps an early Mercian dependency – but which separated East Anglia from two minor kingships (Bilmiga, Widerigga) which occur on the secondary list, implying links with East Anglia and the southern *imperium* (Figure 5). Both Æthelthryth's marriages probably occurred during the period when Northumbrian kings were capable of exercising some influence in the region, since she seems to have been still of child-bearing age during the 670s. It may well have suited King Eadwulf that Ecgfrith should share his concern to stem Mercian domination in this area. Ecgfrith had probably been king in Lindsey – another province touching the Fenland – up to *c.* 679 and the battle by the Trent, and this division of the Fenland margins between Mercia and Northumbria was perhaps also welcome to the East Anglians since it brought potential allies against the Mercian interest in Middle Anglia within effective striking range. Co-operation between the East Angles and Northumbrians against the Mercian interest in Middle Anglia therefore seems to have been a significant feature of the period.

A political accord between the Bernicians, the East Angles and the Kentings was, therefore, a natural one of considerable value to all parties and it is unsurprising that it should have been fortified by a series of dynastic marriages. The common enemy was Mercia and, even with Ecgfrith defeated in *c.* 679, the alliance was sufficiently cohesive, militarily powerful and diplomatically influential to deny the Mercians the overall 'overkingship' that they presumably sought: they were constrained by a deep-rooted political accord between Ecgfrith, his relatives and allies in East Anglia and Kent and the Archbishop of all England. Only with Ecgfrith's death in 685 were Mercia – and Wessex under its new king – freed from the constraints which that alliance had long imposed.

With Northumbria thereafter incapable of effective intervention in the south, Mercian demands were resisted with or without success by these same kingships. In general terms, the great Mercian kings of the eighth century seem to have obtained considerable influence over England south of the Thames, without ever succeeding in swallowing up the entire region. The size, potential wealth and military manpower of Wessex was such that leadership of the south against Mercia would eventually fall to it by default: whether it should be credited or not, the *Anglo-Saxon Chronicle* recalled the

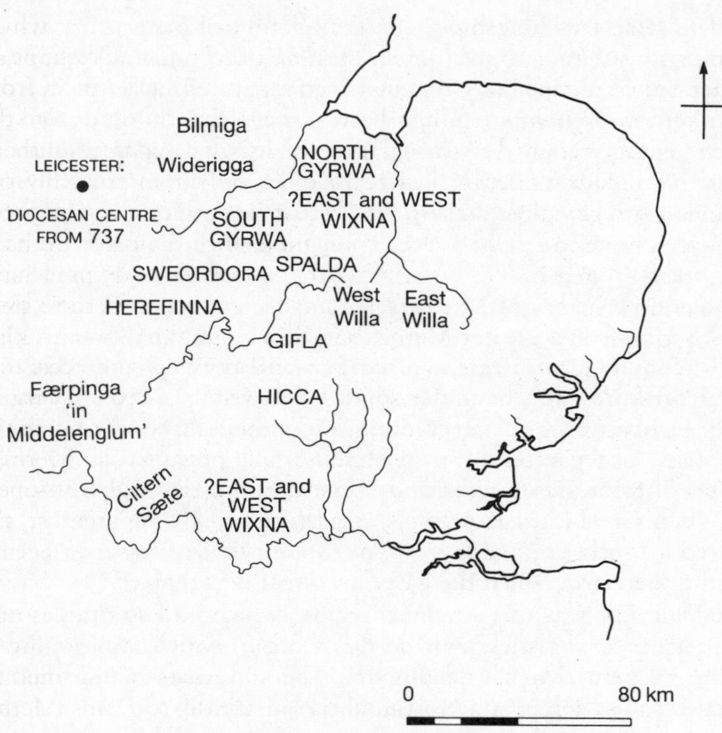

Figure 5 The frontier provinces between the Midland and Southern hegemonies (as the Tribal Hidage), some of which were amalgamated into the subordinate kingship (and eventual diocese) of the Middle Angles in the mid-seventh century. Capitals indicate names on the primary list and lower case names on the secondary list. Several names which may be relevant are omitted (see Figures 3 and 4) and both possible locations for the Wixna are included.

crisis of Mercian control which followed Cœnwulf's death in 819, noting in the year 823 West Saxon victory over the Mercians, a West Saxon invasion of Kent and its satellites (Surrey, Sussex and Essex), an appeal to Wessex for protection from East Anglia and eventual victory by the East Angles over a Mercian counter attack.[38]

The same two kingships – East Anglia and Kent – were, therefore, both still then to the fore in south-east England and capable of independent action and regional leadership. What is more, the southern *imperium* which had been Æthelberht's in the early seventh century retained a strong sense of its own separate identity *vis-à-vis* outside influence, despite the often violent, internal competitions for regional leadership which that had so long encouraged. It is legitimate to emphasise the robustness of the south in the face of Mercia's hegemonic ambitions: the ancient kingdoms of the Midland periphery of Mercia seem not to have resisted their own absorption into a greater Mercia but, despite military defeats, periodic conquest, alien rule and indefatigable political and ecclesiastical pressures, much of the south effectively resisted that same process of absorption and colonisation. That it did so says much for the sense of separateness from Mercia which prevailed in the kingdoms of Kent, East Anglia and Wessex, and their neighbours.[39]

When capable of expressing a preference, all apparently preferred a southern *imperium* – that of Ecgbert of Wessex – to that of the Mercians. When the Mercian threat was replaced by that of the Danes, it was this southern region, which had so much more experience of resisting outside domination, which was to prove more resilient than its neighbours. The conquests of the unitary kingships of Mercia and Northumbria led rapidly to Danish domination of both regions. The difficult experience of the south during the previous two centuries may arguably have contributed to the obstinacy of its opposition to Scandinavian domination in the late ninth century and conditioned acceptance by local communities of the extraordinary social and economic cost of its survival under King Alfred.

The Danish conquests certainly highlight the geography of contemporary English politics: the core of the Northumbrian kingdom was taken over in consequence of a single battle and a Danish kingdom established at York; the Mercian kingship was destroyed, its last incumbent taking refuge in Rome, and it was replaced by a knot of Danish lordships centred in the Mercian heartland of the Trent valley, with at least one dependent English kingship elsewhere within the old Mercian kingdom;[40] the kingdom of Guthrum was only limited to East Anglia and its immediate environs once his attempt to take over the kingship of Wessex (by then all England south of the Thames) had been repulsed by Alfred in the late 870s

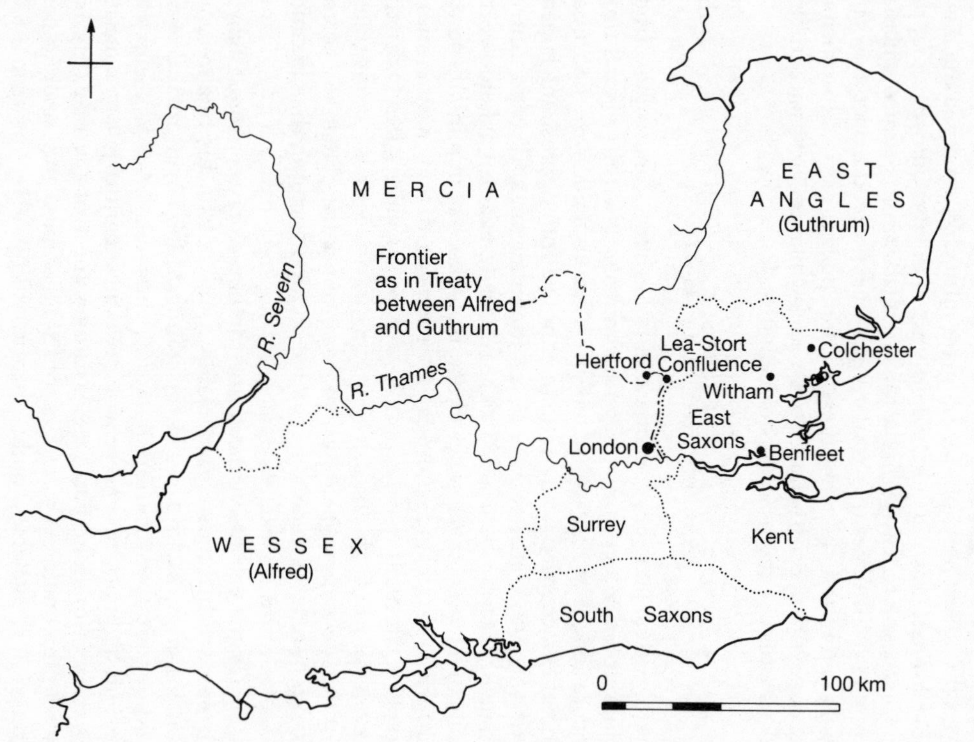

Figure 6 Southern England and the Danes: Alfred, king of the West Saxons and the assorted south-eastern kingdoms, struggled primarily against the Danish king Guthrum, whose kingship was focused on the East Angles but who attempted the conquest of Wessex. Places marked indicate conflicts which are likely to post-date the extant treaty between these two kings.

(Figure 6); a territory defined long since in large part by the southern *imperium* of King Æthelberht seems, therefore, to have been his primary objective.

These recurring clusters of peoples stand out very clearly by the ninth century but it is of more purpose in the present context to trace the origins of these interlocking groups of kingships back into the earliest decades of English history, or even beyond. Our purpose hereinafter must be to test their antiquity and cohesion so as to develop some vision of their origins and interaction, and so establish their position in the geo-politics of Anglo-Saxon England.[41] First, however, it may be appropriate to recall what is by far the earliest of these regional 'overkingships' in Britain which is known to history – that of the kings of Gwynedd over the British kings – and test the robustness of that political system, or vision, through time. British kings have so far played little part in this discussion but they should not be ignored.

A British 'overkingship' in the west

Little discussion has occurred this century concerning 'overkingship' in Wales and its satellites: indeed, it is the political fragmentation of Wales which has been emphasised, with Gwynedd generally accorded no more than a 'hoped for . . . presiding superiority'.[42] Although various source materials make recognition of some interaction between Wales and Anglo-Saxon England practically obligatory, this has been kept to an absolute minimum and the histories of England and Wales written as if they were in most respects mutually exclusive.[43] It will be suggested here that the extent to which the British kingships in the west were integrated within a wider political system has been understated: so too the vigour and persistence of a regional hierarchy among the kingships of the Britons themselves.

By far the earliest evidence for the latter derives from Gildas's assessment of the five British kings (or 'tyrants'): his treatment of Maglocunus, the 'dragon of the island', differs both qualitatively and quantitatively from that of the other four kings to the extent that his higher status and general political superiority seem a matter of reasonable inference.[44] Gildas's awareness of the disparity between the military resources of Maglocunus and some other, greater *dux* ('general') implies that he recognised the existence of an unequal relationship between Maglocunus and a Saxon king – presumably the individual whom he twice identified (in reference to the British clergy who profited by his patronage) as 'their father the devil'.[45] Whatever the precise nature of this relationship, therefore, Gildas's evaluation of the comparative strength of each implies some interaction between them, conditioned presumably by the *foedus* (treaty) which was then still in force and which had delivered peace between Briton and Saxon throughout Gildas's own adult life.[46]

There are insufficient source materials available for the bulk of the sixth century to trace the development of this British 'overkingship' over the following generations but there are signs that it continued to flourish: when Procopius provided his eastern Mediterranean readership with an apparently Frankish-derived excursus concerning a war between the Varni (in Germany) and the Angles (in Britain), he opened with a brief introduction to *Brittia* – the island of Britain – which included the opinion that:[47]

> The island of *Brittia* is inhabited by three very numerous nations, each having one king over it. And the names of these nations are *Angili*, *Frissones*, and *Brittones*, the last being named from the island itself.

If this reflects contemporary perceptions of Britain, *c.* 540–550, at the court of King Theudebald, then it suggests that a single British king was then recognised as the superior of the remainder, at least outside Britain. The precedent provided by Gildas suggests, but does not prove, that this king was the ruler of Gwynedd. Procopius was, however, far removed from Britain and his evidence is at best hearsay. Its admixture with a mass of outright myth must caution all those who look to it for insights into the political structure of contemporary Britain.[48]

It is with the successive kingships of Iago, Cadfan, Cadwallon and Cadafael ap Cynfedw in Gwynedd that this Welsh or British 'overkingship' emerges into history. According to the *Annales Cambriae*,[49] Iago ap Beli died in the year of the battle of Chester. He may, therefore, have been one of those British kings responsible for the protection of the synod of the entire British Church which had occurred at Chester, and so probably marginally inside the territory of the *Wrocensæte*, a (probably British) tributary kingship within the Mercian hegemony.[50] Whether or not these assumptions are correct, the synod should be seen as an event of major political significance: the demands made of the British clergy by Augustine of Canterbury had important implications for relations between the various kings and 'overkings' of the Britons and the Anglo-Saxons; they were probably seen by others as an act of calculated political aggression by King Æthelberht of Kent, in pursuit of influence in, and authority over, his British neighbours. Iago cannot have been impervious to such considerations although his response is not directly documented.

It has often been suggested that Iago died at the battle of Chester, but the author of the *Annales Cambriae* does not suggest this, merely noting his death in the same year: it was Selyf ap Cynan, the king of Powys, who was reputed to have died in the battle itself. The matter is obviously beyond proof but it could have been the death of Iago, the dominant king in Wales – so the temporary disruption of his military leadership of the Welsh – that precipitated Æthelfrith's opportunistic invasion of the Mercian hegemony in that very year. Æthelfrith's purpose was presumably to act against those supporting Edwin, his rival for the throne of the Deiri who had by then been married to the daughter of Cearl of Mercia for most of a decade and so was presumably under the latter's ultimate protection. Æthelfrith had waited for about ten years before invading and he now fought at least one major battle, defeating a Welsh army at the battle of Chester.[51] The death of the king of Gwynedd may, therefore, have represented a shift in the balance of power in his favour and against the Mercian interest sufficient to offer him a window of opportunity and so trigger a violent clash between two of the major English 'overkingships' of the day. If so, Iago was presumably a superior king within Wales and allied to Mercia – but the circularity of such an argument is obvious.

Iago was succeeded by his son Cadfan, Cadwallon's father, who apparently reigned for about a decade. It is this king who was commemorated a quarter century or so later by an inscribed stone at Llangadwaladr, a church reputed to have been founded by his grandson, Cadwaladr. The inscription on this monument is exceptional as regards its language, its message and its deployment of superlatives – this last something which is otherwise reserved on such monuments almost exclusively for God: 'Cadfan King, wisest and most renowned of kings'.[52] The language in which this claim was made suggests that Cadwaladr was concerned to claim for his grandfather, albeit retrospectively, primacy over the other Welsh kings. If so it seems unlikely that his efforts were entirely disinterested: they were perhaps one element in his own attempt to restore his dynasty's authority in Gwynedd, and within Wales as a whole (see below). There is, therefore, considerable potential for a propagandist element in this inscription but it need not have been entirely inappropriate to Cadfan's actual status.

Cadwallon

Bede introduced Cadwallon in a passage which opened with an elegy to Edwin's reign, in which he described him as ruling *gloriosissime* over the *gentes Anglorum et Brettonum* for seventeen years, for six of which he was additionally a 'soldier in the kingdom of Christ'.[53] Edwin's position was, therefore, in the context of Bede's own rhetoric, morally unassailable and his rule entirely virtuous. In contrast, Cadwallon *rex Brettonum* 'rebelled' against Edwin in alliance with Penda, a pagan prince of the Mercian people (*gens*).[54] Association with a pagan Mercian, however brave, was damaging to Cadwallon's reputation and reduced any credit he might otherwise have been accorded by Bede's audience on account of his Christianity. That Christianity was in any case of a kind which Bede repeatedly dismissed as heretical. The contrast with Edwin was even more damning: whereas the latter was acclaimed in language comparable to that with which Pope Gregory had, by letter, addressed King Æthelberht,[55] and associated with Christ as if one of his household thegns, Cadwallon was depicted as the antithesis of the good king and as an immoral rebel both against the virtuous 'overking' and also, by extension, against Christ himself. Through this portrayal, Bede sustained the premise with which he opened his *Historia*, that the English (particularly the Bernicians) – not the Britons – were God's chosen people so the rightful rulers of Britain.

Cadwallon was, therefore, depicted as morally damnable: he 'made very great slaughter among the church and people of the Northumbrians'; he was crueller even than the pagan Penda; despite having the name and profession of Christianity, he was a barbarian in his heart and habits, who spared neither women nor children; he displayed the cruelty of a wild beast and tortured his victims to death, showing no respect even for Christians among the English. Gildas's animal imagery as applied to the Saxons may well have acted as a spur to Bede's portrayal of the Britons.[56] He broke off his attack at this point to direct yet another generalised accusation against British attitudes to English Christianity, so betraying the contemporaneity of his comments concerning Cadwallon's achievements. The entire passage is, therefore, clearly shaped by imperatives which derive from, and sustain, Bede's very specific perceptions of the relative virtues of the English and the Britons *vis-à-vis* God and it is with this fundamental (but contemporary and highly rhetorical) message that he closed book two of his *Historia*.

In the opening chapter of book three, Bede resumed his treatment of Cadwallon but, once again, he focused not on the achievements of the Welsh king but on the Northumbrian kingship. At this crisis the Deiran and Bernician dynasties both attempted to secure their interests under apostate kings. Their prompt destruction by Cadwallon provided Bede with an object lesson in the fate appropriate to prominent apostates; herein the Welsh king was necessarily portrayed as an agent of God. Yet Bede characteristically denied him any moral advantage therefrom: the divine vengeance of which he was the agent was recognised as just but Cadwallon's agency exhibited *impia manu* – 'unrighteous force' – so denying him the credit which might otherwise have been his.

Thereafter Bede maintained a consistent and virulent hostility to his achievements and gloried in his eventual defeat and death:

> he possessed the Northumbrian provinces for an entire year not as a victorious king but destroyed and tore [them] to pieces with terrible bloodshed as if a savage tyrant.

The use of thesis and antithesis stresses his condemnation: so too does his characterisation as *infandus* – 'unutterable', a term which is cognate with the *nefandus* by which Gildas had qualified his only literal reference to the Saxons in the *De Excidio*.[57] There are several hints in this passage that Bede was consciously and systematically reversing the relative virtues of Britons (God's own people) and Saxons (brutal, unspeakable, barbaric, immoral and suited to animal metaphors) which he had found in the *De Excidio*. Certainly Bede adopted the Bible-derived allegory of King David for Oswald – the Christian, Bernician king responsible for Cadwallon's death. Cadwallon's boast that his great army was irresistible was, perhaps, an allusion to the Philistine champion, Goliath.[58]

Cadwallon was, therefore, depicted by Bede as a figure who was little short of demonic: he was the antithesis of King Lucius, that British king of yore who had been obedient to the divinely sanctioned Roman *imperium* and to the papacy;[59] he was similarly but more immediately depicted as the antithesis of the righteous and divinely sanctioned, Christian Northumbrian kings of his own day, whose God-given duty it was to rule the Britons; and by his rebellion he became a rebel against Christ as much as against His agent (King Edwin) and his actions could be placed outside the normal parameters of Christian behaviour. It was he who was bestial and barbaric – not the Saxons as Gildas had averred – and his end was implicitly compared with that of various powerful heathens who had been worsted by the Israelites and their champions in the Old Testament. Like the British rulers with whom Gildas had been familiar, Cadwallon was a *tyrannus*. His moral status was that of his entire race, all of whom were 'barbarians'. So did Bede exploit the career of Cadwallon to sustain his own reversal of the providential treatment of Saxons and Britons which he had found in Gildas's work.

So much for Bede's perception of Cadwallon: what of the historical figure and his role both within Wales and without? Cadwallon apparently succeeded his father Cadfan *c.* 625. Less than a decade later, Cadwallon and a Mercian nobleman – later King Penda – conspired successfully to destroy King Edwin and his household at Hatfield.[60] Despite his invective, Bede's treatment of Cadwallon is sufficiently detailed to enable us to establish with some degree of certainty his status and ambitions as a Welsh king.

First, the evidence for his tributary status *vis-à-vis* King Edwin. According to Bede:[61]

> king [Edwin's] earthly power had grown, so that unlike any of the English before him, he received under his *dicio* ['rule'] *Brittania* to its furthest limits, not only the provinces frequented by themselves [the English] but also those of the Britons. He even *subiugavit* ['annexed'] the islands of Man and Anglesey to the *imperium* of the English.

In Bede's mind there was clearly a close and causal relationship between Edwin's imminent conversion and the expansion of his power to incorporate both Anglo-Saxons and Britons. This was portrayed as part of God's great plan for His people. Beyond the rhetoric, however, there should be no doubt that his superiority was recognised, even before his conversion in 627, in Gwynedd. That Bede singled out Edwin's *imperium* over Anglesey and Man for special comment may reflect the dialectical necessity of sustaining his allegory of Roman rule of Britain as a precedent appropriate to English domination:[62] just as the Romans secured *imperium* over the islands around and even beyond Britain, so too was it necessary that the greater English kings should be seen to exercise similar rule. It may also, however, reflect a valid tradition regarding Edwin's particular concern to impose himself in Gwynedd: there may be a difference in emphasis between the general receipt of all Britain under his *dicio* – which may well reflect the process of lesser kings seeking his protection, or some similar, diplomatic process – and his *subiugavit* of Anglesey and Man, which perhaps implies an act of conquest.[63]

Later Welsh literature singled out Edwin as the archetypal English villain of the period, portraying him as dependent on King Cadfan at some point during his period in exile (*c.* 604–616) and so as an evil ingrate when he subsequently attacked Cadwallon.[64] Whether or not he was ever in Wales prior to 616, he was a close associate of King Cearl of Mercia and so presumably a party to whatever relationship then existed between Wales and Mercia. It does seem probable that he later evicted Cadwallon from his kingdom and drove him into exile in Ireland.[65] If so, this may have been his response to Cadwallon's role as the principal protector of British churchmen, with whom Edwin's bishop, Paulinus, had inherited a feud from Archbishop Augustine.[66] Welsh literature again records (if retrospectively) Cadwallon's victories over Welsh opponents as well as Edwin: upon his return he presumably found it necessary first to restore his own position in Wales *vis-à-vis* Edwin's allies before leading his forces to Hatfield. Bede leaves us in no doubt of his own opinion concerning the relationship between Cadwallon and Edwin at this point: Cadwallon *rebellavit* ('rebelled') against King Edwin.[67] He was, therefore, portrayed as a subordinate ruler who was subject to the overall (and divinely sanctioned) hegemony of the English 'overking'.

If the Tribal Hidage is Edwin's tribute list for the year 625, with additions and a final total attributable to 626,[68] then Bede's insistence on the universality of his *imperium* by that date requires that the British kingships of the west should be represented therein.

None are named but it is suggested (above) that the *Westerne* may be an English rendering of a British 'overkingship' in the far west. This otherwise obscure people have hitherto been postulated as either inhabiting Cheshire and northern Staffordshire,[69] or Herefordshire and its environ,[70] but neither solution is very satisfactory: the first preserves the consistency of the clockwise circuit around Mercia, which seems such a clear characteristic of the primary list of the Tribal Hidage, but requires that an otherwise unknown kingship which was capable of paying a large tribute equivalent to 7,000 hides (equal to Lindsey with Hatfield, for example) existed in this thinly populated and economically backward corner of England which is far easier allocated to the *Wrocensæte*; the second avoids this problem but destroys the geographical rationale inherent in the list.[71]

The only solution which respects the order implicit in the primary list of the Tribal Hidage and identifies the *Westerne* with a known and significant kingship requires that King Edwin's secretary – who was presumably Bishop Paulinus – was referring to the court of a British king in Gwynedd, so probably on Anglesey. Bede noted that Anglesey was assessed at the equivalent of 960 hides, so a tribute of 7,000 hides owed by the king of the *Westerne* presumably reflects his role as a tribute-receiving king among the Britons.[72] Certainly the 'Westerners' would have been appropriate as a term to denote all the western British kings from Dumnonia northwards – and Bede's reference to British control of the Isle of Man in association with Anglesey may imply that that should be included at this date in the kingship, or at least the 'overkingship' of Gwynedd; furthermore, there is no other category appropriate to the Britons on this list. If the Tribal Hidage was King Edwin's and if the *Westerne* is a term used for the western Britons, then it necessarily encompasses all of them. If so, then a single king was presumably responsible for their behaviour, and their tribute, to King Edwin.

If the primary list of the Tribal Hidage was, in essentials (so from entries two to sixteen), a list which had originated as an oral record of tributes payable to a Mercian 'overking',[73] then the *Westerne* had been tributary to dominant English 'overkings' for at least a decade before the Tribal Hidage was written down. The relationship could, of course, have been far more ancient than this, and may even have been continuous, or near continuous, since the era of Gildas, Maglocunus and the *pater diabolus* – the 'father – devil' of the British clergy in Gildas's *DEB*.

Cadwallon was killed by Oswald of Bernicia in either 634 or 635.[74] In the opinion of Bede, Oswald's *imperium* then became as extensive as Edwin's had been.[75] By the time Bede was writing, Adamnan had already termed him '*imperator* of all Britain'.[76] Both writers had good reason to be partisan towards Oswald, the one in favour of a Christian Bernician king and the other of a patron of the Irish Church. However, incidental information offered by Bede substantiates their claims.[77] From *c.* 635, Oswald was, therefore, 'overking' of all *Britannia*, so of Wales as well as the Anglo-Saxon dynasties.

Although Oswald is unlikely to have shared Bede's highly rhetorical – even casuistic – hostility to the British clergy under the protection of the Welsh kings, Cadwallon's kin cannot be expected to have found favour with an 'overking' whose brother he had recently slain – apparently with a degree of treachery.[78] Rather, Eanfrith's death necessarily imposed on Oswald the duty of vengeance. Given the will, he apparently had the power to prosecute a blood feud against Cadwallon's kin.

Once again, details are not available but the predictability and menace of King Oswald's hatred coincides with a period which saw a dynastically obscure king ruling Gwynedd – the otherwise unknown Cadafael ap Cynfedw. Cadafael was later reviled in Welsh Triads as one of three Welsh kings who were 'sprung from villeins',[79] so he was clearly not then believed to have been kin to Cadwallon: circumstances may suggest that he owed his throne to King Oswald. If so, his protector's death in 642 left Cadafael exposed to Mercian pressure and necessitated his co-operation with the 'overking' of the Midlands but his support of Penda was not wholehearted: he withdrew from the Mercian army on the eve of the battle of *Winwæd* (in 655, against Oswiu, Oswald's brother and successor), so earning the alliterative epithet *Catguommed* – 'Battle Dodger'.[80] Whether or not this reflected his sympathy for the Northumbrian dynasty, his action rid Cadafael of a powerful, and presumably unwelcome, English superior. It was, however, a risky step to take which can only have earned the undying enmity of King Penda, whom Cadafael could not know (when he forsook him) would die on the morrow. It seems unlikely, therefore, that his was the act of a minor local king, whose rule was exclusive to Gwynedd: some of the other kings of the Britons who had enjoyed the fruits of Penda's success at the 'distribution of Judeu' may well have followed him, in which case he was acting as 'overking' in the west and as an active and interested participant in the complex relations then existing between Mercia and Northumbria.

Oswiu was reputed to have 'taken plunder' in Wales thereafter,[81] but it is unclear which kingship was the object of his wrath. He may have been reacting to the Welsh participation in Penda's ravaging of Bernicia (in 655) but he may equally well have been active on behalf of his own allies among the Welsh kings, against Mercia's sympathisers. This was, after all, the year in which the Mercians themselves overthrew his direct rule of their own people in favour of the young Wulfhere,[82] so Northumbrian activities in Wales are unlikely to have been independent of the coup which ultimately excluded their influence from the central Midlands.

After 655 Cadafael disappears from history leaving no trace of influential successors: at about the same time, Cadwallon's son, Cadwaladr, attained the throne of Gwynedd and set about re-establishing his position as a patron of the British Church – hence his association with Llangadwaladr. It was there that he chose to publicise the illustrious memory of his own forebears: the grandiose memorial to Cadfan was arguably designed to remind contemporaries of the glories associated with his own royal dynasty of Gwynedd in the past. The precise purpose of these activities is obscure but his return from exile to take over the kingship of Gwynedd would certainly have provided an appropriate context. If so, then the restoration of Cadwallon's heir may well have coincided with that of Penda's son in Mercia (in 658), in both instances at the expense of the Bernician interest.

Later Welsh literature would render Cadwaladr as a British hero capable of delivering Britain from the Saxons.[83] In reality his role was probably less heroic and his position more dependent on the balance of power between the Mercian allies of his house and their Northumbrian enemies. He may, however, have been responsible for the reinstatement of Gwynedd's ruling house following a period of exile precipitated by pressure from Bernicia. As the late and much lamented Professor Dodgson long since opined, one element in the wars of the seventh century was a blood feud between the house of Gwynedd and the Northumbrian dynasty.[84] What

Cadwaladr perhaps achieved was to re-establish the native dynasty after a lengthy crisis which stemmed directly from the disastrous defeat and death of Cadwallon in the mid-630s, far off beside the Tyne.

The British kingships of Cadwaladr's era may not have been identical in strength or extent with those of his father: there are signs that Penda had taken advantage of the temporary weakness of the Welsh 'overkingship', perhaps under the troubled rule of Cadafael, to redraw the boundary with his own hegemony. The Mercian dependency of the *Magonsæte* in the central marches was one result;[85] another may have been the annexation of eastern Powys from the Severn northwards to the Irish Sea.[86] Both, perhaps, reflect the opportunism of an English king of Mercia who was temporarily (642–*c.* 650) free from the danger of attack from his English neighbours so capable of expanding his rule westwards. The subkingships of the western Midlands – such as the *Wrocensæte* – were arguably swallowed up into the Mercian kingship during this same period. Penda's activities are the more understandable if the current king of Gwynedd was a Northumbrian appointee who lacked the moral authority of the native dynasty and yet was (temporarily) devoid of Bernician support.

There are insufficient facts available to make positive statements concerning these affairs but this is at least one viable interpretation of Anglo-Welsh interaction during the period. If it is correct, then it was Penda who was responsible for at last redrawing the frontier between English and British kingship which had been put in place perhaps two centuries earlier, during Gildas's childhood.[87] The Welsh were long to contest these adjustments and it was perhaps this issue which ended the long period of comparatively close co-operation between Mercian and Welsh kings. During the eighth century Welsh successes in Powys are associated with King Eliseg, to whose memory a great pillar was erected near Valle Crucis a century or so later,[88] but his victories are unlikely to have been achieved without the backing of Gwynedd. The *Annales Cambriae* detailed a battle at Hereford in 760 and various Mercian inroads in the 770s through to the 790s. Wat's Dyke may already by this date have been old,[89] but the much longer Offa's Dyke was presumably constructed at some date between 755 and 796. Offa's successors took advantage of a dynastic crisis in Gwynedd early in the following century, seizing Rhufoniog

(816), Degan(n)wy and all Powys and campaigning even in Snowdonia.[90]

It was this same crisis which precipitated a change of dynasty in Gwynedd, bringing Merfyn ap Gwriad to the throne (825–44). Merfyn's family eventually united what remained of Welsh-ruled Powys to Gwynedd but of greater moment is his association with the *Historia Brittonum*, which was apparently composed in Gwynedd, probably at his court and apparently on his behalf, in the fourth year of his reign.[91] An important feature of this work is the propagandist reinforcement of the reputation and authority of Gwynedd over against the other Welsh kingships: 'Vortigern' is portrayed herein as a pagan arch-traitor to the British cause, yet the universal ruler of the Britons.[92] He was associated with Demetia (south-west Wales), where he was portrayed as ultimately perishing through divine intervention via the agency of that orthodox Christian hero, St. Germanus.[93] The attempt by 'Vortigern' to build himself a great fortress in Snowdonia was miraculously and successfully resisted by the very land itself,[94] and the miracle explained by the boy figure of Emrys (Ambrosius Aurelianus, the personification herein of secular virtues who had obviously derived from Gildas);[95] 'Vortigern' was reputed to have subsequently abandoned Wales and the citadel of Snowdonia to Ambrosius, so associating him exclusively with Gwynedd. The claim to 'overkingship' was given maximum authority by terming him *Embreis Guletic* – 'Emrys the Overlord'.

The *Historia Brittonum* derived the rulers of Builth, Gwerthrynion and Gloucester ultimately from the same arch-traitor, 'Vortigern',[96] and the native kings of Powys from a royal servant or slave, one Cadell, servant to King Benlli.[97] Only Gwynedd's kings, therefore, could claim descent from the virtuous Ambrosius, with whom was associated ultimate victory (still then in the future) in the conflict with the Saxons – as exemplified herein through an allegory featuring red and white dragons.

The *Historia Brittonum* contains, therefore, considerable support for Gwynedd's claims to a general leadership of the Welsh nation – so claims to a Welsh 'overkingship' which had now to be re-emphasised and reclaimed on behalf of a new and still insecure dynasty.[98] The author claimed Roman precedents for the British kingship of the present: the Romans had placed *imperatores* in Britain; from it they had taken 'gold and silver and bronze, and all her precious raiment and honey'.[99] Mention of precious metals probably derives from Gildas,[100] but the author has apparently updated Gildas's reference, adding other commodities which would, in his own day, normally form a part of the payments to a king or 'overking'.

Cadwallon: conclusions

The primacy of Gwynedd's kings over their British neighbours was already a matter of fact when Gildas was writing and may then have been up to a generation old. There are insufficient sources to judge the situation over the following century but those which do survive – such as Procopius's *History of the Wars* – suggest that a British 'overkingship' continued. A more or less continuous account is possible from around 600 onwards.

A consistently important influence on the careers of the north Welsh kings was the success, or otherwise, of their several interactions with their English neighbours. At the start of the seventh century, Gwynedd's kings appear to have been acting in close association with pagan Mercia's rulers and were probably themselves tributary 'overkings' within a wider Mercian hegemony: they were necessarily conjoined with them as co-sponsors of the synod which occurred *c.* 601, on the boundary between their respective areas of influence, at Chester; if the primary list of the Tribal Hidage developed out of King Cearl's tribute list,[101] the *Westerne* – so the Welsh 'overkingship' – were already subject to the distant supremacy of a Mercian king even before *c.* 615. Thereafter, perhaps Cadfan and then, more certainly, Cadwallon were successively 'overkings' inside Wales but subject to the oversight of successive English kings.

The combination of Edwin's enthusiastic adoption of Roman Christianity and his universal *imperium* posed a new threat to the Welsh 'overking' and Edwin apparently drove Cadwallon into exile in Ireland. The latter was deprived, therefore, of scope for a diplomatic settlement of any differences between himself and his English superior and was forced into the risky business of invading the heartland of English-ruled territory as the only effective means of regaining his own patrimony. Following his initial success he turned north, leaving his Mercian ally to establish himself in the Midlands. He attempted to destroy English rule in Northumbria, perhaps in favour of a revival of British lordship there, by defeating and killing the Deiran king and murdering Eanfrith of Bernicia. The entirety of this strategy was necessarily of a 'high risk' nature and Cadwallon's defeat and death at Oswald's hands, combined with the latter's immediate and universal *imperium*, probably spelled disaster for his dynasty. Oswald may have succeeded in evicting the enemies of his house from Gwynedd and substituting the otherwise unknown Cadafael as 'overking' in Wales, who famously repaid this debt by abandoning Penda of Mercia on the eve of the battle of *Winwæd*, against Oswiu and the Bernicians. Oswiu was last active in Wales in 658 – the same year as a Mercian rebellion against him reinstated Penda's kin to the Mercian kingship in the person of his son, Wulfhere. It may have been this same period which enabled Cadwallon's son, Cadwaladr, to regain control of Gwynedd and restore the fortunes of his house more widely throughout Wales.

Little of this reconstruction is capable of proof but an interactive interpretation of Anglo-Welsh affairs is made obligatory by Cadwallon's career, which should not be treated as just some temporary and ill-judged aberration disturbing an otherwise virtually self-contained history of Wales. The subsequent crisis within Wales and the temporary demotion of Mercia's old allies there may have been key factors in precipitating Mercian expansion westwards and so the breakdown of the earlier accord between these two neighbours. Whether or not this was the precise occasion for that important process, it certainly began a long history of Welsh opposition to Mercia which led to various wars and the construction of at least two massive frontier systems. These wars in the west seriously inhibited Mercia's expansion on other fronts and contributed ultimately to the collapse of her hegemonal position in Southumbria. At precisely that time, a new Latin text was written in Gwynedd in support of British claims *vis-à-vis* the Saxons, which also contained material which was designed to sustain the claims of Merfyn, King of Gwynedd, to the primacy of all British-ruled Britain. The rhetoric, at least, was a true, lineal descendant of Gildas's treament of Maglocunus, some three and a half centuries earlier.

The Mercian 'overkingship'

The earliest ruler of Mercia named by Bede was King Cearl.[102] An apparently late, and certainly retrospective, process of rationalisation eventually led to his incorporation into the dynasty represented by Penda,[103] but it is all too possible that those responsible had no knowledge of this king that was independent of Bede, in which case his comments are the only valid basis for discussion and later attempts to link him with Penda's dynasty must be rejected as spurious, or at best unproven.[104] Cearl's name does not occur in genealogies of the Mercians which derive from the late eighth and ninth centuries and this fact is probably significant.

The pagan and Mercian Cearl was of no intrinsic interest to Bede, who referred to him solely in the context of a lengthy and semi-hagiographical account of King Edwin, and those of his close kin who had accepted baptism:

> From that time for six consecutive years, that is right up to the end of the reign of that King Edwin, Paulinus preached the word of God, with the King's assent and support, in that province; those who were predestined to enjoy eternal life believed and were baptized, among whom were Osfrith and Eadfrith, sons of King Edwin, both of whom were born in his exile, of Cwenburh, daughter of Cearl king of the Mercians.

Bede's interest in Cearl, therefore, resulted only from his role as grandfather of Edwin's elder sons, whom he distinguished by this reference to their mother and maternal grandparent from the king's second family by Æthelburh of Kent. We can, however, make some progress in reconstructing his role in the inter-regional politics of the early seventh century. Edwin fled *c.* 604 from Æthelfrith's *putsch* in Deira. Æthelfrith's commitment to the extermination of the male representatives of the rival dynasty was a matter of common knowledge in Northumbria in the early eighth century.[105] The poisoning of Edwin's elder nephew, Hereric, when at the court of (British) Elmet, was one highly relevant and violent death for which Æthelfrith should surely bear ultimate responsibility. It may be that Edwin only became politically significant once Hereric (who had already produced at least two children so was of an age to be politically active) was dead. Thereafter, it was Edwin whose death Æthelfrith sought.

Osfrith and Eadfrith, at least, were born during Edwin's exile and the marriage between Edwin and Cwenburh most probably occurred after his flight from Deira,[106] when Edwin was a penniless refugee with nothing except his lineage to offer a marital partner. That, even in such circumstances, he was able to obtain a wife of

Cwenburh's undoubtedly elevated status implies a particular set of conditions:

1 That this marriage had the blessing of King Cearl.
2 Its inequality suggests that Cearl saw Edwin as a political pawn through whom to embarrass his northern neighbour, Æthelfrith – else why allow his own daughter's marriage to a refugee? If so, Cearl's area of influence and governance was presumably interactive with that of Æthelfrith, his rival and approximate equal in power.
3 The birth to this marriage of at least two children suggests that Edwin lived under Mercian protection for some considerable period between *c.* 604 and *c.* 615.[107] If he also spent time in North Wales during this period, that was perhaps likewise under the ultimate protection of the Mercian king, or at least occurred with his approval. That possibility certainly implies that Mercia and Gwynedd were then co-operating one with another.
4 Cearl's autonomy in matters of marital policy and external diplomacy requires that he was outside the 'overkingship' of Æthelberht of Kent, whose hegemony extended *c.* 600 not to the Humber (as Bede repeatedly claimed[108]) but as far as East Anglia, the Hwicce and Wessex.

Cearl emerges, therefore, as a king who was already a force to be reckoned with in England by *c.* 604, who was independent of his neighbours and prepared to confront neighbouring 'overkings', even one with as warlike a reputation as Æthelfrith.

If Cearl had ambitions in Deira, he necessarily already enjoyed a degree of control over the provinces in between his own Mercian heartland (in Leicestershire, Nottinghamshire, lowland Derbyshire and eastern Staffordshire) and East Yorkshire – so in Lindsey, Hatfield and Elmet. If the Tribal Hidage was Edwin's tribute list in the 620s (as argued above), there is reason to think that the primary list was based on an earlier one – albeit an oral one – of Mercia's dependencies. If so (and the logic is necessarily by this point somewhat extended) then it is possible to reconstruct Cearl's Mercian hegemony in some detail (Figure 1). It may be significant that, however tentative the results, this reconstructed hegemony does border Deira, both on the Humber and the Ouse, including as it does both Elmet and Lindsey with Hatfield.

Cearl's demise is undocumented: I have argued elsewhere that he was a victim either of Æthelfrith's Chester campaign or some other unknown but closely related Bernician attack, but the evidence is entirely circumstantial.[109] What is beyond dispute is that Edwin was forced to flee once more, this time from the entirety of Mercia and the putative Mercian hegemony of his father-in-law in the Midlands and Wales, to take refuge beyond the Fens, inside the southern *imperium*, at King Rædwald's court. Edwin's flight certainly implies that Cearl was no longer able to protect him and there is good reason to think that a real disaster had overtaken the Mercian 'overkingship' at Æthelfrith's hands.

There are several factors which suggest that, for a short period prior to his own death, Æthelfrith either himself exercised kingship within Mercia and its erstwhile satellites or substituted his own appointees as client kings of Mercia: that he learned rapidly of Edwin's presence in East Anglia suggests that only a short distance separated Rædwald's court from men who were answerable to Æthelfrith – which seems improbable if Æthelfrith's influence stopped at the Humber; he was likewise enabled to dispatch messengers to Rædwald not just once but three times over what seems to have been a short space of time, so could presumably guarantee their security up to the East Anglian frontier; his threat of war was taken with the utmost seriousness by Rædwald, suggesting that neither side envisaged any undue difficulty in Æthelfrith marching through the Trent valley; finally, he was defeated and killed south of the Humber inside what Bede interpreted as Mercian territory.[110] Bede believed the battle to have occurred inside either what was then Mercia or what had since become recognised as Mercia; and if Hatfield was an extensive territory in the early seventh century which had then been divided between Northumbria and Mercia *c.* 679–80, then the second option seems the more likely. Whichever, Bede's text confirms that Æthelfrith was south of his core, Northumbrian territories without his full campaigning army: this necessarily suggests that he had taken upon himself the rule of Mercia and its satellites, much as his son Oswiu would again do in the 650s.

Once more, there is some evidence which is supportive of Mercia's early role as a regional 'overkingship'. This status was, however, overthrown by Æthelfrith who briefly made himself ruler of two regional 'overkingships'. When Æthelfrith was killed, Bede suggests that Edwin succeeded to Æthelfrith's *regnum* ('kingship'). He certainly secured both Deira and Bernicia but Bede's text is most easily interpreted as implying that Edwin took over, under Rædwald's benign and universal 'overkingship', the entirety of the Midlands and the north, albeit with many subkings beneath him. That would at least explain the considerable extent of his *imperium* over both Angles and Britons even before his victory over the West Saxons and his subsequent conversion – on which point Bede was quite adamant.

Rule of the Mercian hegemony by two successive Northumbrian kings was a disaster both for the Mercian political community and for Gwynedd. It was presumably at this stage that Lindsey, Hatfield and Elmet were detached from their dependence on Mercia and attached to the north – a usurpation that would be hotly disputed for the next sixty years. It required Edwin's death and the destruction of his dynasty for the Mercian 'overkingship' to resume under a native dynasty: it was refounded by Penda and his kin and this was presumably his primary objective when he added his own warband to that of King Cadwallon for the Hatfield campaign. The Welsh presumably reached Hatfield via Mercian territory, so the failure of the Midlanders to alert Edwin to the approach of this army suggests that sympathies there lay with the insurgents, despite the Mercian grandpaternity of Edwin's elder sons.

Penda and his brother thereafter found it politic to recognise the 'overkingship' of Oswald – the slayer of his own close ally, Cadwallon, but his deployment of a powerful army which included a Welsh contingent at *Maserfelth* against the Bernician king in 642 suggests that he had already by then restored the regional hegemony of Mercia – exclusive of Gwynedd and its satellites, perhaps. If so then he had presumably already achieved this during the year or so between Hatfield and Oswald's victory over Cadwallon, since it seems unlikely that Oswald would have countenanced the challenge to his authority which this process must otherwise have posed. Thereafter his recognition of Oswald's *imperium* would surely have curtailed his ambitions. The Mercian hegemony was, therefore, probably reconstructed during the one or two years of political chaos which followed and was consequent upon Edwin's death in 633, during part of which Penda's own close ally, Cadwallon, was in the ascendant and capable of providing political circumstances conducive to that objective. It was the work of Penda and perhaps his brother Eobba.

The first sixteen entries of the primary list of the Tribal Hidage were to constitute the bulk of the eighth-century kingdom of Mercia. Elmet and part, at least, of Hatfield were lost to Northumbria but Elmet's putative association a generation earlier with Urien's northern British confederacy may imply that it had then been part of the north, rather than greater Mercia. Gains made during the seventh century far exceeded these minor losses, including the Hwicce, a people who had appeared on the secondary list of the Tribal Hidage and who had apparently been tributary to King Æthelberht in the opening years of the century.[111] Erstwhile Welsh territory was annexed, primarily from Powys (see above); the *Arosæte* were detached from the south, presumably along with the Hwicce; so too the *Cilternsæte* and London with northern parts of the Home Counties (Figure 7). The annexation of these various provinces to the Mercian interest reflects the poorly documented success of Penda and his sons *vis-à-vis* the more fragmented 'overkingships' in Wales and the south and also the ultimate failure of the Bernicians to hinder the episodic and opportunistic expansion of their hegemony, operating with all the advantages which a central location conferred.

At the date when Cearl makes his one brief passage across the stage of history, he was already middle-aged: old enough at least to have a daughter of marriageable age. He may have already ruled Mercia for anything up to two decades or so, which could push his rule back to the 580s. The true antiquity of this hegemony is, however, lost in prehistory. If the Tribal Hidage can be used in this respect,[112] then it may be significant that Mercia seems to dominate the centre of England by its sheer size: whether one adopts the 12,000 hides to which Bede referred in the context of 655–8,[113] or the (perhaps penal) assessment of 30,000 hides allotted it in this document, Mercia's resources appear to have dwarfed those of its near neighbours, the largest of which paid tribute at 7,000 hides. The Mercian dominance of the Midlands does, therefore, look so well established by *c.* 600 that it may have been in existence for many generations.

Procopius had, of course, referred to a single king of the Angles in Britain (see above) and it is tempting to equate this figure with an Anglian ruler centred in 'original Mercia', whose 'overkingship'

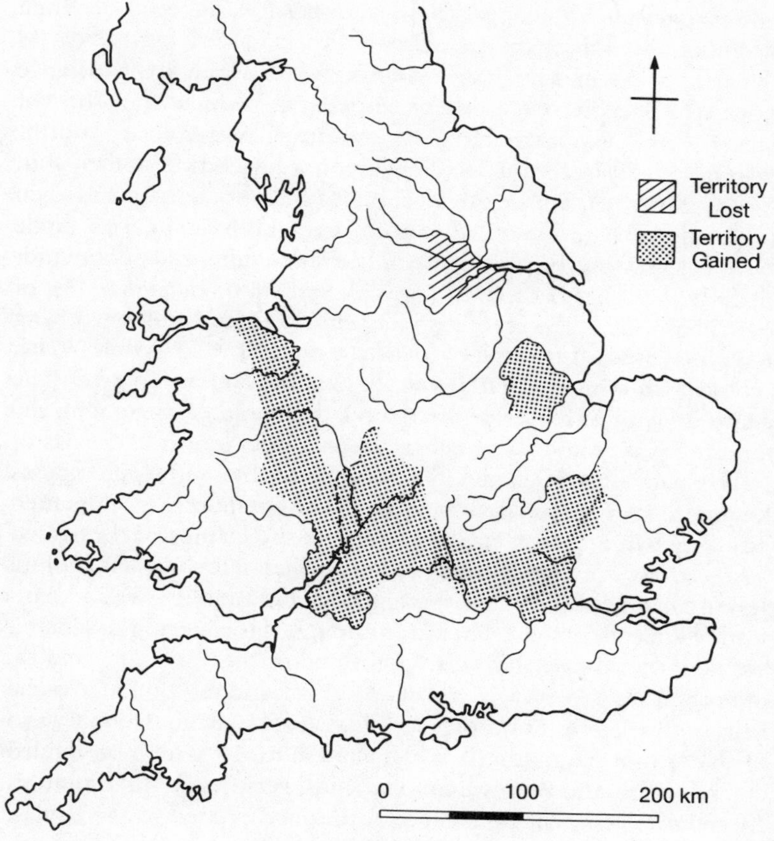

Figure 7 Approximate estimates of the territorial gains and losses of the Mercian kingship from and to other 'overkingships' during the seventh century, including the apparently one-time subordinate 'overkingship' of the Welsh. Long-contested territories which were apparently within the early Mercian hegemony and which they ultimately retained (such as Lindsey) are not marked.

might have extended even to Yorkshire, but this issue is beyond resolution. The bitterness with which the two Anglian 'overkingships' in northern and central England were to compete with one another may imply that they originated as a single entity, although there is no good reason to backdate Ecgfrith's title of *rex*

Humbronensium – 'king of the Humber-folk' – into the early seventh or even the sixth centuries:[114] the term clearly post-dates the dynastic and kingship names Bernicia and Deira by which the northern dynasties were otherwise defined – which are British in origin – and was arguably a new name *c.* 680 coined so as to advertise Ecgfrith's claim to rule on both sides of the Humber, so in the province of Lindsey which he had so recently lost to the Mercians. The title may, therefore, have been original to Archbishop Theodore or his agents. Once that claim had become entirely hollow the northern title was altered to *Nordanhymbri* – 'the Northumbrians'.[115] Procopius's testimony should not be pressed too far. It was commonplace for writers from the sixth to the tenth centuries to refer to even Saxon kings in Britain as 'Angles',[116] so caution requires that his reference to a three-fold division of insular kingship is ultimately beyond reconstruction.

The name 'Mercia' and the locality of the early core of the kingdom has been much discussed.[117] The etymology of the term is not disputed: it derives from OE *Mierce*, the 'people of the march' and seems to have been deeply entrenched already by the end of the seventh century. Why this dominant people should have carried a frontier-related name is unclear, although it is generally associated with an early border between English and British territory and the important role of the Mercians in the conquest of the western Britons. This does not, however, distinguish Mercia from Wessex or Northumbria, both of which had borders with non-English communities, and that is a fundamental weakness of this solution. An alternative might be to suggest that it is related to the Roman provincial structure: the east Midlands lay within the fourth-century province of Flavia Caesariensis, with its capital at Lincoln. This was, effectively, the territory of the Iron Age tribe of the Corieltauvi and their satellites, so a territorial unit of great antiquity.

Flavia Caesariensis was the only province of those which fell under exclusive Saxon control (so excluding Britannia Prima) to have had borders with all three of the other late Roman provinces. If the fifth-century Germanic takeover was, in part at least, conditioned by pre-existing geo-political boundaries,[118] then the name 'Mercia' could have originated from recognition of this province's unique geographical position (Figure 8). Once the western province of Britannia Prima had been divided between British kingships in the far west and the Saxon-dominated lowlands of the east,[119] the opportunity existed for Anglo-Saxon rulers of Flavia Caesariensis and Maxima Caesariensis to attach to themselves the (primarily British) kingships of neighbouring parts of Britannia Prima.

If the Tribal Hidage provides insights into the extent of the Mercian and southern 'overkingships' in the first quarter of the seventh century, then it is the southern one which seems by then to have been the more successful in expanding into Britannia Prima: excluding Mercia's putative influence over the British 'overkingship' of the west, its kings only obtained direct hegemony over the territory of the Cornovii, ruled from Wroxeter, which ultimately became the Mercian province of the *Wrocensæte*.[120]

Such an hypothesis is currently beyond proof but the relevant, very tentative outlines of these organisational units do at least suggest some degree of continuity, so evolutionary processes as opposed to the catastrophic reworking of frontiers in consequence of Anglo-Saxon conquest.[121] Indeed, discrepancies between the geography of governance in the Roman and early Medieval periods are as likely to stem from our ignorance of the actual boundaries of Roman provinces and Anglo-Saxon 'overkingships' as from real differences. At the very least, alternatives to existing notions of Mercia's origins should be canvassed and interaction between the geography of Roman Britain and Anglo-Saxon England explored without preconceptions.

The southern 'overkingship'

It is with Æthelberht's Kentish 'overkingship' that a southern *imperium* first enters history: the visit of Rædwald to his court and acceptance (however reluctantly) of baptism there implies that the East Anglian king was subject to his oversight, and this is confirmed by Bede's comment on the relationship between them in his list of *imperium*-wielding kings;[122] Augustine's meeting with British clergy at Augustine's Oak, on the frontier between the territory of the Hwicce and the West Saxons,[123] requires that Æthelberht's protection was effective on this spot, far distant from his own realm, suggesting that his superiority was recognised by both these kingships. The boundary meeting-place was a trenchant reminder of his interest in contact between two subkingships; additionally, Æthelberht's principal supporter among his neighbours was his

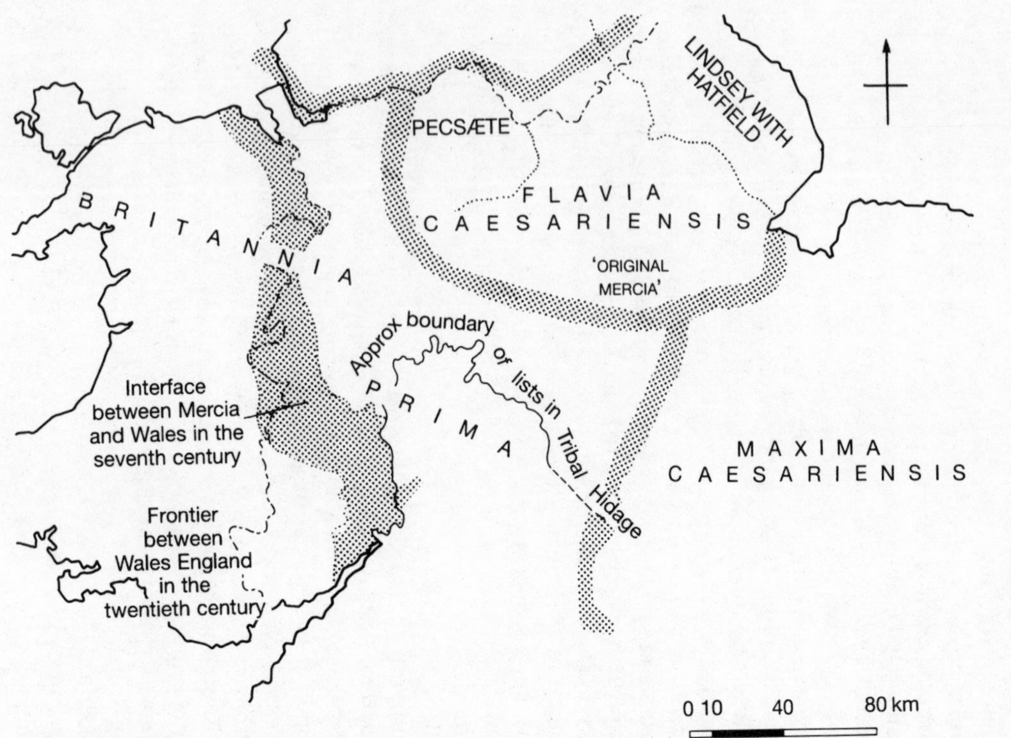

Figure 8 Hypothetical geography of the late Roman provinces in central Britain set against the hegemonal geography of the seventh century.

nephew, King Sæberht of the East Saxons, whom Bede specifically stated was subject to his *potestas* ('power').[124]

These four relationships, which can be reconstructed in detail from Bede's *Historia*, mirror with some precision the geography of the secondary list of the Tribal Hidage: there are numerous peoples to whom Bede made no reference in this context (most particularly the South Saxons) but there is no fundamental discrepancy between these two sources. Complete harmony requires just two emendations: firstly that Bede's repeated assertion that Æthelberht's *imperium* extended to the Humber be set aside as unhistorical, and included by him for highly rhetorical purposes;[125] and secondly, that what were arguably King Edwin's earliest additions to a tribute list which he had otherwise taken over from King Æthelfrith (viz nos. 17–19 of the Tribal Hidage, including Wight) should, to reconstruct Æthelberht's *imperium*, be taken away from the primary list of the Tribal Hidage and added to the secondary list.

With these alterations effected, Æthelberht's *imperium* can be reconstructed (as Figure 1). Its antiquity is, however, obscure. Æthelberht's rule is unlikely to have been as lengthy as Bede supposed since he was not yet even king of Kent when he married the Frankish Bertha, *c.* 580.[126] In 597, Kentish *imperium* over the south may have been comparatively novel. There is, however, material evidence visible in the distribution of imported grave-goods that may imply that a cultural – so perhaps also a political – frontier between the south and the Midlands played a significant role in the patterning of high-level social contacts and exchange.[127]

Bede was familiar with stories concerning at least two, earlier, southern 'overkings', Ælle of the South Saxons and Ceawlin of the West Saxons, but had no good reason to inform his audience of their deeds, their dates, or the extent of their *imperium* – even supposing he knew these things, which is doubtful.[128] Later writers developed a pseudo-historical context for these and other semi-mythical characters but neither the *Historia Brittonum* (of the 820s) nor the *Anglo-Saxon Chronicle* (of the 890s) can be shown to contain material which is both original and reliable pertinent to Kent and its neighbours in the fifth and sixth centuries.[129] The *Anglo-Saxon Chronicle* was deeply committed to portraying West Saxon kings as vigorous warlords already in the late fifth and sixth centuries, who had sprung from an *adventus* which was unique to themselves: that this should have been headed by a leader with a

British name, Cerdic, betrays the pseudo-historical credentials of this origin myth.[130]

There are several pointers to this southern *imperium* having its origins in the geography of Roman Britain: several of the major peoples of the sixth and seventh centuries occupy territories which replicate (as far as can be judged) those of pre-existing Romano-British *civitates*, so may descend directly from them: the 'North *folc*' of East Anglia seem to have occupied an area remarkably similar to the territory of the Iceni;[131] the kingship of the South Saxons replicates the jurisdiction of the Regni, or Regnenses;[132] the territory of the Jutes of Hampshire and Wight seems too similar to that of the Belgae to be entirely coincidental (Figure 9);[133] the Hwicce look very much like the Dobunni as regards their territory (Figure 10); the kingship of the East Saxons replicates the jurisdiction of the *civitas* of the Trinovantes; in the case of Kent, not only does the tribal territory apparently survive more or less intact from one period to the other but the *civitas* name does as well, so a degree of organisational continuity seems almost certain. The antiquity of the Wealden transhumance system and its routeways further underlines the continuity of the basic pattern of settlement and land-use in Kent, Sussex and Surrey from the Roman past into the Anglo-Saxon period.[134]

A second indication of some organisational debt to the Roman past is the interest shown from an early date in controlling London, once arguably both the provincial and diocesan capital. Bede described London in the present tense as the *metropolis civitas* – 'capital town' – of the province of the East Saxons,[135] but in the context of its receipt of a bishop under the protection of King Æthelberht's close associate and kinsman, Sæberht. Its markets apparently attracted the attention of several seventh-century kings and it was eventually wrested from the control of the southern kingdoms by the Mercians, to become the principal *wic* of their 'empire' but the kings of Kent seem to have had an earlier interest in it and the West Saxon kings established temporary control of the diocese at the turn of the century. The bishopric of London was eventually to encompass the bulk of the apparently late and artificial province of the Middle Saxons (hence Middlesex), of whom there is no record under this name in the Tribal Hidage.[136] As becomes the old diocesan centre, therefore, there is some evidence that London lay in the marches between the spheres of influence of

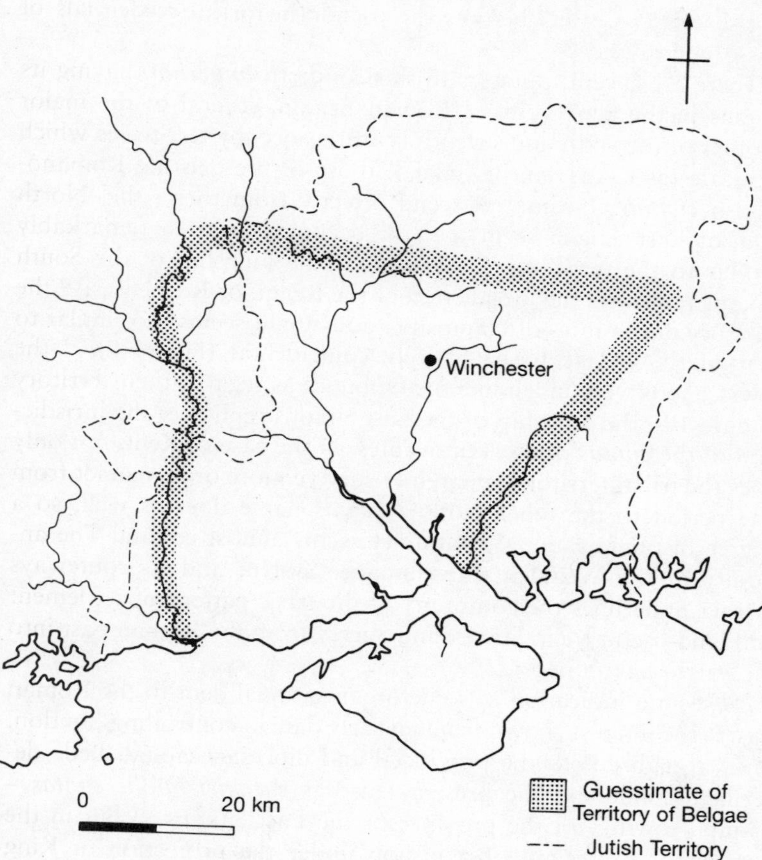

Figure 9 Approximate territory of the Belgae of Roman Britain (after Jones and Mattingley, 1990, p. 154) set against the territory of the Jutes of Hampshire (the *Meonwara*) and Wight (after Yorke, 1989, p. 85).

two of the hegemonies which ultimately succeeded Roman control. Authority thereover was a significant indicator of *imperium* throughout the south during the seventh and eighth centuries, if not before.

The possibility that the southern 'overkingship' developed from the Saxon seizure of the province of Maxima Caesariensis has

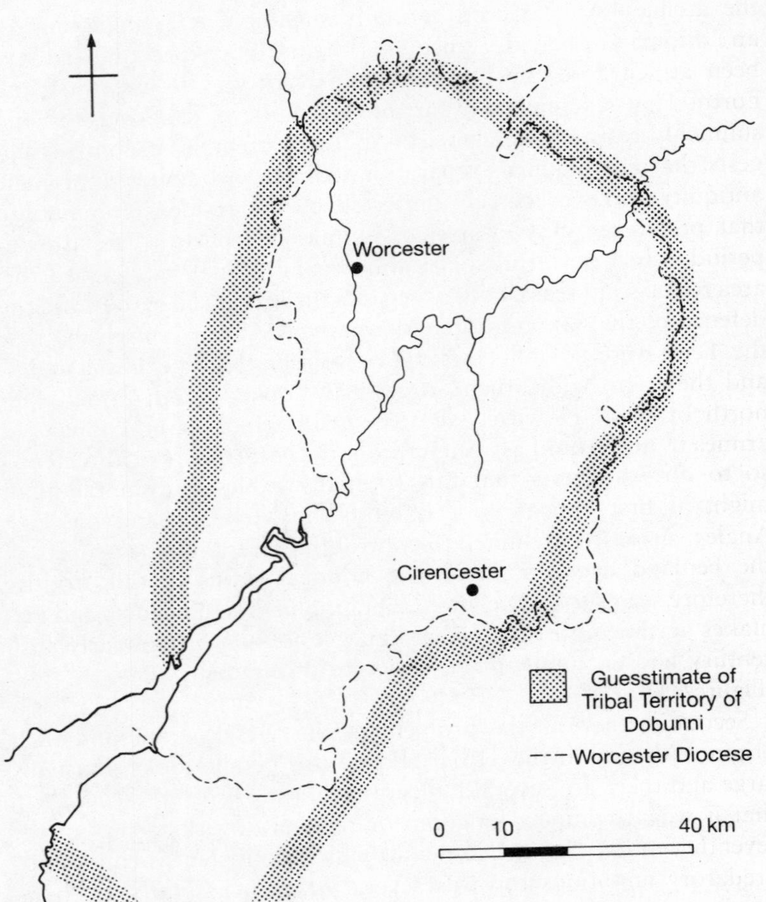

Figure 10 Approximate territory of the Dobunni in the late pre-Roman Iron Age and Roman period (after Cunliffe, 1978, p. 108), set against the territory of the Hwicce, as defined by the medieval diocese of Worcester (after Hill, 1981, p. 81).

already been touched upon. As a theory it is obviously beyond proof but there are several factors which make this idea an attractive one: firstly, East Anglia is the only Anglo-Saxon kingdom which carries an Anglian name within the southern *imperium*. If the name betrays the actual cultural and ethnic affinities of its ruling class (as the archaeological record certainly suggests), it is something of an anomaly therein, since it might be expected to have been attached to the other Anglian territories to the west and north. That it remained a part of the southern 'overkingship' and staunchly resisted Mercian (so Anglian) attempts at control suggests that East Anglia's separation from the Midlands is of some antiquity and was fiercely preferred by the resident community: that preference may even stem ultimately from the late Roman period, when powerful social and organisational factors tied this area to the south-east, both as regards the provincial system and the defence of the Saxon Shore. Alternatively, it may simply be that the Fens were so influential as a frontier that the East Angles, and the Iceni before them, necessarily looked south rather than north or west. However, the ease with which several kings led armies to and from East Anglia from the Midlands – or threatened so to do – suggests that this frontier was less substantial than might at first appear. Indeed, both the Mercians and the East Angles variously attempted to control the several minor peoples of the Fenland between them. The political status of this frontier therefore seems to outweigh its topographical significance, and this makes it the more likely that the geopolitics of the early fifth century had an input to the structure of regional *imperia c.* 600 (Figure 11).

Secondly, there is the problem of the West Saxons and their origins. Already in the Tribal Hidage this people looks unusually large and there are several indications in the *Historia Ecclesiastica* that it was a complex kingdom or regional 'overkingship' in the seventh century. It was also one which consistently entertained predatory ambitions towards several of its neighbours. Such instincts are most marked as regards the Jutes of Hampshire, in whose territory the West Saxons founded their second diocese at what would eventually become the kingdom's capital of Winchester,[137] and West Saxon acquisitiveness here and in Wight could reflect a long and unequal association between two parts of that portion of Britannia Prima which had fallen under Saxon domination in the fifth century. The presence of fifth-century (even early to mid-fifth-century) Anglo-Saxon cemeteries in the upper Thames valley – where the earliest West Saxon diocese was to be established at Dorchester (Oxon.) – suggests that this was the heartland of early Saxon control. If so, what we may be dealing with by the

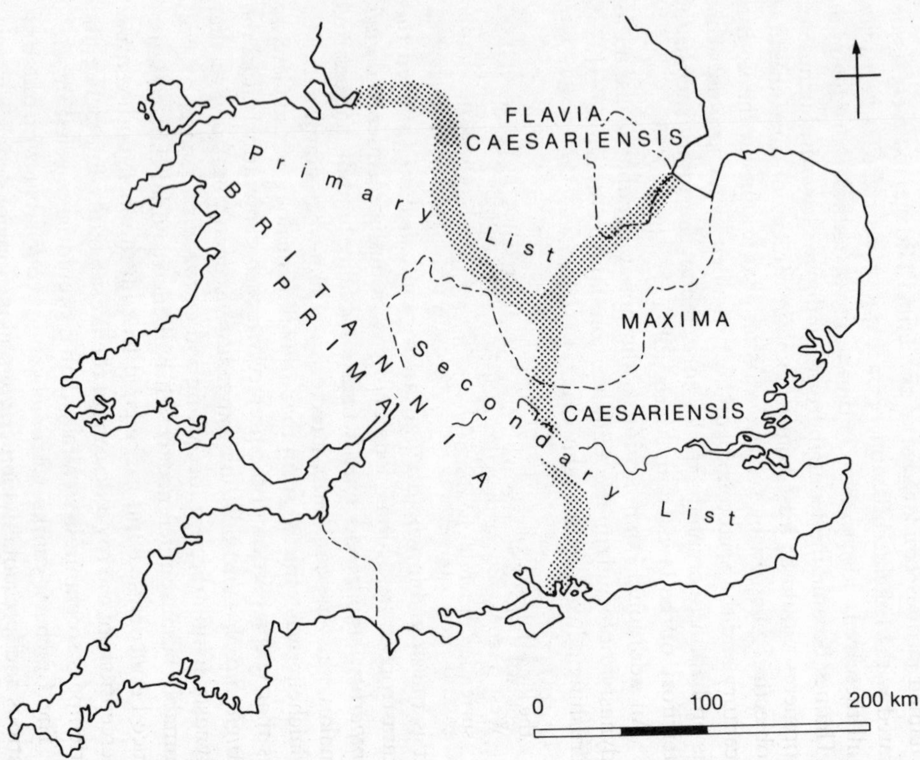

Figure 11 Hypothetical geography of the provinces in the south of late Roman Britain set against the boundary between the primary and secondary lists of the Tribal Hidage.

seventh century in terms of geopolitics may be the consequence of the division of Britannia Prima.

While the British west of the old province seems to have retained a degree of political integrity into the seventh century – and its cultural distinctiveness much longer – the Anglo-Saxon dominated east became split into two, the northern territories of which fell under Mercian influence leaving the south to interact with the south-east. There are indications that the break between these two was still a matter of dispute in the seventh century: while several kingships on the north side of the middle and upper Thames were named in the secondary list of the Tribal Hidage and were associated with Æthelberht's *imperium* (Hwicce, *Arosæte*, *Cilternsæte*), all these were lost to Mercia during the seventh century when the Thames became the frontier from London westwards. Such developments would at least help to explain the vigour and ambitious objectives pursued by successive West Saxon kings in the seventh century and the need to explain away – albeit by an account which is probably apocryphal – the loss of neighbouring areas (such as the territory of the Hwicce) to Mercia.[138]

An additional complication is the possibility that a change of dynasty occurred in the 620s in consequence of King Edwin's crushing defeat of Cuichelm:[139]

> the king [Edwin] collected an army and came against the people of the West Saxons and in the course of war either killed or received in surrender all whom he discovered to have plotted his death.

It is questionable whether Cuichelm's kin can have survived this catastrophe, let alone retained his kingship under Edwin's *imperium*: the blood feud which Cuichelm himself had started makes this appear most unlikely. It may be significant that Cuichelm was omitted from the 'official' genealogy of the Gewisse as that was recorded in the preface which became attached to the *Anglo-Saxon Chronicle*, although he was incorporated into that dynasty within the text, becoming associated with Cynigils,[140] presumably because reference to him by Bede required that his existence be recognised and assimilated to conventional ninth-century perceptions of the royal descent of the West Saxons. In practice, the attempt is so manifestly clumsy that it should be rejected.

The Cuichelm of the Chronicle is irreconcilable with the ambitious and (presumably) *imperium*-seeking king of Bede's *Historia*.

If Cuichelm and Cynigils were in reality unrelated, then Cuichelm's disastrous defeat may have heralded a dynastic revolution in Wessex which enabled a rival dynasty – perhaps the rulers of one of Wessex's numerous subkingships – to obtain power under Edwin's overall *imperium*. If such occurred it may help to explain the duality of Bede's references to both the West Saxons and Gewisse, with the latter dynasty replacing that of Cuichelm in the tempestuous year 626. British or potentially British names (Cerdic and Cædwalla are only the most obvious) recur within this dynasty to an extent that invites the oft-repeated suggestion that its origins were not Germanic but British: if so, a dynasty which was still in some respects in touch with British language and culture may have seized power in the West Saxon subregional 'overkingship' in 626. A dual (and unusually unsatisfactory) origin myth was the result. The suggestion should not be dismissed too lightly, particularly given the presence of at least two British bishops within West Saxon territory and available to assist Bishop Wine's consecration of Chad as bishop of the Northumbrians, in or soon after 664.[141]

Such discussions are beyond resolution but they may nevertheless be informative. Whatever the precise nature and origin of the association between the West Saxons and their eastern neighbours, it does seem to have become well-established already by the early seventh century. What had not by then been decided is just where leadership of the southern *imperium* should rest – whether with the West Saxons or one of several of their eastern neighbours inside what had been Maxima Caesariensis.

It was in large part this multifocal structure of the south which made it vulnerable to intervention from outside during the seventh and eighth centuries. West Saxon leadership, and protection, of its eastern neighbours only became an established fact in the ninth century, by which time much territory which had been within Æthelberht's *imperium* had been lost to the Mercians (Figure 7). Until 685, Bernician and Mercian kings had little difficulty in identifying and exploiting rivalries between the several southern dynasties with the aim of controlling the region in their own several interests, or at least denying such control to their enemies. Thereafter, the intensity of Mercian influence varied through time but was rarely negligible.

One last indication of the antiquity of the southern *imperium* derives from the comments of Procopius, who included a king of the Frisians among his three insular rulers. Either the Jutes (of Kent, Hampshire and Wight in Bede's reconstruction) or the Saxons could be meant, since all three were closely associated on the western periphery of the Germanic homeland (in Holland, Denmark and neighbouring areas of Germany) in the settlement period. Frankish envoys to Byzantium may have had good political motives for suppressing the titles of Jutes or Saxons – if it was they who provided this information to Procopius, although that is by no means certain. The continental homelands of each lay beyond Merovingian control at this date, although Saxon settlements had occurred in the area of Bayeux apparently with Frankish approval. To the Franks the much closer Frisians of Holland and the Rhineland, with whom they necessarily had close links, may have seemed the more appropriate catch-all title for these various warrior communities on both sides of the Channel. Whatever the precise reasoning, this reference to a single king of the Frisians in Britain could be associated with the most southerly *imperium*, where Saxons and Jutes were supposedly intermixed.[142] Concern must remain, however, that Procopius's sources for this point may have been either fraudulent or negligible, in which case the entire construct is unhistorical. The apparent lack of interest of Gregory of Tours in the tribal nomenclature appropriate to Britain's inhabitants denies us any assistance from this much nearer source.

Northumbria

It is generally agreed that the name 'Northumbria' is of late derivation, being formed only in Bede's own lifetime and probably late within it at that, perhaps even by him. Earlier, Ecgfrith had described himself – or been described by his ally Archbishop Theodore – as *rex Humbronensium*, but the two English dynasties in the north were earlier identified by reference to their core kingdoms of Bernicia and Deira, both of which are ultimately British names. Indeed, all the known kingships and kingdoms of the north have indigenous nomenclature – a fact which suggests that English domination may have been a comparatively late phenomenon and have become established within a pre-existing geography of sub-Roman tribal kingships, as opposed to the civil jurisdictions of the *civitates* of the south. There is substantial and comparatively early archaeological evidence for a pagan English presence only in southern and eastern Yorkshire and it seems likely that Germanic settlements were for long confined to that same area. That it had hitherto been the social and economic heartland of the province of Britannia Secunda may be relevant.[143]

Despite their restricted distribution, the political influence of these Germanic incomers may, of course, have been far more pervasive than that even *a priori* and we should be mindful of Gildas's notice of British tribute payments (presumably to the Saxons) in his own day.[144] To take a further example, some of the 'indigenes' whom Bede envisaged that Æthelfrith 'subjugated' were said to have been made tributary, implying that English influence and political superiority might easily have extended considerable distances beyond areas where early graves can be identified, into territories ruled by British elites.[145]

British resistance in the sixth century to English domination of the north was apparently far greater than that experienced either in the south-east or centre of England. The *Historia Brittonum* was later to recall a British campaign led by Urien, whom Welsh poetry associates with Rheged and Catraeth, against Theodoric, Æthelfrith's uncle, whom he besieged on Holy Island. Whether the author was correct or not, he does suggest that Urien was:[146]

> murdered on the instigation of Morcant, from jealousy, because his own military qualities and skills greatly exceeded all the [other] kings.

He was, therefore, being portrayed as if a British 'overking', deploying the forces of several kingships (Elmet, Rheged, Gododdin and Strathclyde are often cited) in combination against the Angles who had already by this date secured Northumberland.

It may be that there was another region in the north which was comparable to Wales and the south-west peninsula in being initially, by treaty, excluded from the English domination of the bulk of the diocese (of Roman Britain), but if so the fact is undocumented. Certainly, the Votadini (later Gododdin and the Lothians) and Damnonii (later Strathclyde) are likely to have lain beyond English control in the fifth and early sixth centuries, as they had earlier been outside formal Roman control. The elegiac poems of the *Gododdin* collection imply heroic warfare between the former, at least, and the northern Angles.

There seem to have been several stages to the establishment of Northumbria: Bede considered that Ida was the founder of the

Bernician dynasty,[147] and his status was emphasised by an improbable twelve sons by one queen in the *Historia Brittonum*.[148] The same source associates Ida with *Din Guaire* – which is generally identified with Bamburgh – as well as both Deira and Bernicia.[149] He was, therefore, perhaps a successful warrior who much expanded direct English control of territory in the far north, whose reputation survived in story and song down to the eighth century. His reign may have ended with division of his territories among several of his sons and Æthelfrith (his grandson) seems to have had to reconstruct a northern 'overkingship' in the late sixth and early seventh centuries. The memorable victories Æthelfrith achieved in the process apparently gave him the kudos necessary to threaten, then seize, the whole of the north and then the Midlands as well. Had a violent death not intervened, he might well have carried Bernician 'overkingship' even to the Channel.[150]

Aspects of his career will be examined elsewhere in this work and in its successor but sufficient has been outlined to this point to be reasonably confident that Bernician military power was a phenomenon exclusive to the late sixth and the seventh centuries. If there had been earlier attempts by English kings to dominate the north, then the initiative lay with what was, on archaeological grounds, a long-established Deiran kingship and the warrior aristocracies which sustained it, but there is no evidence of their having attempted to establish colonies in the lands of neighbouring British kingships. Indeed, outside the East Riding, Northumbria is characterised by a dearth of pagan English burials which predate *c.* 550.

The late appearance of the northern 'overkingship' finds some slender corroboration in Procopius's assumption that a single king ruled the insular Angles. He may, of course, have been misinformed, or have preferred to simplify his account in this respect (so adapting the insular scene to numerical imperatives which were Christian in origin) but it is at least possible that the Anglian settlement and political structure in Yorkshire was at that stage a dependent satellite of the greater Anglian polity in the Midlands and only broke away once English warriors had been able to secure control of one or more of the several British kingships of the region, beyond the reach of control from the Midlands. Certainly (with the honourable exception of Edwin), it was the late-colonised Bernicia, not Deira, which was to be the principal vehicle of Northumbrian expansion and hegemonal ambitions. The long containment of

English communities within Deira may have been as much a consequence of English political control from outside the region as of the vision of British military resistance from the west and north which is more commonly postulated. Mercian interest in Elmet and Hatfield and King Cearl's sponsorship of Edwin in exile would certainly be consistent with this view.

Northumbria did eventually replicate the late Roman province of Britannia Secunda: the southern boundaries of these two entities are either identical or at least close (once more ignorance is our greatest handicap) and the northern expansion of Bernicia to the Forth and even beyond has clear precedents in earlier Roman attempts to control and police southern Scotland. The core of English settlement prior to the conversion coincided with that same region – the Yorkshire Wolds – which had been the most developed economically during the later Roman period. It was probably then the heartland of the provincial system of patronage and social control. Whether or not Æthelfrith's supremacy should be traced back to the Roman and sub-Roman past via some sort of regional hegemony or zone of interaction between English warlords in Deira and British client states elsewhere is presently unknowable and may long remain so. The possibility arises that it was the third-century province of Britannia Inferior, rather than the smaller but later Britannia Secunda, which provided the initial vehicle for 'anglicisation' in the north but Northumbria certainly had close organisational precedents in Roman Britain: its core was the territory of the Parisi and its periphery was that of the Brigantes and their erstwhile clients and neighbours, whose own interactions are likewise a matter of considerable debate.[151] That pre-Roman system was recognised and ultimately ossified in the creation of Britannia Secunda early in the fourth century, which presumably survived at least into the early fifth century. If we credit the *rectores* of Gildas's text as *bona fide* provincial administrators,[152] then the Roman provincial structure survived in some recognisable form at least as late as *c.* 480 – although this point is at its weakest concerning the north, where Gildas offers no specific information relevant to his own lifetime and of which he may therefore have then known practically nothing. We are today barely better placed.

The Bernician 'overkingship' was either established or re-established, therefore, by Æthelfrith. The kudos consequent upon his aggrandisement *vis-à-vis* the Britons and Deira, and what Bede portrayed as spectacular victories over the Dal Riata Scots and the Welsh, gave him the opportunity to carry his *imperium* southwards but his sudden death in battle exposed the personal nature of his 'empire', which lacked the deep roots necessary to sustain it in adversity. His authority was replaced by that of Edwin of the Deiri who would be, for perhaps seven years, a client 'overking' subject to the ultimate *imperium* of Rædwald.[153] Thereafter Edwin allied himself with Æthelberht's son and heir in Kent, King Eadbald. The primary list of the Tribal Hidage arguably reflects the extent of his 'overkingship' at this stage. His victory over Cuichelm of the West Saxons (who was necessarily primarily Eadbald's rival rather than Edwin's) thereafter projected him in turn to the status of 'overking' even in the deep south: the full list of the Tribal Hidage was a result.

Edwin's policies probably reflect the political imperatives facing any ambitious northern king during the seventh century: his primary need was to weaken Mercia and contain the ambitions of its warrior class to restore themselves, around their own king, to the status of a hegemonal power, with all the influence, wealth and privilege which that would collectively bring them. Edwin inhabited a world dominated by the irreconcilable ambitions of the more potent regional hierarchies – consisting of royals, aristocrats and free warriors – to obtain 'overkingship' for their own candidates. Resulting tensions may in some respects have been comparable to those visible between the several regional communities who backed rival power brokers in the conflicts of the late fourteenth and fifteenth centuries.[154] Like them, the motive was arguably both offensive and defensive, intended both to deny hegemonal power to rival communities and at the same time acquire the same for themselves.

By the 620s, Mercia's hegemony had arguably already been dismantled by Edwin's immediate predecessor and its component parts re-orientated towards the northern kingship. The organisation of the Tribal Hidage suggests that this expedient was retained, with the rulers of each of what had been Mercia's dependencies responsible directly to Edwin (as king of the Deiri) for tribute payment – and Mercia was placed at their head. Edwin subsequently expelled Elmet's British ruler and subsumed this marcher kingship directly into his own kingship of Deira, so detaching it from Mercia's erstwhile dependencies. He probably did likewise in Lindsey and Hatfield, and certainly propagated his new religion in Lindsey,[155] thereby creating a land-corridor towards his ally in Kent. His interference in East Anglia may have been intended to secure the remainder of the east coast to his cause.[156] His putative activities in Wales likewise would have struck a blow at Mercia by destabilising what may previously have been her most powerful subordinate kingship, whose religious sensibilities and policies Edwin probably outraged by his espousal of the Christianity of Canterbury, the authority of which the British clergy had earlier rejected. His policies can be explained by religious imperatives but it is equally appropriate to interpret his conversion as a response to essentially political problems: Paulinus's God had given Edwin victory over the pagan West Saxons. Thereafter He could be harnessed to protect the king's interests against the danger of a Mercian resurgence. Christianity gave Edwin an entrée to Merovingian politics: his Kentish wife was half-Frankish and he procured a Merovingian bride for one of his elder sons. For Edwin, like other early English kings, politics and religion were indivisible.

Edwin's downfall and the destruction of his dynasty at the hands of his Mercian and Welsh enemies brought this edifice crashing down. It was Oswald's victory over Cadwallon (see above) that enabled Æthelfrith's sons to re-establish control of the north and reassert a Bernician hegemony elsewhere. Oswald's initial recognition as 'overking' presumably derived from the kudos he had gained as the victor of *Hefenfelth*, over the mighty Cadwallon, but his position was less secure than that of Edwin's before 633 for three reasons: firstly the marriage alliance between Edwin and Eadbald necessarily ruled out any possibility of Oswald establishing close co-operation with Kent, although he certainly exercised influence there since King Eadbald's protection of his rivals – Edwin's children and his own maternal cousins – was deemed inadequate by the dowager queen Æthelburh, who consequently sent her young family to Frankia;[157] secondly, Penda and his allies had already apparently consolidated their position in Mercia by the time Oswald had established himself and could probably be expected to frustrate and bring down his *imperium* at the earliest opportunity – as Penda eventually did in 642; thirdly, his kingship required the reversal of the balance of power, influence and patronage between the warrior communities of Bernicia and Deira which had obtained for the previous decade and three-quarters, a process which presumably left many of Edwin's erstwhile circle dissatisfied and committed to the earliest possible revival of the Deiran kingship under its native dynasty – which was something which Oswine achieved on Oswald's death.

Oswald apparently pursued similar policies to those of Edwin: he seems to have allied himself with Kent's great rival in the south – Wessex – where he stood godfather to Cynigils, but his influence there was not such that it prevented the West Saxons providing honourable sanctuary to Oswald's Deiran rival, the young Oswine. It may be significant that Cynigils accepted a Frankish, not an Irish, mission. Both circumstances suggest that Oswald was overly dependent on Cynigils and that, although the latter was presumably technically Oswald's tributary at some stage during the 630s, in practice Oswald had little authority on the far side of Mercian territory. Oswald may similarly have intervened in Wales against the interests of Cadwallon's kin (see above); like Edwin he also gave enthusiastic patronage to the clergy of the God who had vouchsafed his initial victory, so beginning a vigorous association between Bernician kings and Irish churchmen which was to last 30 years. That this Church looked in an entirely different direction to that of Edwin for its ultimate authority was a factor of considerable significance in the geopolitics of the central decades of the century.

Despite his own military reputation and these various political and diplomatic initiatives, Oswald was overthrown by Penda: if Mercia had previously been overthrown by Æthelfrith, then Penda may have had the deaths of kinsmen to avenge, which might explain his apparent barbarity towards Oswald himself. His capacity to raise large armies (including other Midlanders and Welsh kings) and cut off Bernicia from its southern ally were probably both critical factors in his victory.

Oswiu took over a much reduced northern hegemony which had probably lost all influence in the south (where the West Saxon king was likewise defeated by Penda and expelled). He had lost also control of Lindsey and Hatfield and was forced to accept Edwin's kinsman as king in Deira. Oswiu laid the foundations for his later rule in Deira and co-operation with Kent by marrying Edwin's half-Kentish daughter, Eanflæd, at the start of his reign, and this may have been a central plank in his subsequent survival. Until, however, he was able to encompass the death of Oswine of Deira (651) and reunite the two core northern kingships, he was hopelessly disadvantaged in the competition for power with Penda, who at some stage raided deep into Bernician territory, even attacking Bamburgh.[158] Even thereafter, Oswiu's son Ecgfrith was a hostage in Penda's keeping, so he may have recognised – however reluctantly – the superiority of Penda even into the early 650s, while apparently scheming against him with the Christian kingships of the East Angles and Kent, and ultimately perhaps even with Penda's son Peada – who became his own son-in-law and accepted conversion. Thereafter Penda invaded the north once more and pursued Oswiu even into the northern marches of Bernicia in an attempt to destroy him but was killed at the battle of *Winwæd* whilst retiring south.

Oswiu's three years of unchallenged supremacy thereafter witnessed an attempt to re-orientate the bulk of English Christianity towards Lindisfarne and Iona but the revival of Mercia's native dynasty (in 658), and perhaps too that of Gwynedd, left him little option but to draw closer to his principal allies in the south. Oswiu's regime organised a major *volte face* as regards authority within the Church at the Synod of Whitby in 664 and this should be seen as the final diplomatic coup by which the Bernicians sought to contain Mercia: it brought Oswiu the committed support of the archbishop at Canterbury and much strengthened his ties with the several southern kings, with whom he had already established marital links and who probably held the balance of military power. This policy was comparatively successful at least until 685, bearing fruit most noticeably in the peace process which followed Ecgfrith's defeat on the Trent, *c.* 679.

The Northumbrian hegemony was, therefore, intrinsically the weaker of the two great Anglian 'overkingships'. Æthelfrith's vast but somewhat shadowy achievements died with him, even if they roused ambitions in Bernicia for extensive 'overkingship'. Not until Oswiu's reign did Bernician leadership within the north become deeply entrenched and it was only at that stage that the close association of Bernicia and Deira under a single kingship became a permanent feature. Northumbria's challenge for a wider *imperium* was sustained only by exceptional war leadership during three generations which brought substantial victories over its enemies. In the longer term, it depended on a series of political alliances to contain Mercia. Direct Northumbrian rule of Mercia was always a policy of last resort which was ultimately unsuccessful, owing primarily to the well-developed sense of regional separateness in the Midlands, with the tradition of Mercian control and so the legitimate aspirations of the Mercian ruling classes to govern themselves and others to their own profit. Bernician hegemony may have been preferred by several of the more powerful southern kings primarily because it was both weaker and more distant than that of Mercia. Political alliances between the north and the south were therefore a recurring feature of the period which some Mercian kings sought to offset by establishing their own client kingships in the south (Wulfhere's favouring of the South Saxons is the obvious case in point). These same alliances had a profound effect on the religious policies of successive kings and massively affected the conversion of the English.

General conclusions

There were several regional *imperia* in Britain in the late sixth century: indeed, that of Gwynedd can be traced back to the late fifth century and it seems even then to have been outfaced by a more powerful Saxon kingship. 'Overkingships' were, therefore, already of some antiquity at the stage when they become better known to history, during the seventh century.

The possibility exists, and should be taken seriously, that they derived ultimately from the political geography of late Roman Britain: that geography was clearly much-altered, most markedly by virtue of the treaty which recognised autonomous or near autonomous British kingships throughout the western half of Britannia Prima.[159] Thereafter, although the process is beyond reconstruction, the absorption of the northernmost reaches of the remainder of that province by Mercia (expanding its hegemony out of Flavia Caesariensis) and the combination of the remainder with Maxima Caesariensis would produce a political geography eerily close to that embodied in the two lists of the Tribal Hidage (Figure 4).

Whether this was their origin or not, the resultant regional agglomerations of kingships proved to be comparatively robust over a very long period. Dramatic military victory might enable an *imperium*-wielding king to establish his own hegemony over a neighbouring cluster of kingships and, in extreme cases, even to usurp the central kingship therein (as Oswiu did in Mercia). More commonly such victory enabled the winner to usurp control over border provinces, or parts thereof, which had hitherto been tributary to another 'overking'. But such realignments were hotly contested over long periods: Welsh resistance to Mercian tenure of parts of Powys remained a fact of border life up to the Norman Conquest and beyond; Mercian hostility to Northumbrian control of Lindsey was ultimately successful but had to be sustained for several generations; Hatfield was similarly debated and may have ultimately been partitioned; the West Saxons eventually reversed Mercian aggrandisement around Dorchester but not the Mercian takeover of the Hwicce and *Arosæte*.

There seems, therefore, to have been a broad consensus concerning the normal limits of each hegemony, irrespective of the king or dynasty of the day, and both the regional 'overkings' and their clients apparently preferred, and sought to return to, traditional relationships which recognised the integrity of the entire region, over and against alterations imposed from outside. Bede's comments concerning hostility towards King Oswald at Bardney (in Lindsey) is an instructive example of just such a preference on the part of a major client province for one 'overkingship' (Mercian in this instance) over another, to which it was sometimes attached as the spoils of war.

The patterning of regional and tribal names reinforce the view that these regional *imperia* were already of some antiquity by the seventh century. It is noticeable that particular types of names occur most often along the marches between them. The commonest group are names in *sæte* (or *sætan*), the plural of *sæta*, a 'resident' or 'inhabitant'. This suffix is generally associated with either a place-name or a regional name of topographical origin (e.g. *Ciltern*). In several instances the prefixes are pre-English (as Elmet) and I have suggested elsewhere that this compound may often refer to a tributary kingship (and so a people) which was recognisably British until a comparatively late date.[160] That they congregate along the marches between these several regional *imperia* may imply that they originated as British-ruled localities which became buffer-states protected by Anglo-Saxon warlords in return for tribute (Figure 12). If so, their distribution certainly suggests that those boundaries had not changed dramatically over a very long period.

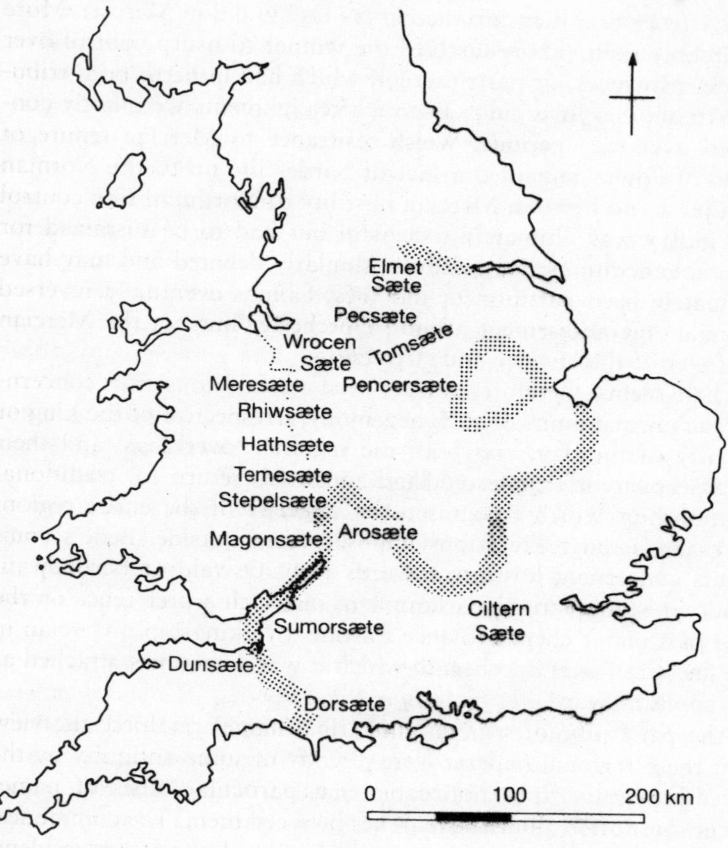

Figure 12 Regional names in *-sæte* and the frontiers of the several 'overkingships' as recognisable in the early seventh century. Such names clearly congregate along these frontiers, and particularly along those between the Celtic west and the two English *imperia* in southern Britain. Pagan Anglo-Saxon cemeteries are notoriously difficult to identify in almost all these areas.

The youngest of the regional 'overkingships' was the northern one, which apparently stemmed from the political and military achievements of an aggressive border dynasty in the second half of the sixth century. Mercia's hegemony in the centre of Britain was necessarily at least one generation older than Penda – who is all too often perceived as its originator. It may (but need not) have been that Anglian kingship remarked on by Procopius. It certainly seems well-established by the time it enters history and it is probably significant that it is never known to have been challenged by any other kingship within the region, many of which arguably had British origins. Co-operation with the British 'overkingship' of Gwynedd may have long been a factor in its stability, at least until Mercian kings (perhaps primarily Penda) encroached upon Wales. The south, too, was probably a single 'overkingship' earlier than was Northumbria but competition for control between Wessex and several of its eastern neighbours apparently weakened its unity and left it vulnerable to outside intervention during the seventh century and thereafter.

Imperium seems not to have been wielded by more than one king at any one time within a traditional area of 'overkingship' – with the possible and occasional exception of the south, where West Saxon kings exercised a limited *imperium* within an agglomerate state from an early date. Otherwise these units seem to have been comparatively discrete. There were apparently four, although more than one could be (and often was) dominated by a single individual.

These regional communities were highly interactive on two levels: within the area of *imperium*, the 'overking' of the day presumably levied tribute on his clients (hence the Tribal Hidage, Bede's references to Æthelfrith's levying tribute and comments on Wulfhere in the *Life of Wilfrid*), provided military leadership (as in Penda's thirty 'legions' at *Winwæd*) and protection, and exercised a degree of control over marital and diplomatic activity between client dynasties;[161] while externally he was responsible for relations with neighbouring 'overkingships', both diplomatically and in war, and generally mediated on behalf of the total regional community with other kings and with the gods.[162] It seems likely that a state of tension was normal between the three English regions at least and, after Penda, also between Wales and Mercia. A degree of military unity under single rule was probably the only effective deterrent to raids in force from outside, such as Cadwallon and Penda both perpetrated in Northumbria. The loss of some autonomy in warfare and diplomacy, and the payment of tribute, was probably considered by most kings (and particularly the kings of minor peoples), most of the time, to be an acceptable price to pay for security.

Relations between the various 'overkingships' appear to follow well-established patterns, throughout the seventh century at least: there were two dominant dynasties which regularly and opportunistically interfered in the other 'overkingships' in their own interests and contrary to those of their rivals.

Regional hegemonies played a very significant role in the conversion process, with 'overkings' who had chosen Christianity in one form or another foisting it onto other kings under their patronage (despite resistance), as well as onto their own peoples. Conversion was a political statement and a series of powerful 'overkings' from Æthelberht onwards used the Church and its authority as a means of expanding or solidifying their own power.

So pervasive do interactions of various kinds seem to have been that it is inadvisable to write the history of any individual kingship without taking account both of its role within a regional system of interlocking peoples and their rulers, and of the impact of interactions on a higher level, between this and other systems. Regional clusters of peoples and dynasties did therefore have an important function, as well as a remarkable robustness, in early Britain. This is not, however, to suggest that some sort of office of *bretwalda* ever existed:[163] that may have been the invention of a West Saxon chronicler in the late ninth century who was keen to associate Alfred's grandfather with Bede's famous list (in *HE*, II, 5) but had no word in the vernacular by which to translate *imperium* (or more strictly *imperator*); alternatively it was simply a consequence of our misunderstanding of his intentions. Universal *imperium* did occur – indeed, it was not uncommon between *c.* 616 and 685 and may have developed at an earlier date without our knowledge – but it did not at this stage develop constitutional dimensions and was never inherited, as regional 'overkingship' could be among, for example, the Mercians and Bernicians. It was, in practice, nothing more than the combination of the various regional *imperia* (normally in part at least by war), with or without subordinate 'overkingships', under the ultimate control of a single king.

There were several such kings who could realistically have claimed to be 'kings of Britain' but the political structure of the world in which they lived was fundamentally different from that of 'Vortigern', with whom the unity of pre-Saxon Britain apparently failed. Kingship had proliferated and the most to which even the most powerful seventh-century king could reasonably aspire was to be a universal 'overking'. He might control several key kingships in person (with or without the committed support of the warrior classes of them all) but the bulk of what had been Roman Britain would necessarily be ruled beneath his ultimate protection by numerous client kings, most of whom exercised authority which derived not from him but from their own dynastic descent and identification with the local elite. To the collective political interests of such men a successful 'overking' had necessarily to pay considerable attention.

The earliest such universal 'overking' known to history is Rædwald, king of the East Angles, and it is to him that we turn next as a detailed exemplar of the politics of the conversion period. Before doing so, however, we should recall that this discussion has been conditioned by Bede's dialectical purposes. Just as those required that the English people and their kings should have exercised *imperium* over all Britain, so too did he envisage this process at its most virtuous under Bernician leadership. Yet there is a reality behind the rhetoric: his arguments would have been a notorious sham had such kings not, on occasion at least, exercised extensive 'overkingship' over large parts – even all – of erstwhile Roman Britain, and even beyond. The reality of political hierarchies (of however temporary and crude a nature) is as much a part of the seventh century as Bede's pursuit of his own providential purposes is a part of the eighth.

Notes

1 E.g. F. M. Stenton, *Anglo-Saxon England*, 3rd ed., Oxford, 1971, pp. 202–38.

2 E.g. S. Bassett, ed., *The Origins of Anglo-Saxon Kingdoms*, Leicester, 1989; B. Yorke, *Kings and Kingdoms of Early Anglo-Saxon England*, London, 1990; D. P. Kirby, *The Earliest English Kings*, London, 1991, is the exception.

3 As the *Origins of the Shire* series, currently in production through Manchester University Press; J. Blair, *Anglo-Saxon Oxfordshire*, Stroud, 1994.

4 E.g. J. N. L. Myres, *The English Settlements*, Oxford, 1986.

5 See discussion in N. J. Higham, *Origins of Cheshire*, Manchester, 1993, pp. 191–202.

6 *Ibid*, pp. 73–5.

7 See above, pp. 76–99.

8 Of which archaeological evidence implies that Lindsey was by far the more prosperous and anglicised, as well as being the larger. It was hidated at 7,000 in the Tribal Hidage (admittedly incorporating Hatfield), versus only 600 hides for Elmet. These figures suggest that the division of provinces reflected Mercian victory. All three were in that sector of the circuit which was dependent on Mercia in the Tribal Hidage, so had presumably been attached to the north by Edwin, who was considered responsible for the expulsion of at least one British subking.

9 Depending on the extent of early Hatfield: for a minimalist interpretation see N. J. Higham, *The Kingdom of Northumbria: AD 300–1100*, Stroud, 1993, pp. 87–9, but this may be superseded by M. S. Parker, 'The province of Hatfield', *Northern History*, XXVIII, 1992, pp. 42–69. A location for the battle of Hatfield in territory subject to Æthelred of Mercia (died 704) late in his life, so probably outside medieval Yorkshire, is implicit in the *Whitby Life*: B. Colgrave, *The Earliest Life of Gregory the Great*, Cambridge, 1985, XVIII.

10 For Hatfield in Herts., see B. Colgrave and R. A. B. Mynors, edd., *Bede: Ecclesiastical History of the English People*, Oxford, 1969, p. 385, fn. 3; Stenton, *Anglo-Saxon England*, p. 137. If the *regio* of Hatfield had only been divided in *c.* 679, then location of the synod there *c.* 680 would have reinforced the Archbishop's triumphant role as peace broker. See *HE*, IV, 7. For discussion, see Higham, *Northumbria*, pp. 138–9; for the date, see J. M. Wallace-Hadrill, *Bede's Ecclesiastical History of the English People, A Historical Commentary*, Oxford, 1988, p. 157.

11 For recent discussion of which see N. J. Higham, 'The Cheshire burhs and the Mercian frontier to 924', *Transactions of the Antiquarian Society of Lancashire and Cheshire*, LXXXV, 1988, pp. 212–14. This was arguably a major tribal boundary in the late pre-Roman Iron Age and a provincial boundary in the late Roman period.

12 *HE*, IV, 21. He was termed *rex* in *ibid*, IV, 22, so was perhaps a subking of Deira under his brother.

13 *Life of Wilfrid*, XX: 'Wulfhere . . . stirring up the southern peoples against our kingship (*regnum*), intended not merely to go to war but also to take tribute . . .'

14 *Ibid*, XIX–XX.

15 Hence his attacks on the Irish and Picts: *HE*, IV, 24.

16 *Life of Wilfrid*, XL.

17 *HE*, V, 24.

18 Indeed, it was virtually ignored by Stenton, *Anglo-Saxon England*, but see *HE*, IV, 19.

19 Bede, *Letter to Ecgbert*.

20 As W. Levison, 'Bede as Historian', in *Bede, his life, times and writings: essays in commemoration of the twelfth centenary of his death*,

ed. A. Hamilton Thompson, Oxford, 1935, p. 148.

21 Eorconwald, bishop of London, 675–93.

22 F. L. Attenborough, *The Laws of the Earliest English Kings*, Cambridge, 1922, pp. 18–23; D. Whitelock, ed., *English Historical Documents: I, 500–1042*, London, 1955, pp. 360–61.

23 *HE*, IV, 26.

24 B. Yorke, *Kings and Kingdoms of Early Anglo-Saxon England*, London, 1990, p. 32.

25 Compare the joint action of a Northumbrian 'overking' and subking as patrons of Wilfrid at Ripon: *Wilfrid*, XVII, or the role of Œthelwald (son of Oswald) as subking of Deira under his uncle (Oswiu), who likewise opposed his superior and close relative: *HE*, III, 14, 23, 24.

26 Described as *princeps* in *HE*, III, 21.

27 *ASC(A)*, 853: at King Æthelwulf's death, his sons succeeded, Æthelbald to Wessex and Æthelberht to Kent, Essex, Surrey and Sussex.

28 *HE*, IV, 15.

29 *HE*, IV, 16.

30 *HE*, IV, 26.

31 Yorke, *Kings and Kingdoms*, p. 137; Kirby, *Earliest English Kings*, pp. 118–24.

32 *HE*, IV, 19; for a map, see P. Stafford, *The East Midlands in the early Middle Ages*, Leicester, 1985, p. 31.

33 *HE*, IV, 22.

34 A. Williams, A. P. Smyth and D. P. Kirby, *A Bibliographical dictionary of Dark Age Britain*, London, 1991, p. 161.

35 Stenton, *Anglo-Saxon England*, p. 135.

36 *HE*, III, 25; *Life of Wilfrid*, X.

37 F. M. Stenton, 'The East Anglian Kings', in *Preparatory to Anglo-Saxon England: being the collected papers of Frank Merry Stenton*, ed. D. M. Stenton, Oxford, 1970, pp. 394–402.

38 *The Anglo-Saxon Chronicle: MS 'A'*, ed. J. M. Bateley, Cambridge, 1986, p. 41.

39 For discussion of Mercian and West Saxon policies towards Kent, see S. Keynes, 'The control of Kent in the Ninth Century', *Early Medieval Europe, II*, 1993, pp. 111–31.

40 That of Ceolwulf, *ibid*, 877.

41 For which, at the level of individual kingships, see Bassett, ed., *Origins*, but note that this work generally minimises the impact of 'overkingship' on the development of individual kingships or peoples and some contributors place excessive reliance on very late sources of questionable historicity, such as king lists, royal genealogies and the *Anglo-Saxon Chronicle*, none of which offer a sound basis for the exploration of the sixth or (in some instances) the early seventh centuries.

42 W. Davies, *Wales in the early Middle Ages*, Leicester, 1982, p. 112.

43 *Ibid*, p. 113. The exclusive treament of Anglo-Saxon England is best exemplified in Stenton, *Anglo-Saxon England*, *passim*.

44 N. J. Higham, 'Medieval "overkingship" in Wales: the earliest evidence', *Welsh History Review*, XVI, 1992, pp. 154–9; Higham, *The English Conquest: Gildas and Britain in the Fifth Century*, Manchester, 1994, pp. 180–86.

45 *DEB*, LXVII, 2; CVII, 4; see Higham, *English Conquest*, for recent, detailed discussion. Gildas's references to the 'devil's' influence on Maglocunus *may* have been a coded reference to such a relationship: *DEB*, XXXIV, 4, referring to the 'wolf' and the 'ill-omened father of all the damned', both of which are metaphors for the Saxons which Gildas had already established by this point in his work.

46 *DEB*, XXVI, 2; XCII, 3.

47 Procopius, *History of the Wars*, ed. and trans. H. B. Dewing, London and New York, 1928, VIII, 20.

48 For general discussion of Procopius, see A. Cameron, *Procopius*, London, 1985, pp. 213–16; for *Brittia*, see E. A. Thompson, 'Procopius on Brittia and Britannia', *Classical Quarterly*, XXX, 1980, pp. 498–507.

49 Which is not anything like a contemporary annal but which *may* be historical by this date: 613, generally corrected to 615.

50 See discussion in Higham, *Origins*, pp. 85–7.

51 For more detailed discussion, see N. J. Higham, 'King Cearl, the battle of Chester and the origins of the Mercian "overkingship"', *Midland History*, XVII, 1992, pp. 1–15.

52 V. E. Nash-Williams, *The Early Christian Monuments of Wales*, Cardiff, 1950, p. 57.

53 *HE*, II, 20.

54 Note that the term *gens* can have pagan associations as in 'gentiles' in the Bible: contrast the use of *ecclesia vel gens* for the Northumbrians, invoking the common use in the Vulgate of *ecclesia* for the Israelite nation.

55 *HE*, I, 32.

56 Higham, *English Conquest*, pp. 53–6.

57 *DEB*, XXIII, 1.

58 Compare Penda at *Winwæd*: J. McClure, 'Bede's Old Testament Kings', in *Ideal and Reality*, ed. P. Wormald, Oxford, 1983, p. 89.

59 *HE*, I, 4.

60 *HE*, II, 20; both *HB*, LXI and *AC*, 630 omit reference to Penda.

61 *HE*, II, 9. See also II, 5, but see comment thereon above, p. 82.

62 See above, pp. 23–4.

63 I have reconsidered this point since writing '"overkingship" in Wales', p. 150, and would prefer to replace the comment therein with this view. Bede used the verb *subiugo* in only two further instances: in I, 3,

Vespasian *Romanorum dicioni subiugavit* ('subjugated to Roman rule') the Isle of Wight; in I, 34, the '(British) indigenes had been subjugated' by Æthelfrith. Both relate to military activity but not necessarily active conquest. The contrast with Edwin's victory over Cuichelm (II, 9) remains sustainable.

64 *Troedd Ynys Prydein: the Welsh Triads*, ed. R. Bromwich, Cardiff, 1961, p. 339 and nos. 26w, 55.

65 *Ibid*, p. 57, no. 29.

66 See discussion in Higham, *Northumbria*, pp. 120–24.

67 *HE*, II, 20.

68 As argued above, pp. 98–9.

69 Stenton, *Anglo-Saxon England*, p. 296; M. Gelling, *The West Midlands in the early Middle Ages*, Leicester, 1992, pp. 83–5.

70 W. Davies and H. Vierck, 'The contexts of Tribal Hidage: social aggregates and settlement patterns', *Frühmittelalterliche Studien*, VIII, 1974, p. 231; D. H. Hill, *An atlas of Anglo-Saxon England*, Oxford, 1981, p. 76; Yorke, *Kings and Kingdoms*, p. 13; P. Sims-Williams, *Religion and literature in western England, 600–800*, Cambridge, 1990, p. 18.

71 Higham, *Origins*, pp. 70–72.

72 For discussion, see Higham, ' "Overkingship" in Wales', pp. 152–3.

73 See above, p. 86.

74 *HE*, III, 1–2.

75 *HE*, II, 5.

76 *Adamnan's Life of St. Columba*, ed. M. O. Anderson, London and Edinburgh, 1961, I.

77 *HE*, III, 7, for his sponsorship of King Cynegils of the West Saxons and association with the grant of Dorchester to the church. That his power was significant (and considered inimical) in Kent is implicit in *HE*, II, 20.

78 *HE*, III, 1.

79 *Troedd Ynys Prydein*, pp. 289–90, no. 68.

80 *HB*, LXV.

81 *AC*, 658.

82 *HE*, III, 24.

83 *Armes Prydein: the prophecy of Britain*, ed. R. Bromwich, Dublin, 1972, lines 81, 91.

84 My gratitude to the late Professor John McNeil Dodgson for his comments on this matter which I recall from a decade ago but which were never published in any detail.

85 K. Pretty, 'Defining the Magonsaete', in Bassett, ed. *Origins*, pp. 171–83.

86 Higham, *Origins*, pp. 98–101.

87 Higham, *English Conquest*, pp. 164–6.

88 Nash-Williams, *Christian Monuments*, pp. 123–5.

89 Higham, *Origins*, pp. 99–101.

90 *AC*, 813–22.

91 *HB*, XVI.

92 Compare *DEB*, XXIII, wherein the 'proud tyrant' was similarly apparently a universal ruler: see discussion, Higham, *English Conquest*, pp. 155–7.

93 *HB*, XLVII.

94 *HB*, XL.

95 *HB*, XLVIII.

96 *HB*, XLVIII.

97 *HB*, XXXV: note that the inscription on the pillar of Eliseg claimed his descent from Magnus Maximus via 'Vortigern', suggesting that its author had a much higher regard for 'Vortigern' than the author of *HB*. It is important to remind ourselves that the *HB* is a piece of literature which is subject to specific and highly contemporary political imperatives of a distinctively Gwynedd-centric kind.

98 In general, D. N. Dumville, 'Sub-Roman Britain: history and legend', *History*, LXII, 1977, pp. 173–92.

99 *HB*, XXX. See also the reference to Lucius and his *subreguli* in XXII, for comment on which see above, p. 25.

100 *DEB*, VII.

101 See above, p. 86.

102 *HE*, II, 14.

103 *Henrici Archidiaconi Huntendunensis Historia Anglorum*, ed. H. Arnold, 1879; *Rogeri de Wendover Chronica, sive Flores Historarum*, ed. H. O. Coxe, 1841–4; see discussion in W. Davies, 'Annals and the origins of Mercia', in A. Dornier, ed., *Mercian Studies*, Leicester, 1977, pp. 20, 25; N. Brooks, 'The formation of the Mercian kingdom', in Bassett, ed., *Origins*, pp. 159–63.

104 For detailed discussion, Higham, 'King Cearl', pp. 1–5.

105 *HE*, II, 12.

106 Higham, 'King Cearl', p. 3.

107 For doubts concerning the accuracy of the various regnal years offered by the *HB*, see Higham, *Northumbria*, p. 77.

108 See pp. 48–50.

109 Higham, 'King Cearl', pp. 6–7.

110 *HE*, II, 12. For discussion of Rædwald's role, see pp. 195–7, below.

111 *HE*, II, 12.

112 It cannot, of course, be used too literally in reconstructing Mercian hegemony given the political factors which have apparently influenced some at least of the figures but this exercise is probably still valid at a rather crude level.

113 *HE*, III, 24.

114 Myres, *Anglo-Saxon Settlements*, pp. 174–5, 182; for a more cautious approach, see Kirby, *Earliest Kings*, p. 77.

115 First used by Bede in *HE*, I, 15.

116 Wormald, 'Bede, the *Bretwaldas* and the origins of the *Gens Anglorum*', in *Ideal and Reality*, pp. 122–4.

117 Most recently by Brooks, 'Mercian kingdom', p. 160.

118 Higham, *English Conquest*, pp. 151–3.

119 *Ibid*, p. 192.

120 For different views on which see Gelling, *West Midlands*, pp. 83–5; Higham, *Origins*, pp. 68–77.

121 Contrast the assumption of catastrophic discontinuity in K. R. Dark, *From Civitas to Kingdom: British Political Continuity 300–800*, Leicester, 1994, p. 50.

122 *HE*, II, 15; II, 5.

123 *HE*, II, 2; I propose to deal with this event in detail in the last volume of this intended trilogy which will focus on the conversion of the English.

124 *HE*, II, 2.

125 See above, p. 57.

126 N. Brooks, 'The creation and early structure of the kingdom of Kent', in Bassett, ed., *Origins*, pp. 66–7.

127 See the seminal work of J. W. Huggett, 'Imported Grave Goods and the Early Anglo-Saxon Economy', *Medieval Archaeology*, XXXII, 1988, pp. 63–96.

128 See above, pp. 52–4.

129 P. Sims-Williams, 'The settlement of England in Bede and the Chronicle', *Anglo-Saxon England*, XII, 1983, pp. 1–41; Brooks, 'Kent', pp. 60–64; Yorke, *Kings and Kingdoms*, pp. 25–8 and *passim*.

130 *ASC(A,E)*, years 495–534. For Ælle, see *ibid* for the year 477.

131 Most recently, see T. Williamson, *The origins of Norfolk*, Manchester, 1993, pp. 32–48.

132 M. Welch, 'The kingdom of the South Saxons: the origins', in Bassett, ed., *Origins*, pp. 75, 83.

133 For the former, B. Yorke, 'The Jutes of Hampshire and Wight and the origins of Wessex', in *ibid*, fig. 6.1, p. 85; for the latter, see the tentative reconstruction in B. Jones and D. Mattingley, *An Atlas of Roman Britain*, Oxford, 1990, p. 154.

134 J. Blair, 'Frithuwold's kingdom and the origins of Surrey', in Bassett, ed., *Origins*, pp. 97–107; N. J. Higham, *Rome, Britain and the Anglo-Saxons*, London, 1992, pp. 129–32.

135 *HE*, II, 3; his choice of terminology perhaps betrays Bede's awareness that London had been chosen as the southern metropolitan see by St.

Gregory: *HE*, I, 29, as well as his determination to write up Æthelberht, for which see above, pp. 49–50.

136 K. Bailey, 'The Middle Saxons', in Bassett, ed., *Origins*, pp. 108–22. Any one of several entirely obscure peoples therein *could* have been located in this area.

137 *HE*, III, 7.

138 That the Hwicce were part of Æthelberht's *imperium* before *c.* 616, but thereafter emerged as a satellite of Mercia, may have led to the apocryphal reconstruction in *ASC(A,E)* for 628 of a battle at Cirencester between Cynigils, Cuichelm and Penda.

139 *HE*, II, 9.

140 E.g. *ASC(E)* for the years 626, 628 and 636.

141 *HE*, III, 28.

142 In which case the king of the insular Angles whose troops attacked the Varni cannot have been Ælle, as very tentatively suggested by myself in *Rome*, p. 149, but could have been some anonymous contemporary.

143 For recent discussion, see D. N. Dumville, 'The origins of Northumbria: some aspects of the British background', in Bassett, ed., *Origins*, pp. 213–22; D. Powlesland with C. Haughton and J. Hanson, 'Excavations at Heslerton, North Yorkshire, 1978–82', *Archaeological Journal*, CXLIII, 1986, pp. 53–173; Higham, *Northumbria*, pp. 76–104.

144 *DEB*, I, 5.

145 See discussion in Higham, *Conquest*, pp. 170–71.

146 *HB*, LXIII.

147 *HE*, V, 24.

148 *HB*, LVI, LVII; use of the apostolic number arguably betrays the influence of later Christian rewriting of early Bernician history so as to promote comparisons between the Bernicians and the early Church of the New Testament. Bede's claim that Ida reigned for twelve years is probably related and both items seem designed to sustain the opinion which Bede expressed in *HE*, I, 22, that the English (of whom Bede considered the Bernician kings to be the proper rulers) were foreknown by God and a chosen people.

149 *HB*, LXI.

150 See below, p. 196.

151 See, for example, W. S. Hanson and D. B. Campbell, 'The Brigantes: from clientage to conquest', *Britannia*, XVII, 1986, pp. 73–89; N. J. Higham, 'Brigantia revisited', *Northern History*, XXIII, 1987, pp. 1–19.

152 Higham, *English Conquest*, pp. 152–3.

153 See below, p. 199.

154 Most recently, see C. Richmond, 'An English Mafia?', *Nottingham Medieval Studies*, XXXVI, 1992, pp. 235–43. I am grateful to my colleague Dr. R. G. Davies for discussion of this subject.

155 *HE*, II, 16; see discussion, p. 95.

156 *HE*, II, 15.

157 *HE*, II, 20.

158 *HE*, II, 16.

159 Higham, *English Conquest*, pp. 175–6.

160 Higham, *Origins*, pp. 85–91.

161 It may have been Oswiu's marriage alliance with Peada, and the latter's baptism in Bernicia, which reignited Penda's hostility towards him.

162 Hence Edwin's, then Oswiu's, dealings with Rome concerning Canterbury: *HE*, II, 17–18; III, 29.

163 B. A. E. Yorke, 'The vocabulary of Anglo-Saxon overkingship', *Anglo-Saxon Studies in History and Archaeology*, II, 1981, pp. 171–200.

5

Rædwald: a pagan 'overking'

By the standards of early England, Rædwald of the East Angles was a great king. Victorious in battle over a formidable opponent, his influence stretched during the latter part of his life from southern Britain to Bernicia.[1] Only a generation ago, his greatness was secure. As one of the *imperium*-wielding kings named in book two, chapter five of Bede's *Historia Ecclesiastica*,[2] he was widely credited with the title of *Bretwalda* or *Brytenwealda* and seen as the overlord of all the kings of southern England.[3] Re-examination of this 'bretwaldaship' has, however, found it wanting.[4] As an institution and as a title it must now be abandoned but recent re-examination of Bede's use of *imperium* to describe the rule of the greater English kings threatens to create a new and minimalist consensus view of early kingship which accords Rædwald a much reduced role.[5] This chapter will re-examine Rædwald's career and his ultimate status as the champion of religious conservatism and political orthodoxy in an England already touched by the new Christian monotheism, contact with which was to have fundamental implications for the social fabric of the English nation as well as the ideology which had hitherto sustained it.

The comparative obscurity of Rædwald's life is due to the scarcity of surviving references to him in literature written even within a century and a quarter of his death. The earliest occurs in the anonymous *Life of Gregory the Great*, written in the very early years of the eighth century at Whitby;[6] his name then appears in four separate passages of Bede's *HE*, including one which derived from the same story concerning Edwin's conversion as that recorded in the Whitby *Life*.[7] His defeat of Æthelfrith was later entered into the *Anglo-Saxon Chronicle* under the year 617,[8] but there is no good reason to think that this derives from a source which is independent of Bede.[9] Excepting only the deaths of Archbishops Lawrence and Mellitus, there were no other entries in the Chronicle within the period of his supposed supremacy, so no reason to think that the author thereof had access to detailed accounts of these years which have since been lost. On the contrary, later Christian writers were concerned to portray the English conversion as a seamless progression from Augustine's arrival ever onwards and upwards towards the glorious and universal triumph of Roman Christianity. They therefore had little reason to dwell on the several years of conservative reaction under a pagan 'overking' which followed Æthelberht's death. No reference occurs in the *Annales Cambriae* or *Historia Brittonum*,[10] implying that Rædwald's *imperium* had little direct or deleterious impact in Wales or on British interests in the north.[11]

Bede and pagan kings

Our knowledge of Rædwald depends heavily, therefore, on his treatment by Bede. His purposes in writing the *HE* are consequently central to the problem of reconstructing Rædwald's career. His historical *magnum opus* should, of course, be treated not as a history but as a piece of dialectic composed for purposes which were immediate, pastoral and propagandist.[12] In this context, Bede was a committed exponent of Roman Christianity, writing at a time when that branch of the faith was still battling for the hearts and minds of the Anglo-Saxons and their distant cousins in Germany against paganism and other branches of Christianity.[13] The *Historia* was a carefully crafted contribution to this ideological struggle. It was written so as to lay before the reader or listener a particular version of the inexorable rise and spread of the true faith under God's guiding hand among His chosen people.[14] It was, therefore, both polemical and rhetorical.

The criteria governing Bede's selection and organisation of information concerning early English kings were not such as would commend themselves to a modern historian researching seventh-century English kingship. Unless their careers conformed to one of several stereotypes which Bede sought to illustrate, he accorded even mighty kings no more than the passing mention necessitated by some other aspect of his account. Excluding only British kings, he exercised his most active discrimination against successful pagans, recognition of whose achievements posed a serious threat to his fundamental message concerning the relationship between the English and God. Bede's purposes here are clarified by his treatment of kings Osric of the Deirans and Eanfrith of the Bernicians, the northern kings who succeeded to Edwin's kingdom.[15] Both apostatised in the crisis of 633–4 but disaster overwhelmed them almost immediately. Bede was thereby enabled to use them as exemplars through which to illustrate the inevitable consequences of apostasy. Because they failed, they suited his purposes well. Their destruction could be portrayed as self-inflicted while their apostasy both polluted and destroyed them. Even at the hands of the 'impious' Cadwallon, whom Bede otherwise castigated, their fate could be portrayed as just. Bede therefore felt justified in denying to both the fame and honour which meant so much to Anglo-Saxon warrior society, peremptorily writing them out of history and transferring their regnal years to the righteous and successful Christian, King Oswald, who was one of his especial heroes.[16]

These reigns were short and came to a bloody end, so they posed no threat to the dynamics of Bede's Christian message but he faced greater difficulties in explaining away the careers of more successful pagan kings. Important casualties of his neglect were kings Cearl and Penda of the Mercians, great kings who had probably at times exercised wide hegemony.[17] Cearl's existence was mentioned only as an indirect consequence of Bede's elaboration of the Christian members of King Edwin's dynasty (see above). This was done in terms which were morally neutral,[18] perhaps because he was such an early figure that he posed no threat to the onward development of Christianity after Æthelberht.[19] Since Bede was almost as dependent on existing Christian views of the past as we are upon him, it may be that such uninteresting subjects as the pagan (and Mercian) Cearl had already been discarded from memory by the time that Bede was collecting his information, particularly given the poverty of his Mercian sources. He may, therefore, have known little else about him. Whether or not, he had every reason to ignore Cearl's putative hegemony, and credit the Christian Æthelberht with what was arguably Cearl's quite separate regional 'overkingship' between the Wash and the Humber.[20]

Penda's successes against Christian kings consistently excited Bede's opprobrium[21] but he was never centre-stage in the *Historia*, only appearing when the author could find no way to avoid mentioning his influence on events. Then he creeps from the shadows as a satanic figure bent on wicked deeds against more virtuous (Christian and predominately Bernician) kings. His eventual destruction was described by Bede in terms which recall that of Cadwallon's at the hand of the heroic King Oswald,[22] and ultimately that of Goliath at the hands of the virtuous David. In Bede's final chronological summary, only Penda's death was recalled, linked with the advent of Christianity among the Mercians in a fashion that implies that Bede considered him the principal obstacle to the conversion of this people and all their neighbours or tributaries.[23] Bede's characterisation of Penda was, therefore, generally negative, but his primary weapon against the reputation of so great a king was neglect.

The only king who died a pagan but whom Bede on occasion treated more generously was Æthelfrith of his own native Bernicia, whose military achievements were probably crucial to the foundation of the Bernician dynasty as a major force in Britain.[24] Where he saw fit, Bede circumvented the moral dilemma posed by his paganism by finding Old Testament analogies for Æthelfrith, picturing him as an English champion versus the Scots and as the unwitting agent of God versus the heretical Britons at Chester.[25] He appears to have been able to do this to his own satisfaction for several reasons, not the least of which was the sympathy which he and his immediate audience shared for this Bernician hero, the true architect of a Bernician-ruled Northumbria, concerning whose deeds tales were presumably still circulating in the eighth century.[26] More compelling intellectually were two literary parallels to his own work which seem to have influenced Bede's perception of the English conversion. The more basic of these was the structure of the Bible, with the pre-Christian Old Testament of the non-Christian, but still God-chosen, Jews serving as a precursor to the Christian era. The *HE* also has an opening section, albeit a short one (the first twenty-two chapters), which prefaces the arrival of Christianity among the English much as the Old Testament prefaces the life of Christ. There are many parallels between the two, which include prophecy which only the arrival of Christ (or in England of Christianity) would bring to fulfilment. Bede ended this section by laying emphasis on the ultimate moral failure of the Britons[27] and looking towards the Christian era among the God-favoured Anglo-Saxons whom the wicked Britons had neglected to convert. His choice of Saul for comparison with Æthelfrith was a subtle one. Bede was clearly aware of the conflicting value judgements concerning that Old Testament king in *Samuel*,[28] and took advantage of this ambivalence in his own treatment of the Bernician hero.

The second extended analogy which Bede employed was with Rome and his perception of its empire. The Romans were portrayed by Bede, an advocate of Roman Christianity, as morally superior to their British subjects[29] and Romans were not damaged morally by their paganism until they began to persecute the Christians.[30] Bede took this opportunity to highlight the martyrdom of St. Alban, a Roman soldier, so claiming the front-ranking British martyr for the Roman Church, prior to Britain's lapse into error, initially through Arianism,[31] then through the peculiarly British Pelagianism.[32]

If it was the Old Testament Jews and the pre-Constantinian Romans, rather than the Britons, to whose moral status Bede looked to establish analogies for the English, he was free to portray early English pagans (i.e. before the arrival of Roman Christianity in 597) as no worse than morally neutral. Only with Æthelberht's conversion were pagans to be condemned. Hengist, Horsa and Ida escaped censure altogether.[33] He was, therefore, enabled to treat Æthelfrith, the father of the heroic Christian Bernicians, Oswald and Oswiu, in generous terms, at least until his career collided with the rise and spread of Christianity. As conqueror of the heretical Britons he could be characterised as an instrument of God's will in bringing to fruition the prophecy or curse pronounced by Augustine at the final collapse of his negotiations with the Britons over a decade before.[34] Only in his last mention of the Bernician king, when treating of his persecution of Edwin (whom he here portrayed, quite apocryphally, as already on the path towards conversion), did Bede feel constrained to pronounce the great Bernician king *infestus* ('harmful') and a *peremtus* ('murderer').[35]

Bede was able to write the more freely concerning Æthelfrith since the current ruler of Northumbria, that King Ceolwulf to whom he dedicated and presented his work, was not Æthelfrith's lineal descendant, claiming instead to have sprung from another branch of the Bernician royal house.[36] Æthelfrith's great-grandson,

King Osred (died 716), had been associated with the Wilfridian camp within the Northumbrian church to which both Bede and Ceolwulf were apparently opposed,[37] and this factor may have given him some valuable leeway in referring to Æthelfrith in such pejorative terms.

Rædwald's dynasty and dates

When dealing with Rædwald of the East Angles Bede faced rather different circumstances. The dynasty still incumbent in 731, the Wuffingas,[38] descended directly from the grandson of the putative and eponymous Wuffa, Rædwald's brother Eni.[39] At least one member of the Northumbrian royal house, St. Hild's sister Hereswith, had married into this dynasty and her grandson, Ælfwald, was king in the 630s.[40] The last really powerful Northumbrian king, Ecgfrith, had married Æthelthryth of the East Angles, Ælfwald's cousin, while her sister Seaxburh, was wife to Eorcenberht of Kent (died 664). Both were honoured in this work and Bede noted that Imma, a Northumbrian thegn, was ransomed with East Anglian money after the battle of Trent on account of this connection. St. Hild too had spent time in East Anglia.[41] Were any Bernician king in the future to revive the northern challenge for supremacy over southern Britain it would probably require the assistance of kings in either or both of East Anglia and Kent.[42]

Close links therefore existed between the current king of the East Angles, Rædwald's reputation and the hopes and aspirations of the Northumbrian leadership. There were, potentially at least, significant constraints on Bede's freedom to comment on Rædwald, despite his death more than a century earlier. His prominence in East Anglian politics was such that his omission from the *Historia* would presumably have been such a flagrant breach of the general historical knowledge of powerful contemporaries that total neglect of his role offered no solution. Bede clearly faced a serious challenge in determining how he should deal with this powerful East Anglian king.

Despite these circumstances, it was essential that Bede register his abhorrence of Rædwald, whose baptism had proved to be *frustra* ('to no purpose').[43] He was the earliest recorded English apostate, so in Bede's eyes worse even than a pagan.[44] He had, however, to proceed warily. It was presumably with this in mind that he minimised the potential for political embarrassment by emphasising that responsibility for his apostasy lay not primarily with the king but with his anonymous wife and 'certain perverse *doctores*'[45] by whom he had been 'turned'.[46] He did this while stressing the king's own *natu nobilis* – 'noble birth'. That nobility was, of course, shared by all the *Wuffingas*, so was a matter of political sensitivity at the date of composition. Bede contrasted it with Rædwald's *actu ignobilis* – 'inglorious deed'. The literary device is a subtle one and far from accidental, serving to separate Rædwald as an individual from the inherent nobility which (as Bede was keen to emphasise) was the general condition of his dynasty.

In combination with his several vindicatory comments concerning Rædwald's Christian relatives,[47] this treatment amounts to a neat circumvention of a potential hazard. The strategy adopted enabled Bede to air his own strictures against Rædwald as an individual while reassuring those who counted themselves his close kin that they were quite divorced from the opprobrium attaching to their most powerful antecedent. It was the conversion of Rædwald's nephews which was Bede's principal interest in this chapter of the *HE* and Rædwald's apostasy was contrasted to great effect with their virtues.[48]

Bede was, then, actively hostile to Rædwald, whose achievements and long and fruitful reign were inimical to his dialectical purposes. In consequence we should not expect him to offer gratuitous information on this subject. Even where noted, the effects of his deeds are likely to have been minimalised, if not actively distorted. True to form, Bede made no attempt to offer dates for the end of his rule, as he did for Kings Æthelberht and Edwin.[49] Yet it is clear that his reign was a long one, overlapping with both these Christian kings. Æthelberht is generally considered to have died in February 616,[50] so Rædwald – who was baptised at his court – was necessarily on the throne of the East Angles by this date. It is unclear how long he had then reigned but he must have been well-established and have already built up sufficient kudos to head a risky military enterprise against the mighty Æthelfrith apparently in the same year,[51] so he had presumably then been king for a significant period.

Even the date of his baptism was omitted by Bede, whether or not it was known to him. It occurred *iamdudum* – 'a passage of time before now' (with apparent reference to the period 627–33).[52] Nor does he offer any clue as to the gap between this baptism and his subsequent apostasy. Rædwald apparently faced a dilemma which was common to other subordinate kings in the conversion period:[53] if he should reject the God of his 'overking', the latter might be antagonised and ensure that his interests suffered in consequence; conversely, overly enthusiastic acceptance of the 'foreign' God at home had implications for his own role as a sacral king, and so his capacity to operate as an intermediary between his people and the gods who were their protectors. Such might place in jeopardy the very essence of his kingship. The course that Rædwald adopted suggests that he fully appreciated this dilemma: his construction of an altar to Æthelberht's God within a pagan temple amounts to a balancing act of some subtlety by which he protected his own role as king of his people without overtly antagonising Æthelberht.[54] It seems likely that this situation prevailed from shortly after his own baptism until Æthelberht's demise, so until February 616, when Rædwald was free to dispense with his allegiance to Christ.

Æthelberht was at his most active in support of the Christian mission at Canterbury in the first few years of its existence. It was then, for example, that he lent his weight to Augustine in his dealings with the British Church in the west.[55] The establishment of dioceses at Rochester and London both predate Augustine's death (*c.* 604) and subsequent correspondence of Augustine's successors with the Scots is far less acerbic and dictatorial than Augustine was portrayed as being when treating with the Welsh.[56] After *c.* 604, Æthelberht, like Cearl of the Mercians,[57] may have felt threatened by the expansion of Æthelfrith's hegemony in the far north.[58] The Chester campaign of *c.* 615 certainly established Æthelfrith in a position from which he was very capable of threatening the southern *imperium* and it may have brought his 'overkingship' into direct contact with that of Æthelberht.[59] Such was not the best time for an ageing king to impose his own, novel religion on a powerful and well-established tributary whose territories marched with those of mightier co-religionists on the outer edge of his own *imperium*.

While there is no means of establishing it as fact, it does seem probable, therefore, that Rædwald's baptism occurred much closer to 600 than 615. In that case he was presumably already king of the East Angles by the opening years of the century and was forced to prevaricate concerning Christianity for a decade or even more. There can be no doubt that Rædwald was already mature in years by the turn of the century. Bede noted that his son, Rægenhere, was slain in battle beside the River Idle, apparently in 616,[60] so he must have been born by 600 at the very latest, and could easily have been a decade or so older. Sigeberht was described by Bede as brother of Eorpwald, son and successor of Rædwald,[61] rather than as Rædwald's son, but this curious choice of terminology need not imply that Sigeberht was entirely unrelated to Rædwald. Bede's phraseology was rather perhaps conditioned by his approval of Sigeberht, whom he described as *homo bonus ac religiosus* – 'a good and religious man'.[62] He had, therefore, no cause to compromise his reputation by reminding his audience of his closeness to the iniquitous Rædwald. Unlike the latter, Eorpwald was Christian at his death. Bede's choice of words need not, therefore, imply that Sigeberht was only half-brother to Eorpwald via his mother, although this has been a recurring interpretation of the passage.[63]

Sigeberht took refuge in exile during the latter part (at least) of his father's reign.[64] Assuming he was Rædwald's son, his flight from the *inimicitia* of his father is an interesting detail. Parallels from the next generation might imply that this fission within the dynasty derived from the son's rapprochement with a rival one in the hope that this would provide him with support against his several brothers to further his own succession on his father's death.[65] If this were the case, then Sigeberht's alliance had presumably been with Æthelberht, which would explain his choice of Frankia as a place of exile and his decision to receive baptism there, even after the death of his erstwhile protector.[66] This is so much speculation but the fact remains that Sigeberht was presumably at least close to maturity by 616, at latest, so had been born before 600. That Eorpwald succeeded his father in the mid-620s implies that he, too, is unlikely to have been born much after 600.[67] Rædwald was, therefore, already married and producing children before *c.* 600, so then at least in his twenties. There is no necessity for him to have been so young: for him to have then been in his forties is entirely feasible.

Æthelberht's *imperium*

That he was baptised in Kent so in the core of Æthelberht's *imperium* must imply that he was then tributary to Æthelberht,[68] and subject to that *imperium*. The nature of this *imperium* is of fundamental importance to any assessment of Rædwald, if only because his name follows Æthelberht's in Bede's list of English kings wielding it.[69] That list was apparently compiled so as to lend substance to the reputation of the first English king to convert by comparing him favourably with great leaders who were, unlike Æthelberht, remembered as having been victorious in war, as was of course King Rædwald.

It was as a tributary ruler subject to Kentish *imperium* that Rædwald spent his early years as the king of the East Angles. He was then, as Bede remarked, 'conceding the leadership in war of his own people' to the Kentish king.[70] Æthelberht's power rested not merely on his own Kentish resources but was bolstered by at least two dynastic marriages. His father had arranged that of Æthelberht himself to Bertha, daughter of King Charibert of Paris, who was in receipt of papal correspondence in 601,[71] so presumably then still alive. During the same period the archaeological record suggests a very real rise in Frankish influences in Kentish metal-working. Close cultural contact was therefore mirrored by cross-Channel political co-operation. If Procopius's account of an Anglian expedition to the continent a generation or so earlier be taken seriously,[72] this alliance may have been capable of delivering military support to one or other of its respective partners at need.

The Frankish alliance may therefore have been of great potential benefit to Æthelberht's dynasty: it presumably reinforced their control of both the Kentish kingdoms, the Kentish ports and the nascent *emporium* at London. It may thereafter have been a significant factor in Æthelberht's own rise to *imperium* in the south where his father was apparently, at the date of this marriage, only a Kentish king;[73] it may have contributed to his control of the flow of high-status goods into Britain from Frankia and that flow may well have increased during his reign under the impetus of profits stemming from his own political superiority inside southern England. The political weight of the Frankish connection should not, however, be overexaggerated. By the time the marriage took place, Bertha was already fatherless and power within northern Frankia had fallen into the hands of rival branches of the family who may have had little interest in supporting Bertha's husband:[74] indeed, her marriage overseas might have been a convenient means of neutralising the potential to cause trouble of the sole descendant of King Charibert. In that case, Æthelberht is unlikely to have obtained anything more from this connection than the kudos naturally attaching to a Christian Frankish bride from beyond the seas, who will have seemed an exotic within the insular world.

The second dynastic alliance was that which had brought his nephew, Sæberht, to the kingship of the neighbouring East Saxons. Like Æthelberht's marriage, this was also presumably an arrangement made by his father which bore fruit in his own reign. Of all Æthelberht's subordinates, Sæberht was the most committed to his policies: only he quickly and (apparently) willingly followed his uncle's lead in religious matters, enabling the 'overking' to establish the only see outside Kent in this generation, at London.[75] It was presumably, therefore, an unequal alliance cemented by close kinship which brought Æthelberht the unqualified support of a second major war band outside Kent, in return presumably for favoured status for its king, his own nephew, within Æthelberht's extended system of patronage.

Æthelberht's power rested therefore on the rich east Kentings (who were perhaps the people with whom his family were primarily associated), his kingship of the west Kentings, his marital alliance in Frankia and the unqualified support of his nephew, king of the East Saxons. This combination was sufficient for his *imperium* to be recognised, and his protection sought, as far as the Wash and the Severn, and there is no evidence that he had had to fight to establish, or thereafter to sustain, his superiority.[76]

That Æthelberht lacked the confidence natural to a proven warleader finds some support in his receptiveness to Christianity, which reached him as part of the many social, diplomatic and cultural contacts between the ports of Kent and those of northern France. As he may well have realised before Augustine's arrival, Christianity offered potential means to enhance the diplomatic foundations on which his 'overkingship' was based, and at the same time strengthen his position both within Kentish society *per se* and *vis-à-vis* his clients. If such considerations were significant in Æthelberht's conversion, then it seems likely that his position was more dependent on diplomatic, dynastic and political considerations than was normal among 'overkings' of the period.

Whatever the reality, Rædwald remained outside this inner core of Æthelberht's supporters but not, perhaps, that far outside it. That one of Rædwald's sons, Sigeberht, bore a Frankish name may imply that the East Anglian king was sensitive to Kentish and Frankish opinion and keen to ingratiate himself with Æthelberht and his continental allies even before the arrival of Augustine.[77] Moreover, Bede apparently knew of no attempts by Æthelberht and Augustine to convert the South Saxon or West Saxon kings, or at least he kept silent on the subject if he did.[78] Yet both these dynasties had produced famous 'overkings' in the past (and perhaps the recent past). If either had ambitions to do so again in the near future, they are unlikely to have willingly worshipped a God whose rites in England centred on a high priest housed at the principal *burh* of the current 'overking', at Canterbury. Rædwald was, however, persuaded to accept baptism when in Kent at his overlord's court and was baptised, suggesting that his relationship with Æthelberht lay somewhere between the extremes represented by Sæberht, on the one hand, and the West and South Saxons on the other.

Bede gives the impression that there was considerable debate at the East Anglian court concerning this conversion.[79] Unless there was a member of the Canterbury mission present, and Paulinus is the individual most often suggested,[80] this debate was undertaken without an advocate for the Roman Church, so largely on grounds of political expediency. The solution adopted is best understood as an entirely pagan response to a diplomatic problem, if only because the positioning of a Christian altar and pagan idols in such close proximity inside a temple are unlikely to have proved acceptable to a Christian priest of whatever sort, let alone Paulinus. The presence of a cleric therefore seems unlikely.

Up to Æthelberht's death Bede implied that Rædwald remained his subordinate as regards military matters,[81] but that event freed the East Anglian king from the oversight of an *imperium*-wielding Christian superior. There appears to have been no recent instance of the son of such a king in the south being able to sustain his father's *imperium*,[82] so no reason why Rædwald should, in 616, concede pre-eminence to Eadbald. It was probably unclear in February 616 who would emerge as the next 'protector' of southern Britain.

Æthelfrith's *imperium*

There was, however, one impressive candidate already in the ring. Æthelberht's death occurred only shortly after a major upheaval in the Midlands,[83] and it was arguably this upheaval which brought

Cearl's Mercian kingship crashing down. In consequence, Æthelfrith of Bernicia was able to extend his 'overkingship' as far as the Fens. At the time of Æthelberht's death, the Bernician king apparently exercised hegemony over far more tributaries, and more territory, than the Kentish king; and their *imperia* probably abutted.[84] Æthelfrith's campaign in the Midlands was presumably what precipitated the flight of Edwin of Deira to Rædwald. It is the fact of Edwin's marriage to Cearl's daughter and the birth of his several sons during his exile which implies that he had hitherto been protected primarily at the Mercian court.[85]

When Edwin reached Rædwald's court he received royal protection but the East Anglian king had second thoughts when a series of embassies from Æthelfrith reached him soon afterwards with offers of silver for the exile's death and threats of war should he refuse.[86] Rædwald was king of a large and prosperous people,[87] but his indecisiveness at this juncture implies that he was not yet an 'overking' and as yet doubted his own military competence.[88] Unless they travelled by sea, the successive arrivals in East Anglia of Æthelfrith's several embassies demonstrate his capacity to protect them as far south as Rædwald's borders, so through what had hitherto been the Mercian hegemony. The seriousness with which Rædwald reacted to the threat from the north implies that Æthelfrith had access to the road system through the heartland of Mercia in the Trent valley and was capable of attacking East Anglia at will. When he was eventually surprised and killed, Æthelfrith fell inside what Bede construed as Mercian territory.[89] Unless he had *imperium* over Mercia, he had no business there except if on campaign and his small forces and lack of preparation make that most unlikely.

There can be no real doubt, therefore, that Æthelfrith was, in the summer of 616, the 'overking' of the Midlands. Given his vastly superior resources and awesome military reputation,[90] it seems most unlikely that the southern kings would, on Æthelberht's death, have looked to Rædwald or any other untried southern king for protection against him (Figure 13). Had he invaded Rædwald's territories with his full army the outcome should have been in little doubt.[91]

These diplomatic exchanges and their eventual outcome are of cardinal significance to Anglo-Saxon history. Had Rædwald given way he would have obtained the friendship of a powerful

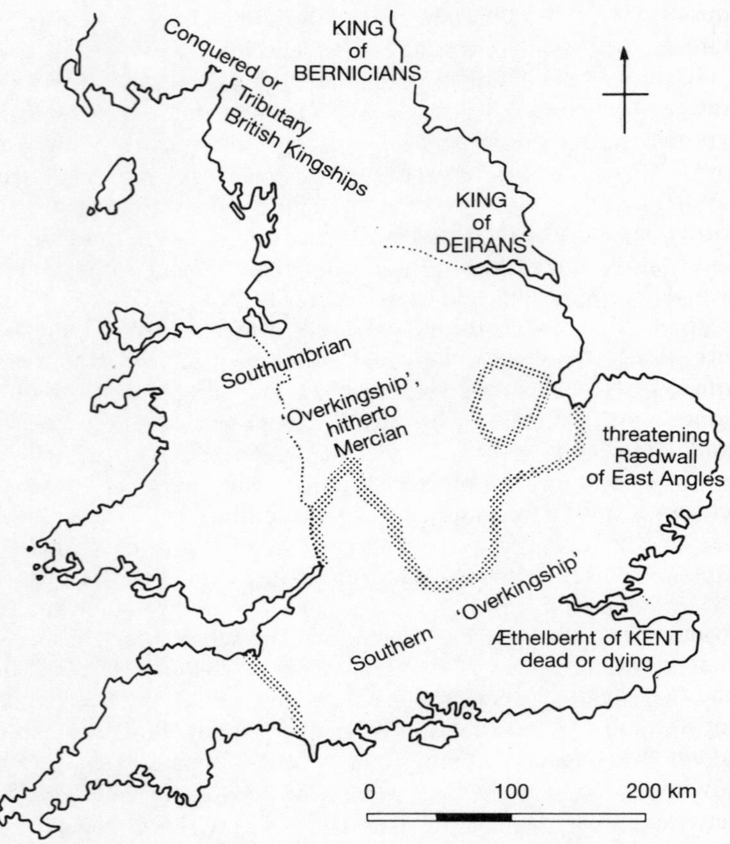

Figure 13 Core and periphery: the structure of Æthelfrith's kingships and conquests to the eve of his death (*c.* 616).

neighbour but tacitly recognised his military superiority. From there, acceptance of his *imperium* would have been but a short step away. Had Æthelfrith thus broken into Æthelberht's erstwhile *imperium*, it seems unlikely that any other southern king would have withstood him. Æthelfrith might, therefore, have aspired to a universal 'overkingship' as extensive as that of Edwin after 626.[92] That is not, however, what occurred. After apparently agreeing to Æthelfrith's demands at the third time of asking, Rædwald reconsidered and, reputedly on his wife's advice once again,[93] decided to honour his own obligation to protect his guest. He therefore marched on Æthelfrith, took him by surprise and killed him.

His success probably owed much to Æthelfrith's lack of preparation. It owed even more to his own decisiveness. One might hypothesise that Æthelfrith had been overconfident of his ability to cow Rædwald, an erstwhile mere tributary king who is unlikely to have had a military reputation of his own. The latter's rapid march north seems to have been the last thing the victor of *Degsastan* and Chester was expecting. His own earlier victories had been achieved by marching out against his enemies with forces which were at least as prepared as theirs and probably often more so. Æthelfrith paid with his life for underestimating his opponent's willingness (or his wife's, perhaps) to seize the initiative in a similar fashion. That alone compensated for the inequality of the military resources available to each of them, so enabling Rædwald to win a victory as spectacular and decisive as that which Cadwallon would later achieve over Edwin in 633.

Rædwald restores Edwin

So much can be reconstructed from Bede but his testimony, like that of the *Life of Gregory the Great*, derived from a Christian tradition the purpose of which was not to record Rædwald's deeds but to construct a semi-miraculous prologue to the conversion of Edwin. Bede focused, therefore, on a vision supposedly seen by Edwin at Rædwald's court which he then linked with an interview between Edwin and Paulinus which reputedly occurred about a decade later.[94] Rædwald was named, and his changing attitude recorded, only to the extent that either provided a context appropriate to the first of these prophetic episodes. Rædwald's subsequent victory over Æthelfrith was, in Bede's view, a mechanical process through which God's long-conceived purpose was brought to fulfilment, so no credit to the victor.

In Christian and Northumbrian opinion, divine favour towards a virtuous king was made manifest in Oswald's victory over Cadwallon,[95] Oswiu's over Penda[96] and Ecgfrith's over the Mercians and Picts[97] by the relatively small numbers with which each overcame the vast hosts of a less favoured opponent. Comparable treatment was not accorded Rædwald by Bede. On the contrary his force was portrayed as greater than Æthelfrith's. His victory did not, therefore, imply divine support for his cause *per se*, but its use by the Lord as a means to achieve quite separate objectives. Rædwald's triumph was, moreover, minimised by notice of a significant loss, the death in battle of his son, Rægenhere.[98] Thus this great victory added the less to the reputation of Rædwald himself.

Additionally Bede minimised Rædwald's role by the order in which he mentions these events. Edwin's marriage (about 625), his conversations with Paulinus, the baptism of his daughter and his own conditional promises to convert (in 626) were all described in *HE*, book two, chapter nine. Boniface's letters to Edwin and Æthelburh then follow (chapters ten and eleven). Penultimately a heavenly vision was incorporated before Bede referred in the briefest possible terms to Rædwald's victory and its role in establishing Edwin in power (chapter twelve). Much of the credit due to Rædwald was, therefore, transferred via careful construction of his narrative by Bede to God and his agents, both human and heavenly. This can hardly have been an accident. Rather it betrays the keen intelligence of Bede and the subtlety of his purposes once more.

Bede rounded off his description of these events with the sentence:

> And so Edwin, in accordance with the prophecy which he had received, not only survived the ambushes laid by his inimical king [Æthelfrith], but also succeeded to the glory of the kingship of that same murderer.[99]

As an assessment of the causes of Edwin's triumph this is lamentable. As a piece of Christian writing designed to place Edwin's conversion in the providential context appropriate to it, it is outstandingly effective. Rædwald's responsibility for the establishment of Edwin's kingship was effectively transferred to God.

According to Bede, Rædwald assisted Edwin in recovering his *regnum* – 'kingship'. This use of the singular probably reflects the political reality of his own times, when the Northumbrians constituted a single kingship.[100] As Bede was well aware, Edwin was of the Deiran royal house, not the Bernician,[101] but it is clear from the flight of Æthelfrith's sons to the far north that, under Rædwald's protection, Edwin became king of the Bernician people as well.[102] As king of the Bernicians and Deirans he also seems to have stepped into Æthelfrith's role as 'overking' of the Britons of northern England and southern Scotland,[103] and of the Midlanders,[104] all of whom were arguably subject to Æthelfrith's *regnum* at the time of his death (Figure 13).

Rædwald had protected Edwin and, at great risk to himself, furthered his interests. He had been outstandingly successful and brought down his enemies. It is difficult to find a greater obligation owed by one king to another in Anglo-Saxon history than that owed by Edwin to Rædwald. There can be no reasonable doubt that Edwin both recognised, and relied upon, the *imperium* of his saviour in the task confronting him in the north. The difficulties inherent therein should not be ignored: the flight of Æthelfrith's sons meant that Edwin's northern borders were threatened *ab initio* by what was to all intents and purposes a government in exile and the fact that many young Bernicians accompanied them suggests that they had the power to harm his regime should their Scottish and/or Pictish hosts allow them so to do;[105] even those of the Bernician nobility who remained are likely to have been of doubtful loyalty to a Deiran king; royal patronage had probably to be rebuilt virtually from scratch. This had moreover to be undertaken by a king who had been severed from most of his own folk for over a decade and had been no more than a youth when he had fled the wreck of the Deiran kingship, *c.* 604. During the intervening years many Deirans may have become comparatively complacent concerning Æthelfrith's regime. Edwin was, therefore, in great need of stability and support and that was available in the short term only through his relationship with Rædwald. In return for security and the protection that Rædwald's reputation could confer, Edwin would presumably have been prepared to pay him tribute,[106] to honour him by his occasional visits to the East Anglian court[107] and to serve with his own troops in his army, should the need arise.[108]

This was a relationship which benefited both parties. Rædwald gained thereby the unqualified support of a second major war band funded from the resources of northern and central Britain. With such backing and with the kudos derived from his own decisive victory over the mighty Æthelfrith, it is hardly surprising that his protection was sought and his *imperium* recognised by his peers in southern Britain.[109] Rædwald's *imperium* was, therefore, far more extensive than that which Æthelberht had wielded, encompassing all the great 'overkingships' which had existed in Britain south of the Antonine Wall at the turn of the century (Figure 14).[110] He deserves to be recognised as the first king in history to achieve this status,[111] although others may have done the same unbeknown to us in the fifth and sixth centuries.[112]

The existence of a large tributary 'overkingship' (Edwin's) beneath Rædwald's general superiority insulated many lesser dynasties beyond the Fens from direct contact with Rædwald. It may be this factor which led to his omission from later literature emanating from British courts and looking back to this period. Edwin's career was, in contrast, a matter of great concern to them.[113] Nonetheless, albeit by proxy, Rædwald's influence and protection extended across all of Britain. Given his apostasy and Bede's consequent hostility, the latter's reluctant and guarded recognition of Rædwald's *imperium* and his use of it to bolster that of Æthelberht is a clear indication of his exceptional status. The new 'overking' was unassailable after the battle by the River Idle. It is the reputation of such kings as this which lived on beyond their deaths for many generations in Anglo-Saxon England.

The apostasy of Rædwald and Eadbald

It is obvious that Rædwald did not share Bede's perspective on these events. Given both his later reputation as an apostate and his ambivalence towards Christianity before 616, we can be reasonably certain that it was not Christ whose aid he invoked on the eve of battle beside the River Idle. Their victories in perilous enterprises under what they believed to be Christ's protection were cogent factors in persuading Edwin, Oswald and Cædwalla, respectively, of the efficacy of the Christian God as a god of war.[114] Supposing this logic to be general at the time, Rædwald presumably saw in his own victory confirmation of the power of whichever god he believed had sustained him in his hour of need.[115] Knowledge of his success may also have inclined other kings towards the same god, so away from Christianity. If he had not already rejected the worship of Christ prior to the battle, from the moment of his victory he was free to do so. Æthelberht's death and his own great victory define the brief period within which Rædwald decided to turn his back on Christ.

Rædwald's ability thereafter to intervene in the affairs of specific kingships under his protection differed little from that of his im-

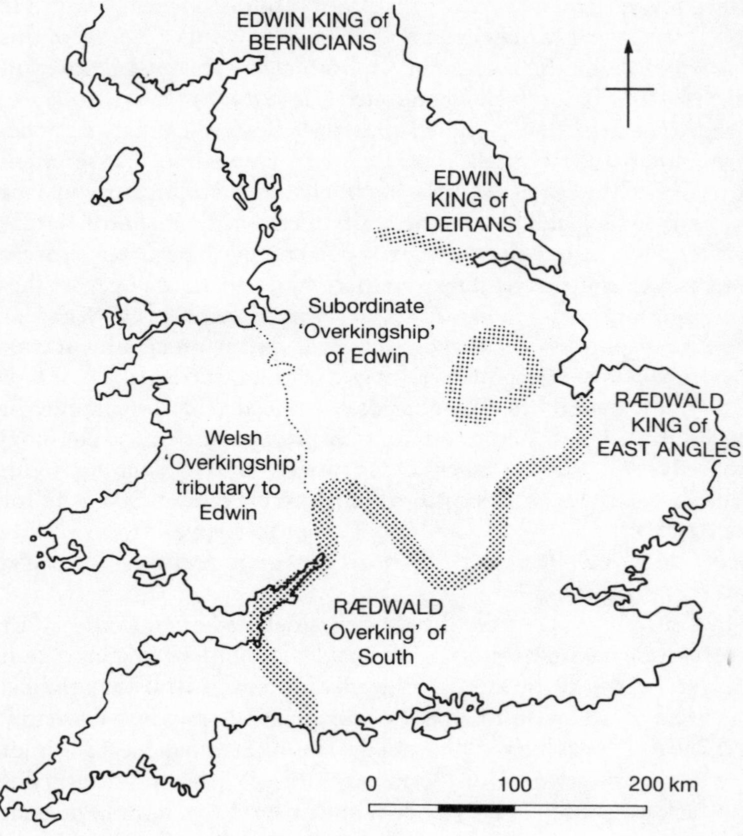

Figure 14 The kingship and tiered 'overkingship' of Rædwald, king of the East Angles (*c.* 616–*c.* 624), encompassing the subordinate hegemony of Edwin of Deira in central and northern Britain – which in turn incorporated a tributary 'overkingship' in Wales.

mediate predecessor as 'overking'. Æthelberht had established the worship of his new deity in both his own kingdoms in Kent and had required, or persuaded, his nephew to accept a similar mission in London (where the kings of Kent had substantial influence, if not rule) but his very limited success in persuading Rædwald to change gods, his failure among the Welsh and apparent lack of initiative elsewhere presumably reflect the practical limits of his power over the generality of his client kings.

With Æthelberht and Sæberht both dead in *c.* 616, the sons of the latter promptly abandoned Christianity and drove out Bishop Mellitus. Bede argued that they 'had remained pagan . . . throughout their father's reign but had seemed to discontinue a little while he was alive'. His treatment of them, and particularly the story which follows of their arguments with Bishop Mellitus, implies that Bede believed them never to have been baptised, in which case they were pagan rather than apostate. Even a little 'discontinuity' may however have involved baptism.[116] Whatever the circumstances, their religious *volte face* coincided with the inception of a new pagan 'overkingship' and this is unlikely to have been coincidental. It is more likely to reflect the recapture of the political heights by a committed pagan than the strength, or otherwise, of their earlier commitment to Christianity. With Kentish Christian 'overkingship' replaced by pagan East Anglian, the East Saxon rulers naturally took steps to shed all traces of their erstwhile involvement with the former regime and the God which had sustained it.

In Canterbury, the new situation was debated at a meeting of the three insular Italian bishops, probably later in 616,[117] and their analysis of the prospects for the mission was so gloomy that all purposed to abandon England. Mellitus and Justus actually left,[118] and Bede's Canterbury sources had to invoke (or concoct) a miracle to explain the survival of the mission at its core site.[119] Eadbald's apostasy was not linked by Bede with Rædwald's triumph, presumably because to do so would be to admit to Rædwald's *potestas* over a king whom Bede had cogent reasons to present as free-standing and of exceptional virtue. It should be remembered that Bede was careful to minimise Rædwald's influence and detract from his reputation wherever possible, as in book two, chapter five.[120] To admit to Rædwald's power over Eadbald at Canterbury would have been tantamount to admitting Woden's superiority over Christ.

Bede claimed instead that Eadbald's apostasy derived from his marriage to his step-mother.[121] This practice is known to have occurred among German pagans[122] and may have been adopted so as to reunite the widow's political influence and her dower with the portion of the dominant heir, to the advantage of both. In the case of the Varni the decision was reputedly made on grounds of political expediency and this may also have been important in Eadbald's case. Unlike Eadbald's Frankish second wife, we do not know the identity of Æthelberht's widow but, since her marriage to the old king was comparatively recent,[123] it probably reflected a political alliance which remained relevant in 616, and one perhaps which was aimed at Æthelberht's enemies. Although her first marriage must imply that she was Christian, her subsequent match with her stepson implies that Æthelberht's widow, at least, apostatised in 616. There is, of course, the outside chance that the lady in question was a member of Rædwald's kin, in which case Eadbald's marriage to her becomes the more understandable, as does her anonymity, but that can be no more than the wildest speculation. It seems likely, however, that both Eadbald's religious policies and his choice of wife at this dangerous time were influenced by the rise of the inimical Rædwald to supremacy.

Despite this setback for the Canterbury mission, its survival even under an apostate or pagan king implies that his protection of it continued in the heartland of his power, since Æthelberht's own law code makes it abundantly clear that the Church relied heavily on the crown for its security. In other words, despite his personal compliance with the religious policies of his new overlord and his making a marriage which was inimical to the Christians, Eadbald did not entirely abandon the priests with whom his father's power had become so closely associated. To do so would have been as damaging to his own prospects of future greatness as Rædwald's over-enthusiastic espousal of Christianity would have been to his kingship a generation earlier. The two cases have much in common.

As soon as Rædwald's influence was removed, Eadbald re-emerges as a Christian king, the groom of a high-born Frankish lady and the protector of the Canterbury mission, who was keen to insist that Christianity should prevail within the marriage between his own sister and Edwin of Deira.[124] The miraculous (re)conversion as told by Bede may have a basis in reality (it equally may not) but it is inadequate as an explanation of Eadbald's oscillations concerning his own religious preferences. His position shadowed the shifting balance between pagan and Christian 'overkingship' with such accuracy that a causal link is almost obligatory.

It may be that some members of Eadbald's family maintained their commitment to Christianity even despite Rædwald's *imperium*. Bede never suggests that all the Kentish Christians lapsed at this stage but only those who had previously converted solely in deference to Æthelberht.[125] Æthelburh, Edwin's bride, may have been one who remained Christian,[126] in which case patronage of the Canterbury mission may have continued even within the royal family. Parallels from later in the century imply that an 'overking' might be satisfied by far less than the wholesale conversion of a tributary people, provided only that the king and perhaps his immediate household acquiesced.[127] With Kentish Christianity shorn of its bases outside Eadbald's core territory in eastern Kent and with the king at least resuming pagan sacrifice, Rædwald could be satisfied that he had achieved what was feasible in the course of taming and rebutting the aggressive and self-assertive religion sponsored by his predecessor as 'overking'.

If Eadbald chose to experiment in the striking of coinage,[128] it seems unlikely that Rædwald would have immediately recognised that as a challenge to his own authority.[129] Coining was something quite new in England at this date and unknown outside Kent. It was several generations before English kings would see it as an important facet of the language of power and seek to restrict the capacity of lesser men to produce their own coins. The presence of Frankish coins in the Sutton Hoo ship burial implies a degree of complacency among the rulers of the East Angles concerning the origins of whatever gold coins were reaching them.[130] The continuing existence of an emasculated mission at Canterbury may have been viewed from East Anglia with a similar degree of tolerance.

If Rædwald's *imperium* was much like Æthelberht's in quality, there was little else he shared with the deceased Kentish king who had lent his political weight to religious changes of revolutionary proportions. Rædwald's attitude towards these changes and his ultimate rejection of the Frankish and Kentish religion label him a conservative in matters spiritual and ideological, who wished to restore the traditional Anglo-Saxon customs and forms of worship.

After Æthelberht's reign one might envisage difficulties in restoring the pagan *status quo* to health. The Kentish king had, for almost twenty years, placed his support behind an alien priesthood which strenuously denied the very existence, let alone the potency, of the pagan gods; yet he had survived and apparently even prospered, eventually dying (most probably of natural causes) with his supremacy still intact. That the gods whom he had declined to propitiate had shown themselves incapable of harming him can have only undermined confidence in their powers. Since Rædwald's victory over Æthelfrith was that of one pagan over another, the new regime could not claim that its traditional gods had been matched against the Christian God in the ultimate proving ground of divine efficacy, on the battlefield. Its ideological stance was, therefore, less secure than that of Edwin or Oswald, the former of whom had been victorious over a pagan king and the latter over a British Christian who had himself recently destroyed one Roman Christian and two pagan English kings.

Rædwald did what he could in the circumstances to renew faith in the potency of traditional rites. By corralling its priests in an impotent mission at Canterbury and throwing his own political weight as 'overking' behind paganism, he created conditions in which the worship of indigenous deities could resume with some confidence but Æthelberht's Roman mission had administered a profound shock to the ideological and religious world of the southern English. If the traditional world was to be fully restored, it needed reinforcement of the sort that the Christian mission had drawn from their Italian heartland and Frankish co-religionists. The obvious direction for Rædwald and his *doctores* ('teachers' or 'priests') to turn was the Baltic littoral whence the English believed, with good cause, that they had originally derived. There lay the heartland of Germanic paganism, secure in the continued commitment to it of communities sharing the Vendel culture. There too lay the fount of English cultural and racial identity.

Pagan supremacy

If the *Beowulf* poem was in any way typical of the context and characterisation which more traditional English poets preferred during the conversion period,[131] then the geographical and historical context in which it was set may well reflect the attractions which the continental motherland offered to pagan kings in their search for reassurance within a pagan ideology. The possibility that *Beowulf* derives from East Anglia adds something to this suggestion,[132] but it is not essential to the argument.

East Anglia also offers a unique body of archaeological evidence for links at approximately this date with the Baltic and Rhineland. To mention only the most obvious parallels at Sutton Hoo and Snape, English communities borrowed the rite of ship burial which was then popular with the leaders of southern Sweden.[133] This is not the place to add further comment to the voluminous literature on Sutton Hoo but there are several factors which imply that this royal cemetery should be identified quite specifically with Rædwald and his immediate affinity, irrespective of the attribution of any particular grave to the 'overking'. No other East Anglian leader is likely to have had the resources, political freedom and status to engage in a sustained intercourse with the distant Baltic kingships; nor did others have such a need to invest in the more extreme and expensive rituals of contemporary continental paganism in order to reassure English pagans and face down Christianity; no other had access to the exceptional wealth and diplomatic leverage of a tribute-taking king, which was an essential precursor to securing such extraordinarily rich goods, let alone depositing them in the royal cemetery. It is the political context, as much as the evidence of the Frankish coins,[134] that makes Rædwald's claims on Sutton Hoo so impressive. It would seem to be the cemetery in which were interred his closest and richest adherents, perhaps with members of his own family and household alongside himself, dating from the years of his own supremacy but perhaps continuing, if on a less profligate level, into the renewed pagan leadership instigated by Ricberht's murder of the Christian King Eorpwald. It was most probably a monument conceived and used entirely within a single generation: with the succession of the Christian and Frankophile Sigeberht, the 'Age of Sutton Hoo' was surely over.[135]

In 1993 a challenge was issued to the hitherto near-universal association of Sutton Hoo with the East Anglian dynasty, a challenge which provides a valuable opportunity to re-consider the evidence.[136] While arguments for caution over the dating evidence provided by the coinage seem very proper, the case presented for Sutton Hoo being an East Saxon cemetery, and the rich ship burial under mound one being Sæberht's, is less than convincing. The presence in that grave of what was probably a specifically Christian set of silver bowls does not favour Sæberht over Rædwald, since their surrender by Sæberht's sons to the new 'overking' in, or shortly after, 616 would be at least as apt a means of disposing of them as their interment with the deceased East Saxon king. Their ultimate incorporation in Rædwald's own grave might have been thought to symbolise his triumph, and that of his pagan gods, over Christianity; nor does the presence of what may have been East Saxon spears suggest that Sæberht was the likelier interred, since an expected feature of the hoard of an 'overking' must surely be the preponderance of items which had reached him from beyond the frontiers of his own people. This interesting exploration of circumstantial evidence which might be thought to favour Sæberht's candidacy does not detract from several features of the grave-goods, such as the possible gold-foil wolf on the 'ceremonial wand' and more certain wolf-decorated mounts from the purse-lid, which are peculiarly well-suited to identification of mound one with the East Anglian dynasty.[137]

If the east bank of the Deben had at some point lain marginally inside East Saxon territory,[138] it seems most unlikely that this was the case when the Sutton Hoo cemetery was developing. If the graves were (as seems very probable) intended to act as a boundary marker, then it was surely the Deben itself that was the physical frontier, implying that the cemetery was sited on the East Anglian side of that boundary. If this marginal block of land was in dispute between the kings of the East Angles and East Saxons, then it may well have been in East Saxon hands during the reign of the Kentish 'overking's' closest associate, with control resumed by Rædwald once Sæberht's sons acknowledged his supremacy. The construction of his sepulchre here would then have advertised his triumphant rule by virtue of its location within disputed territory which he had successfully regained in the latter part of his reign. Although certainty still eludes the modern commentator, Rædwald's responsibility for the cemetery remains by far the most likely interpretation.

Rædwald's influence may also be divined in the genesis of an *emporium* at Ipswich, where a significant expansion in trading contacts occurred in the early seventh century.[139] The site lay only some twelve miles from his palace at Rendlesham and the cemetery at Sutton Hoo.[140] As behoves a king whose ideological stance drew him towards the Baltic homelands, his *emporium* specialised (to a far greater extent than did London and the Kentish ports) in contacts with the Rhineland, where Frisian carriers probably provided the necessary links to establish and sustain contacts with the

North.[141] This is not to suggest that such contacts were entirely new. There is plentiful archaeological evidence of cultural exchange between Germans in the new, insular world and the old homelands throughout the fifth and sixth centuries and no obvious sign of a break.[142] The archaeology of Ipswich does, however, suggest a significant if temporary shift of emphasis away from the growing dependence of Kentish ports on links with Frankia in favour of renewed intercourse with pagan Germany.

Bede and his Christian sources would have revelled in the downfall in battle of the apostate Rædwald, had that occurred, and would surely have sought dialectical advantage therefrom. That he had nothing to offer concerning Rædwald's end does, therefore, imply (but does not prove) that the great pagan king died, like Æthelberht, of natural causes. His *imperium* died with him and his heir was forced, within a year or so, to recognise the 'overkingship' of that same Edwin whose fortunes had been made by Rædwald.[143] The expansion of Deiran power across the south was facilitated by a Kentish alliance but the critical factor was Edwin's decisive victory over the powerful Cuichelm of the West Saxons.[144] Edwin thereafter placed a heavy tribute on the East Angles[145] and interfered to an unusual extent in the internal affairs of this tribute-enriched kingship, where many presumably still hankered after the benefits derived from Rædwald's erstwhile East Anglian *imperium*. None of Rædwald's successors succeeded in regaining his pre-eminence but, among the middle-ranking dynasties of seventh-century England, East Anglian kings thereafter demonstrated an unusual willingness to risk their lives in battle against more powerful opponents.[146] Perhaps they anticipated that they, like Rædwald, might win victory against the odds over a mighty 'overking', so in their turn be recognised as the divinely favoured ruler whose protection would be sought, and bought, by their peers.

If so, then that often suicidal aspiration, together with his own impressive reputation and (probably) the most splendid burial ground so far identified in the Anglo-Saxon world were ultimately Rædwald's principal legacies. The traditional paganism which he had defended and sought to restore was by 700 without political support of any consequence in England and the archpriests of Christianity were firmly in control of religious trends. In this respect Rædwald undoubtedly failed but, by the standards by which kings were measured in contemporary Anglo-Saxon literature, one can hardly deny that his failure was heroic.[147]

Notes

1 His great victory was over Æthelfrith on the banks of the River Idle: *HE*, II, 12; his influence over Bernicia was via the rule there of his protégé Edwin.

2 See above, pp. 57–8.

3 On the basis of Bede's repeated claim of a Southumbrian *imperium* on behalf of Æthelberht: *HE*, I, 25, 32; II, 5. For discussion, see E. John, *Orbis Britanniae*, Leicester, 1966, pp. 6–8; F. M. Stenton, *Anglo-Saxon England*, Oxford, 3rd ed. 1973, p. 53; R. Bruce-Mitford, *Aspects of Anglo-Saxon Archaeology: Sutton Hoo and other Discoveries*, London, 1974, p. 73.

4 B. A. E. Yorke, 'The Vocabulary of Anglo-Saxon Overlordship', *Anglo-Saxon Studies in History and Archaeology*, II, 1981, pp. 171–200; S. Fanning, 'Bede, *Imperium* and the Bretwaldas', *Speculum*, LXVI, 1991, pp. 1–26; S. Keynes, 'Rædwald the Bretwalda', *Voyage to the Other World: the legacy of Sutton Hoo*, Medieval Studies at Minnesota, V, edd. C. B. Kendall and P. S. Wells, Minneapolis, 1992, pp. 103–23.

5 E.g. D. P. Kirby, *The Earliest English Kings*, London, 1991, pp. 65–6; Fanning, 'Bede', p. 16.

6 *The Earliest Life of Gregory the Great, by an Anonymous Monk of Whitby*, ed. B. Colgrave, Cambridge, 1985, XVI; the notice of *Redvald* as *rex Westanglorum* is presumably a mistake by a continental scribe: *ibid*, pp. 69, 149–50, n. 65. Supposing this to have been a misguided addition rather than an error of the clumsiest sort, the original is most likely to have read *rex Anglorum*, which would bring this text into line with contemporary references to *imperium*-wielding kings: see the letter of Gregory to Æthelberht, quoted by Bede, *HE*, I, 32, and see his description as *rex Anglorum* in *HE*, II, 12, which equates with the nomenclature that Bede considered appropriate to the near universal, insular kingship of Edwin.

7 The latter is *HE*, II, 12. The remainder are *HE*, II, 5; II, 15; III, 18.

8 *ASC(E)* for the year 617.

9 The elaboration of Edwin's succession in the same entry is obviously derived from a compilation of information obtained from *HE*, II, 5 and II, 12.

10 The listing of the Wuffingas in *HB*, LIX includes Wuffa, Tytill and Eni but omits Rædwald. This is an eighth-century genealogy, not a king-list, so the omission is unremarkable. For discussion, see S. Newton, *The origins of Beowulf and the pre-Viking Kingdom of East Anglia*, Woodbridge, 1993, pp. 105–31.

11 In contrast with that of Edwin: *HB*, LXI, LXIII; *Trioedd Ynys Prydein*, ed. R. Bromwich, Cardiff, 1961, p. 339.

12 As is quite clear from the numerous value judgements in his text: see above, pp. 10–15, 198.

13 The British Church remained 'schismatic' in 731 but Iona had conformed in 716: *HE*, V, 22. There were no pagan kings in England after the 680s although individual pagan practice was probably then still widely prevalent, hence the penalties in the Penitentiary reputedly of Archbishop Theodore.

14 *HE*, I, 22: 'But nevertheless divine pity did not desert his people, whom he foreknew . . .'. The parallel between the pagan English and the Old Testament Israelites is compelling.

15 *HE*, III, 1.

16 *HE*, II, 1–6, 9–14. See also III, 9.

17 For the former, N. J. Higham, 'King Cearl, the battle of Chester and the origins of the Mercian "Overkingship" ', *Midland History*, XVI, 1992, pp. 1–15; for the latter, *HE*, III, 24. Note the parallel between Penda's royal *duces* here and Rædwald's *ducatus* in II, 5.

18 *Ibid*, II, 14.

19 Or because Cearl was unrelated to the Mercian dynasty of the present, which descended from Penda.

20 See above, pp. 145–6.

21 Although his comment in *HE* II, 20 is neutral or even complimentary: Penda was portrayed as a *vir strenuissimus*, albeit a heathen one. This physical prowess may have helped Bede circumvent a major *lacuna* in the logic of his *Historia* by helping to explain away the defeat and death of the divinely supported Edwin at the hands of those whom he dubbed pagans and heretics. Additionally, it is implicit that even a pagan Mercian king was, in Bede's eyes, morally superior to a Christian British one. Thereafter his presence is fleeting but inimical, as in *HE*, III, 9, wherein he was anonymous so not personally credited with victory, and III, 16, wherein the impact of his successful campaign was mitigated by the device of portraying God, through Aidan, prevailing against him. In both these references his characterisation is implicitly demonic.

22 Compare *HE*, III, 24 with III, 1–2.

23 *HE*, V, 24, yet Bede considered that Penda had no objection to individuals adopting Christianity: *HE*, III, 21.

24 *HE*, I, 34.

25 *HE*, II, 2.

26 Both these passages (*HE*, I, 34 and II, 2) may betray elements derived from heroic songs or poems, as in the numbering of the monks at Bangor which is too stereotyped to be realistic.

27 *HE*, I, 22, where Bede summarises Gildas, *DEB*, XXVI.

28 J. McClure, 'Bede's Old Testament Kings', in *Ideal and Reality in Frankish and Anglo-Saxon Society*, ed. P. Wormald *et al.*, Oxford, 1983, pp. 82, 87, 90–91.

29 Albeit that their virtues were principally military ones: *HE*, II, 2, 3, 12. Under Roman control the British became virtuous Christians (I, 4; I, 6), but contrast Bede's comments concerning British heresies after the rise of tyrants in Britain: I, 8; I, 17.

30 *HE*, I, 3; I, 6.

31 *HE*, I, 8, following Gildas, *DEB*, XII, 3.

32 *HE*, I, 10; I, 17: Bede probably did not realise that Pelagianism began at Rome, not in Britain: B. R. Rees, *Pelagius: A Reluctant Heretic*, Woodbridge, 1988, *passim*.

33 *HE*, I, 15; V, 24.

34 *HE*, II, 2.

35 *HE*, II, 12.

36 Descended from Ida, of course: D. N. Dumville, 'The Anglian Collection of Royal Genealogies and Regnal Lists', *ASC*, V, 1976, p. 30.

37 Goffart, *The Narrators of Barbarian History*, Princeton, 1988, pp. 325–8.

38 *HE*, II, 15.

39 The seminal work on this dynasty is F. M. Stenton, 'The East Anglian Kings of the Seventh Century', in *Anglo-Saxon Studies in some aspects of their History and Culture presented to Bruce Dickins*, ed P. Clemoes, London, 1959, reprinted in *Preparatory to Anglo-Saxon England*, ed. D. M. Stenton, Oxford, 1970, pp. 394–402; see also B. Yorke, *Kings and Kingdoms of Early Anglo-Saxon England*, London, 1990, pp. 58–71, and see note 10, above.

40 *HE*, IV, 23, naming Hereswith and her son, King Ealdwulf.

41 *HE*, III, 8; IV, 22; IV, 23.

42 As had apparently sustained the *imperia* of Edwin and Oswiu, and perhaps also of Ecgfrith.

43 *HE*, II, 15.

44 *Ibid*: 'his later condition was worse than his first'.

45 *Ibid*: *quibusdam peruersis doctoribus*, but the normal meaning of *doctores* in Bede's work is as Christian teachers. These 'perverse teachers' were offered as the antithesis of virtuous clergymen, so implicitly represented disciples of the devil.

46 *Ibid*: *seductus est*.

47 *Ibid*.

48 *Ibid*: Sigeberht was a *vir per omnia Christianissimus ac doctissimus*.

49 *HE*, V, 24. Later attempts to date Rædwald's death are embedded in texts which clearly derive from the *HE* and presumably stem from interpretations thereof: e.g. *Flores Historiarum*, ed. H. Richards Luard,

London, 1890, I, p. 302, which offers AD 624. Although this cannot be far wrong, it is not authoritative.

50 *HE*, V, 24, but see the debate concerning Bede's dating: D. P. Kirby, 'Bede and Northumbrian Chronology', *English Historical Review*, LXXVIII, 1963, pp. 514–27; M. Miller, 'The Dates of Deira', *Anglo-Saxon England*, VIII, 1979, pp. 35–61; S. Wood, 'Bede's Northumbrian Dates Again', *English Historical Review*, XCVIII, 1983, pp. 280–96.

51 Already victor of *Degsastan* and Chester, Æthelfrith was described by Bede in language implicit of a great military reputation and 'overking': *HE*, I, 34; II, 2.

52 *Ibid*, II, 15.

53 Compare the situation of Æthelwealh, King of the South Saxons, baptised under Wulfhere's patronage and rewarded for his compliance with Wight and Meonware, but who had made no effort to spread Christianity outside his own household before Bishop Wilfrid arrived: *HE*, IV, 13. The killing of Eorpwald, Rædwald's son and heir, after his conversion may also be significant: *HE*, II, 15.

54 *Ibid*.

55 *HE*, II, 2.

56 *HE*, II, 4.

57 Higham, 'King Cearl', p. 7.

58 Æthelfrith's conquests among the Britons and Scots need have had little impact on southern England but his usurpation of the Deiran kingship, *c.* 604, brought the direct rule of a great war-leader into contact with kingships which were apparently tributary to the Mercian king, in Elmet, Lindsey and Hatfield and the Peak. *HE*, II, 12 and *HB*, LXIII.

59 See above, p. 195 and Higham, 'King Cearl', pp. 6–9.

60 Although this event was not dated in any contemporary or near contemporary text the sequence offered by Bede (*HE*, II, 12) allows little room for departure from this date, although the *Laud Chronicle (ASC(E))* preferred 617 for a highly derivative conflation of the battle, Edwin's succession and his rise to a near universal 'overkingship'. See also *AC*, 617.

61 *HE*, II, 15.

62 *Ibid*, III, 18. See also note 48.

63 Stemming initially from William of Malmesbury, who is unlikely to have had access to relevant information independent of *HE* and probably made an ill-founded deduction: *Willelmi Malmesbiriensis Monachi De Gestis Regum Anglorum*, ed. W. Stubbs, London, 1887, I, p. 96, XCVII: *Sigeebertus successit Eorpwald, vir Deo dignus, frater eius ex matre . . .*; Stenton, 'East Anglian Kings', p. 49, footnote 2.

64 *HE*, III, 18.

65 Compare the career of Œthelwald, Oswiu's nephew and subking of Deira, in 655: *HE*, III, 24; or Peada's *rapprochement* with Oswiu from

653: *HE*, III, 21, 24. Both suffered political eclipse or death thereafter.

66 *HE*, II, 15. I. Wood, *The Merovingian Kings, 450–751*, Harlow, 1994, p. 176.

67 *HE*, II, 15.

68 *Ibid.*

69 *HE*, II, 5. For a detailed discussion of this text and Bede's purposes, see pp. 57–8.

70 Hence his baptism in Kent: *HE*, II, 15. See also II, 5: 'who while Æthelberht lived, conceded to him the military leadership of his people'. For discussion of this translation see N. Brooks, *The Early History of the Church of Canterbury: Christ Church from 597 to 1066*, Leicester, 1984, p. 63; P. Wormald, 'Bede', p. 106, footnote 30; T. Charles-Edwards, *Addenda*, in *Bede's Ecclesiastical History of the English People: an Historical Commentary*, by J. M. Wallace-Hadrill, Oxford, 1988, pp. 220–22; Keynes, 'Rædwald', pp. 106–7; above, pp. 57–8.

71 *Gregorii papae registrum epistolarum*, ed. P. Ewald and L. M. Hartmann, *MGH Epistolae*, II, xi, p. 35; Colgrave and Mynors, *Bede*, p. 74, footnote 1; Wallace-Hadrill, *Bede's Ecclesiastical History*, p. 39; D. P. Kirby, *The Earliest English Kings*, London, 1991, pp. 31–5.

72 Procopius of Caesaria, *History of the Wars*, tr. H. B. Dewing, London, 1914–40, VIII, xx.

73 Gregory of Tours, *Decem Libri Historiarum*, ed. B. Krusch and W. Levison, *MGH, Scriptores Rerum Merovingicarum*, Hanover, 1951, IX, 26: 'the son of a certain king of Kent' may imply that Æthelberht's father was only one of two (or more) such kings.

74 N. Brooks, 'The creation and early structure of the kingdom of Kent', in *The Origins of Anglo-Saxon Kingdoms*, ed. S. Bassett, Leicester, 1989, p. 67.

75 *HE*, II, 3, where he was described as *sub potestate* of Æthelberht.

76 *HE*, II, 2.

77 This supposes Sigeberht to have been born already before 597 and also that this was his original name rather than a later baptismal name given him in Frankia. For the latter possibility, recall that Æthelburh, the Kentish princess, was known also as Tata: *HE*, II, 9. It may have been commonplace for converts to adopt a new name upon baptism, as clergy often did either then or at consecration – as, for example, James the Deacon and Archbishop Deusdedit.

78 Despite Augustine's meeting with the British clergy on the borders of the West Saxons: *HE*, II, 2. Attempts by the authors of the *ASC* to place Ælle and Ceawlin in a more precise chronological and historical context than Bede offered must be rejected as unhistorical.

79 *HE*, II, 15.

80 This hypothesis depends entirely on Bede's use of *autem* in the opening line of *HE*, II, 16, as referring back specifically to his treatment of the fortunes of Christianity in East Anglia in II, 15. This is far from compelling. Bede used *autem* elsewhere to mean 'moreover', 'additionally' or as a simple conjunction. See, for example, *HE*, II, 1: *Rexit autem ecclesiam . . . Secundo autem. . . .* Had Bede meant to infer Paulinus's presence in East Anglia he would arguably have established it far less ambiguously than this.

81 *HE*, II, 5 and see notes 69 and 70.

82 Æthelberht is not known to have inherited his *imperium* from Eumenric, his father, although it was the latter's diplomacy which apparently initiated links between Kent, Frankia and the East Saxons, so Eumenric's claims are far from nebulous. See *HE*, II, 5 for Ælle and Ceawlin.

83 Higham, 'King Cearl', pp. 6–10.

84 *Ibid* and see below.

85 *Ibid*, but note Bede's reference to the many *loca vel regna* through which he wondered in exile, all of which, until his arrival in East Anglia, were presumably under Cearl's influence: *HE*, II, 12.

86 *Ibid.*

87 Or at least one which is known to have produced exceptional numbers of Anglo-Saxon cemeteries and graves.

88 *Contra* Kirby, *Earliest Kings*, pp. 72–3, who based his supposition that Rædwald exercised a kingship which was autonomous of Æthelberht before 616 on a very different interpretation of *HE*, II, 5.

89 *HE*, II, 12: *occidit in finibus gentis Merciorum*, but see note 34, pp. 104–5, above.

90 As recounted by Bede, *HE*, I, 34; II, 2.

91 Compare Penda's attacks on Cenwealh, Sigeberht or Anna: *HE*, III, 7; III, 18.

92 *HE*, II, 5; II, 9.

93 *HE*, II, 12.

94 *Ibid.*

95 *HE*, III, 1.

96 *HE*, III, 24.

97 *The Life of Bishop Wilfrid by Eddius Stephanus*, ed. B. Colgrave, Cambridge, 1927, XIX, XX.

98 *HE*, II, 12. Compare Bede's use of a miracle to reduce, for rhetorical purposes, the impact of Ecgfrith's defeat (which he never actually admits) by the Mercians by the River Trent: *HE*, IV, 21; IV, 22.

99 *HE*, II, 12.

100 The *Nordanhymbri*: e.g. *HE*, I, 15; II, 20; III, 26. Bede's explanation of the term in the first of these implies that it was novel in 731. For earlier use of *Humbrenses*, see *HE*, IV, 17 and *Life of Gregory*, XIX, but

this title is most unlikely to pre-date Æthelfrith's conquests south of the Humber. It was not, therefore, a 'folk-name' of great antiquity but a name given to a new grouping of what had been separate kingships which had neither name nor identity prior to his usurpations. The name was subsequently redefined by a generation grown accustomed to the loss of Lindsey – the principal 'Southumbrian' kingship held by the Bernician royal house during much of the seventh century. *Regnum* could here be a synonym for *imperium*.

101 *HE*, III, 1; III, 6.

102 *HE*, III, 1.

103 If Bede's claim that he was Æthelfrith's *successor* was literally true: *HE*, II, 12.

104 My own interpretation of the Tribal Hidage certainly points to that conclusion: see above, pp. 86–7.

105 *HE*, III, 1: *magna nobilium iuventute*.

106 As Edwin would himself take tribute from his own subordinates.

107 As had Rædwald honoured Æthelberht: *HE*, II, 15, and as other kings would honour Oswiu: *HE*, III, 21.

108 As did various *duces regii* ('royal warleaders') serve under Penda in 655: *HE*, III, 24.

109 For parallels, see above, pp. 22–30.

110 N. J. Higham, *Rome, Britain and the Anglo-Saxons*, London, 1992, p. 230.

111 Bede very pointedly conferred this status on the Christians, Edwin, Oswald and Oswiu, but not the pagan Rædwald.

112 As, for example, in the case of the powerful king whose forces routed the Varni: Procopius, *History of the Wars*, VIII, xx.

113 *HB*, 61, 63; *AC*, 617, 630 and, by implication, 629; *Trioedd ynys Prydein*, ed. R. Bromwich, Cardiff, 1961, nos. 55, 62, 69.

114 *HE*, II, 9; III, 1; IV, 16.

115 Perhaps Woden, if the descent of the East Anglian kings recorded in *HB*, LIX, is other than a stereotype. See also Dumville, 'Royal Genealogies', 31, which ends with *Woden Frealifing*.

116 *HE*, II, 5. Note that Bede contrived their punishment by God by invoking a later defeat at West Saxon hands: cf. his use of the battle of Chester as divine punishment of the Britons. That punishment should have seemed appropriate may imply apostasy. Whether or not, the coincidence of the deaths of Sæberht and Æthelberht enabled Sæberht's sons to revive paganism among the East Saxons while Rædwald's victory and rise to *imperium* arguably raised expectations that this policy would reap handsome rewards.

117 *Ibid*.

118 *Ibid*.

119 *Ibid*, II, 6.

120 By highlighting Rædwald's subordination to Æthelberht until the old king's death.

121 *HE*, II, 5: the translation of Colgrave and Mynors offers 'apostate' for *perfidus*: p. 151, as does L. Sherley-Price, *Bede: A History of the English Church and People*, London, 1955, p. 109. It could be as well translated 'treacherous', so avoiding the very specific term above but the inference of apostasy must stand (*contra* Colgrave and Mynors, p. 151, note 5). Bede's assertion a few lines before that 'he had refused to receive the faith of Christ' is inconsistent with this. It may be that Bede's Canterbury sources were on this matter either confused or contrived: Christian tradition probably preferred an Eadbald who had resisted baptism but, once converted, had been consistent, to a king who had apostatised and then been re-converted. Bede depicted Eadbald elsewhere in virtuous terms: *Ibid*, II, 8; II, 11; II, 20. That he was here seen as vulnerable to divine *corrigendum* and afflicted by fits of madness underlines the dialectical content of this passage, which detailed even worse punishments for his East Saxon cousins. Eadbald's precise condition must remain in doubt but it is not easy to reconcile Æthelberht's enthusiastic support for Christianity over two decades, his enshrining of royal protection for its priests in a law code and the numerous baptisms in Kent with his heir's intransigent paganism throughout.

122 Procopius, *History of the Wars*, VIII, xx.

123 Post-dating 601, at least; see note 71.

124 *HE*, II, 5; II, 9. See discussion in Kirby, *Earliest Kings*, pp. 40–42.

125 *HE*, II, 5.

126 The appointment of Paulinus as bishop at least implies as strong a commitment on her part as on her brother's in 625: *HE*, II, 9.

127 *HE*, IV, 13, for the case of Æthelwealh of the South Saxons.

128 I. Stewart, 'Anglo-Saxon gold coins', in *Scripta Nummaria Romana. Essays presented to Humphrey Sutherland*, ed. R. A. G. Carson and C. M. Kraay, London, 1978, pp. 147, 153, 162–5. The earliest issues occur at London and in East Kentish cemeteries – a mix which would accord well with the known sphere of influence of the Kentish kings in the early seventh century.

129 As eighth-century kings might have done: *contra*, Kirby, *Earliest Kings*, pp. 42, 65–6.

130 Or a preference for a particularly wide selection of Frankish coins, the very diversity perhaps having its own, now obscure meaning: R. Bruce-Mitford, *The Sutton Hoo Ship Burial: A Handbook*, London, 1979, pp. 84–92; A. C. Evans, *The Sutton Hoo Ship Burial*, London, 1986, pp. 88–9. This reasoning supposes Sutton Hoo to be East Anglian, for which debate see above, p. 206.

131 Despite its Christian content and imagery, the setting is profoundly traditional and pagan.

132 S. Newton, *The origins of Beowulf and the pre-Viking Kingdom of East Anglia*, Woodbridge, 1993, *passim*.

133 R. Bruce-Mitford, *Aspects*, pp. 55, 114–40; 'The Sutton Hoo Ship Burial: some foreign connections', *Angli e Sassoni al di qua e al di la del Mare*, Spoleto, 1986, pp. 196–210; W. Filmer-Sankey, 'The Snape Anglo-Saxon Cemetery and Ship Burial: Current state of knowledge', *Bulletin of the Sutton Hoo Research Project*, 2, 1984, pp. 13–15.

134 Evans, *Sutton Hoo*, p. 109.

135 *Ibid*, pp. 108–10.

136 M. Parker Pearson, R. van de Noort and A. Woolf, 'Three men and a boat: Sutton Hoo and the East Saxon kingdom', *Anglo-Saxon England*, XXII, 1993, pp. 27–50.

137 Newton, *Origins*, pp. 106–9.

138 *Ibid*, pp. 34–5.

139 S. Dunmore, V. Gray, T. Lauder and K. Wade, *The origin and development of Ipswich: an interim report, East Anglian Archaeology*, I, 1975, pp. 59–60; R. Hodges, *Dark Age Economics: The Origins of Towns and Trade, AD 600–1000*, 1982, pp. 70–73.

140 Yorke, *Kings and Kingdoms*, p. 65.

141 Hall, *Dark Age Economics*, pp. 87–94, interprets the insular distribution of European pottery in terms of competition between rival trading nations; but shifting and ideologically distinctive preferences within the high-status households which controlled their markets in England are at least as plausible a factor.

142 J. Hines, *The Scandinavian Character of Anglian England in the pre-Viking Period*, Oxford, 1984, *passim*.

143 See above, pp. 91–2.

144 *HE*, II, 9.

145 For a tribute of 40,000 hides, see the 'Tribal Hidage': D. N. Dumville, 'The Tribal Hidage: an introduction to the texts and their history', in *Origin of Anglo-Saxon Kingdoms*, ed. S. Bassett, Leicester, 1989, appendix I.

146 *HE*, III, 18.

147 That they took exceptional risks must be preferred to the view that they were 'an unlucky house': Stenton, 'East Anglian Kings', p. 49. Their high death rate in battle has been seen as indicative of the general riskiness of early kingship: e.g. J. Campbell, *The Anglo-Saxons*, London, 1982, 56, but it does seem exceptional rather than the norm.

6

An English empire: status and ethnicity

The unfree

Both the several law codes, and the literary works of English priests written in the early eighth century, focus primarily on law-worthy sections of the population. The law codes embody relationships and regulate interaction. Clerical texts recount conversions and single out individuals with some special role in the workings of divine providence in human history.

In the law codes, the lower sectors of society (those who did not have direct access to customary tribal law) are barely referred to, apart from their value to their masters as possessions or in recognition of their potential to harm their betters. The few references to them which do occur were therefore related to the control of subgroups who had no redress at law as individuals, in accordance with the over-riding self-interest of the free population, who did enjoy such rights.

Bede and his contemporaries wrote primarily about clerics (most of the better known of whom originated either from abroad or from well-to-do households) or kings, their *comes* and *milites* (*thegns* or *gesiths*, the warrior classes) and *nobiles* and *duces* (*ealdormen* and other sectors of the nobility at the top end of the landholding classes). Given the sheer bulk of the *Historia Ecclesiastica*, it may at first sight appear that there are remarkably few references to the common man. On consideration, however, the suspicion begins to emerge that the rural proletariat and unfree population were quite legitimately beneath Bede's attention, since they were without influence in the political struggles and religious debates of the day and quite inappropriate for individual attention. What is more, it is far from certain that Bede would have recognised their collective membership of the *gens Anglorum*, whose conversion he had taken upon himself to narrate. It is the social, ethnic and cultural identity of this massive but rarely recorded underclass that will be addressed in the first part of this chapter.

Terms describing the proletariat

Bede simply did not use many of the standard Latin terms appropriate to the rural population. The word *agricola* (farmer) does not appear in this work (other than as a personal name); *cultor* (husbandman or labourer) is nowhere used in its literal sense, although it occurs as a metaphor for a Christian worshipper, a priest or a bishop; likewise, *cultura* is used only for 'religion' or 'worship'; *paganus* (literally 'country-dweller') occurs a total of twenty-nine times in the *Historia Ecclesiastica* but only in a context which requires it to convey its secondary meaning of 'pagan'. It is worth noting in passing that it was used disproportionately often – and presumably intentionally so – of the Mercians, so forms a subtle part of the apparatus of detraction and condemnation by which Bede sought to undermine the moral status of the principal English rivals of his own people, both in the present and in retrospect. *Paganus* occurs in this same sense in the *Life of Wilfrid*, as does *gentiles* ('gentiles', so 'pagans', used in similar contexts herein).

In the *Historia Ecclesiastica*, *vulgus* ('the vulgar') occurs six times but is not restricted to a specific class: it was used pejoratively of evil spirits in a vision of hell, of British commoners, pagan East Saxons, and the Deiran country folk (perhaps in a pagan context) who witnessed Coifi's putative profanation of his own pagan shrines.[1] It occurs only once in contrast to *nobiles* (the warrior class: see below, p. 225). Its usage has, therefore, a demonstrably rhetorical dimension. *Rusticitas* and *rusticus* ('rusticity', and 'rustic' so 'peasant') are similarly used in a variety of contexts, so for example in condescending comments appropriate to those ignorant of, so not conforming to, Roman methods of computing Easter, but they otherwise occur in contexts specific to rurality and country dwellers in general, sometimes in combination with poverty, or as an antithesis to *urbs* ('town'). In only one passage does Bede contrast the term with *miles* ('warrior') in a context which implies that he has in mind a clear distinction of class, and this is that same instance as is reserved above for later discussion.[2] The term *plebs* occurs thirteen times but was used as loosely as is the word 'people' today, variously denoting the rural community, those sections of free society which were neither royal nor noble (so perhaps the *ceorl* population), Christian congregations (in contrast to the clergy), or as an equivalent to *gens* for the entire English race or a significant part thereof.[3] *Servus* (literally 'slave') occurs in all twenty-six times but twenty-five of these are conventional references to members of the clergy (as 'servant(s) of God') and only one to the unfree rural population.[4] *Famulus* ('servant') was used exclusively in reference to the clergy, and most famously of Bede himself, occurring in all twenty-five times.

It is in his use of the term *vicanus* that Bede seems most consistently to be making reference to the rural population: the term derives from *vicus*, a word which he seems to use only of rural settlements and primarily of estate centres, but it occurs only three times in this text. In the first, Bede was rehearsing a miracle story designed to enhance the reputation of the martyred King Oswald[5] and it was a significant feature of this tale, which implicitly lent weight to it, that it was one of the British race (whose utter iniquity he had already established) who was therein instrumental in demonstrating the potency of Oswald's sanctity. This Briton supposedly collected soil from what was, unbeknown to him, the place of Oswald's martyrdom and continued his travels until evening when he arrived at a *vicus* (so 'rural settlement') where he found *vicani* enjoying a feast in a *domus* ('house' but in this context apparently a 'hall') which had a central fire, wall-posts, a roof of wattles and hay thatch. That the Briton was welcomed to the feast implies that a degree of mutual understanding and respect existed between himself and the masters (*domini*) of this hall. They may also, therefore, have been Britons. If not, they were apparently perfectly complacent about the fact that he was, so were presumably well-used to visits from Britons of whatever status. If this traveller was a servant or slave, then a parallel exists between this story and the opening chapter of the *Life of Wilfrid* (see below), wherein Wilfrid's hagiographer claimed that, as a boy, Wilfrid's virtues included his deferential treatment of visitors whether these be *regales socii* or *servi eorum* ('friends worthy of a king' or 'their servants/slaves').

The locality of this alleged incident immediately becomes significant. Conventional wisdom concerning Oswald's martyrdom has long placed it in the vicinity of Oswestry and so reduced any interpretational difficulties inherent within this passage to a minimum, since the Briton and his hosts could all legitimately and quite appropriately be considered Welshmen in such a context. However, recent reconsideration of this point has established the poverty of the evidence by which it has hitherto been sustained and it should probably therefore be discounted.[6] One alternative would be to equate *Maserfelth* with Makerfield (in Lancashire),[7] which is at least appropriate to the political context in which it was fought, so for example identifying the Mercians as the likely aggressors.[8] Against this must be placed the apparent ease with which the Mercian Queen Osthryth, and her husband, King Æthelred (675–704), subsequently recovered what they claimed to be Oswald's remains and translated them to Bardney in Lindsey, without apparent hindrance from, or reference to, the Bernician kings. This detail would seem to tell against a site which was, during Æthelred's reign, inside Northumbria (as southern Lancashire then surely was), in favour of one which had been subject to Oswald in the past but was then (at the date of this translation) securely under Mercian control. On these grounds, a site in Lindsey itself, or that part of Hatfield which may have become attached to Mercia once more *c.* 680, would offer the closest fit with the small amount of information available to us: such would accord with the evidence for the clustering of the sites of battles between Northumbrian kings and their opponents in the strategic corridor running along the Roman roads from central Yorkshire to the Trent;[9] it would also better suit the political contexts of the relevant periods, to the extent that these can be reconstructed; it would likewise fit better with the role which the Mercian crown expected Bardney to perform *vis-à-vis* Oswald's remains if it proved to be the minster within whose *parochia* the battle had been fought. Place-names in *-felth* likewise cluster hereabouts, most noticeably in southern Yorkshire, with only a small number of outliers occurring west of the Pennines in medieval Lancashire and Cheshire.

The locality appropriate to this miracle obviously remains unknown, but we are here confronted by the probability that Bede was referring to *vicani* somewhere in the marches between Northumbria and Mercia, and a distinct possibility that they were somewhere in the north-east Midlands, at some date between 642 and 731, who were either themselves Britons or at least very familiar with Britons. The actual veracity of Bede's story is inconsequential. It is the fact that he told it in this way that is significant, with a particular set of assumptions concerning the life-experience and reactions of his own audience, without apology, explanation or comment. That nearby Elmet was certainly under British kings as late as 616 × 630 is certainly pertinent to, and helps sustain, the conclusion that an early eighth-century audience would have expected the countryfolk in this part of England to have been British, or at least prepared to entertain British travellers at their feasts, *c.* 680. The rank which Bede imputed to the masters of this feast is unclear from his text but it may be that it was the estate reeve or steward whom he here had in mind (on whose ethnicity more below). It must be noted that the north-east Midlands have yielded quantities of Anglo-Saxon (or, in current archaeological parlance 'Anglian') material remains, sufficient to be considered to have been an integral part of England and heavily settled by Germanic immigrants.[10] This anecdotal evidence from the literature does not sit easily with such views.

Vicani were generally of low status and subject to the governance of others. They were consistently portrayed as reactive, rather than proactive, in their behaviour. In book three, chapter twenty-six of his *Historia*, Bede depicted such people congregating together in a most humble fashion should a priest of the Hiberno-Northumbrian Church happen to come to their *vicus*, so as to benefit by his teaching. If this is anything more than mere rhetoric, his comment may bear the construction that such *vicani* might often have been British Christians who were eager to hear the preaching of a Celtic priest of whom their English political masters approved, but this remains only one of several possible interpretations of this passage. Whatever their precise ethnic and cultural context, these *vicani* were clearly being portrayed as receptive to the wishes of men of higher rank within the social hierarchy.

Similarly, Bede used the term for estate-dwellers in the Old Saxon homeland:[11] the two Hewalds, who were English missionaries, made contact with a *vilicus* ('reeve' or 'steward') and were accomodated in the guest-house (*hospitium*) on the *vicus* for which he was responsible while they awaited access to his patron or master (*satrap* was the appropriately foreign term which Bede used which occurs only in this passage of the *HE*, albeit five times therein). But they were murdered by the *vicani* who feared the consequences for their own religious practices of the introduction of their new religion to the *satrap*. The *vicani* were themselves later killed and the *vicus* burnt by order of that same *satrap* in retribution for their violation of his protection of these missionaries, despite their never having progressed further towards his presence than a guest-house on an estate from which he was at the time absent. This unusual initiative undertaken by the *vicani* therefore brought down upon themselves the full force of the *potentia* ('power') of the owner of the estate; and this concept of 'secular power' was one to which Bede made frequent reference elsewhere. It seems most unlikely that the *vicani* were expected to have had recourse to any court or legal process exclusive of the estate on which they lived. Against the *potentia* of the estate owner they had, therefore, no legal redress and they were, at least to this extent, unfree.

Bede referred in similar terms, but in slightly different language, to masses of the rural population in his description of Paulinus's ministry at Yeavering:[12]

> In those days he did nothing else from morn until dusk but instruct the *plebs* who converged on him from all the little settlements [*viculi*] and places [*locae*, so perhaps 'small estates' or 'farms'] around in the teaching of Christ, . . .

The access of such *plebs* to Yeavering and the king's own bishop may imply that they were predominantly freemen but it is generally considered that northern Bernicia was still fundamentally British as regards the grass-roots of local society in the early seventh century, so these up-country, *viculi*- and *locae*-dwelling *plebs* from the hinterland of Yeavering arguably included many who were likely to be identifiable at this date as Britons in their culture and language. Their behaviour was once again fundamentally reactive, being dependent on the will of the king and his nobility, whose baptism preceded and conditioned their own.

Other evidence

Unfree tenants and labourers could be present on a large royal estate in some numbers. The figure of 250 slaves of both sexes (*servi et ancillae*) on the eighty-seven hide estate of Selsey is arguably an approximation, perhaps even a guess,[13] but Bede did not imagine that this was the only population on the estate, the servile contingent being only part of the *homines* (men) mentioned, all of whom were granted by the king to Wilfrid with the estate so were apparently tied to it. That problematic late Anglo-Saxon document, the *Rectitudines Singularum Personarum*, details precisely this type of mix of servile and free workers and tenants on a comparably large, but anonymous, estate *c.* 1042–1066.[14] It may well be that similar gradations of freedom existed, if largely unbeknown to us, on the large estates of the seventh century, with a complex balance of different types of tenant and estate labourer, some of whom were specialists and some generalists, and only some of whom had the right to choose, so leave, their lord and the estate on which they were resident.

Other English writers of the same period offer a similar picture. The anonymous Whitby monk writing of St. Gregory likened his role, in death, through a biblical allegory, to that of a 'faithful and sagacious slave' (*servus* but this can translate as 'servant') of God's household, one of whose duties would be to dole out wheat, probably as food but conceivably as seed corn.[15] His use of *servus* here obviously owes something to its conventional use for a clergyman (see above), but the role which he envisaged Gregory performing is more elaborate than that and implies that different ideas were coming into play. His model may have been a servant of his own monastery perhaps, or the steward of a household of high status, that of a king, nobleman or bishop. Whichever, the image of Gregory as a servile (or at least relatively unfree) household manager implies that households of high status and equivalent complexity might then be overseen by an unfree steward. This suggests that even men of low status (at law) could occupy as responsible a position in seventh-century English society as they had in the Roman Empire. Slaves were not, therefore, necessarily just labourers or peasant farmers but could be active in such key activities as the central control, storage and allocation of grain. As noted above, the opening chapter of the *Life of Wilfrid* records that the young Wilfrid was wont to 'minister skilfully to all who came to his father's house, be they friends fit for a king or their slaves (*servi*)'. Such *servi* are again unlikely to have been drawn from the rural proletariat, whose freedom to move and indeed whose need to move may have been comparatively limited, but were presumably either estate managers travelling on business or personal retainers of the English *nobiles*, but who were themselves of low status and unfree (as the passage in the *Life of Wilfrid* implies). The probability of such men being recognisably British is unquantifiable but Bede's British traveller at least opens the door to the possibility.

The anonymous author of St. Cuthberht's first *Life* recognised a distinction between 'food fit for a king' (*cibo regali*) and 'food fit for a slave' (*cibo servili*), both of which he imagined would have been present in the camp of an army on campaign.[16] St. Gregory, as a ghostly steward, might have been expected, therefore, to have been concerned not only with quantities of provender, but also with the allocation of food of the appropriate quality to different sectors of the household: the leaders of the *gens Anglorum* ate food of one quality and the servile masses who attended on them, or carried provender to them, ate another.

The story that Bede included concerning the miraculous inability of the Mercians to bind the *miles* Imma, whom they had captured after the battle by the Trent, provides crucial evidence for the fundamental separation of the warrior society of the English nation from the peasant mass by whom they were supplied in precisely this sort of situation. Imma was one of the *militia* ('soldiery' so 'warriors') of the Northumbrian King Ælfwine who was captured on the battle field, where he lay wounded, by the men of a *comes* of King Æthelred of the Mercians:[17]

> He feared to confess that he was a warrior [*miles*]; he replied that he was a peasant [*rusticus*] and a poor man and bound to a wife, and declared that he had come on the expedition with other like men to bring food to the warriors.

By implication, as is clear for example from Bede's subsequent *Letter to Ecgbert*, a military retainer attached to a superior household would not be married but he would be a man of free or even gentle birth. That he claimed to be married was, therefore, as much an impediment to his being a household warrior as was his claim to be poor and a *rusticus*.

The deception was intended to avoid the fate which Bede makes it clear that a *miles* might normally expect in such circumstances: that is, death in vengeance for the losses sustained by the opposing army. That the *miles* was considered by both parties to be an appropriate object of such vengeance, but the *rusticus* not, implies that the former, but not the latter, was considered to be a full member of the appropriate *gens* (people) – so vulnerable to a blood feud which that *gens* had incurred *en masse*. If Imma were not a member of the warrior class, he was, according to the viewpoint which Bede was here adopting, not a member of the Northumbrian *gens* at all. The ruse failed, however, being uncovered by his captors' observation of their prisoner:

> those who watched him closely noticed from his appearance, his apparel and his speech that he was not of the poor common stock [*de paupere vulgo*], as he had said, but of noble stock [*de nobilibus*].

There were, therefore, recognisable differences between a *miles* and a *rusticus*, even given that the *miles* concerned had just fought and been wounded in a great battle, so was unlikely to be looking his best. That the free and noble sectors of society had long hair may have been one distinguishing mark (see below); the impact of hard labour on the hands would have been an obvious indicator; the quality of clothing was perhaps another and the accent, even the vocabulary and language used, the last.

Ethnic divisions

It is a matter of logic, even of definition, that the rural proletariat was far more numerous than the remainder of society. Bede was here making perhaps his most explicit comment concerning this mass of population beneath the ranks of the law-worthy and weapon-owning to whom his text otherwise primarily refers, in terms which distinguish the mass from their masters. Those distinguishing marks were a matter of physical culture and language. They were reinforced by the exclusion of that mass of the rural and unfree population from the myth of kinship and group identity which sustained each of the English peoples, so ultimately the *gens Anglorum* in its totality. That the *rusticus* was considered by both a Northumbrian *miles* and a Mercian *comes* to belong outside the *gens* to which Imma himself belonged, even while loyally serving that *gens* when in arms, implies that he would have been expected, by Bede and his audience, to have had an entirely separate sense of group identity. He was, therefore, presumably a Briton as well as being a member of the unfranchised and unfree proletariat at the base of English society.

A similar conclusion may be appropriate to a miracle story told in favour of the young Cuthberht in the third chapter of Bede's version of his *Life*. The story is a familiar one: monks attempting to float rafts carrying building timber down the lower Tyne were caught by the tide and in danger of losing them, much to the delight of 'a not small crowd of the vulgar (*vulgaris turba*) on the north bank among whom Cuthberht was stood'. The crowd:

> began to mock their monastic life as if they deserved to suffer, having spurned the common law of mortal men and broadcast new and unknown rules for living. Cuthberht prohibited their shameful derision, enquiring, 'What are you doing, brethren, reviling those whom you see being even now borne away to destruction? Would it not be better even and more humane to pray to the Lord for their safety, than to rejoice at their dangers?' But they were angry with him with boorish hearts and words and said, 'Let no man speak up for them and may God have no mercy on them who have robbed men of the religious practices of old and how they ought to observe the new no-one knows.'

That Bede imagined Cuthberht's response to such a crowd of countryfolk would have been to urge them to prayer requires that they could be portrayed as Christians, not pagans. Their reply confirms this: Bede had them referring not to many gods or demons but to one God, so the Christian God. It was new practices to which they objected, not Christianity itself. If these *rustici* were conservative-minded Christians of the old school then logic dictates that their Christianity had British roots and that they were British countryfolk, not pagan English peasants.

It is possible to pursue the perceptions of the early eighth-century *literati* just a little further concerning this issue, and particularly concerning the mechanisms which brought this particular social and political system into existence and which then sustained it. It is that to which we shall turn next.

Bede brought the first book of his *Historia Ecclesiastica* to a close with a short chapter devoted to the deeds of an early Bernician, King Æthelfrith. This king was to appear once more, and as an influential figure, in the second book,[18] so perhaps could be considered to need some introduction, but Bede's comments were less innocent than this. As a Bernician himself, he chose to invoke the reputation of a local royal hero and warrior-king, who was apparently still remembered by his own people at the time of writing, so as to compare (albeit implicitly) the conversion of the English with the coming of Christ himself. Just as the wide conquests and subsequent peace inaugurated by Augustus had been seized upon by Christian writers as a context peculiarly appropriate to the coming of the Messiah, so too did Bede provide a warrior king of the English who conquered his foes and imposed himself upon them to create a context which was similarly appropriate to Augustine's mission,[19] and his conclusion of book one with this image much strengthened its impact.

Thus did Bede for the first time claim primacy for his own people and its kingship within the framework of his providential history (just as he was to do in *HE*, II, 5), but the terms in which he described the deeds of his hero must in general terms embody his perception of the subordination of the Britons to the *gens Anglorum* in the present, and to the Romans in the distant past. What he wrote translates as follows:

> During this period Æthelfrith, a very brave king and most desirous of glory, presided over the *regnum* of the Northumbrians, who ravaged the *gens Brettonum* more than others of the English, so that he might indeed be compared with Saul, once king of the Israelite *gens*, excepting only this that he was ignorant of the divine religion. For no military commander or king made more lands of theirs either tributary to the *gens Anglorum* or habitable by them, having first exterminated or subjugated the indigenes.

Given that Bede perceived the English as God's chosen people and as His agents within Britain throughout their stay therein, he was implying that Æthelfrith had exceeded all others in a task which was both entirely commendable and divinely ordained, that of establishing English supremacy over the Britons. This passage therefore offers an eighth-century perspective on the mechanics of English supremacy, as that was supposed to have been established some four generations previously. There are several important insights into this process. It was initiated, in Bede's view, by war and the ravaging of enemy territory. Two options confronted the antagonists thereafter: the victorious king could either *exterminare* the Britons or subjugate them. By either means he was obtaining political control over them, but the extent and depth of that control was a variable. The term *exterminare* literally means 'to drive out' but Bede, who used it in four separate passages of the *HE*, does seem to have had in mind something of the more murderous meaning of the present day, using it otherwise in the context of the Saxon revolt against the Britons, Penda's attack on Northumbria and the West Saxon seizure of Wight. In each instance he clearly envisaged considerable violence to have taken place. The term must, therefore, carry at least some of the weight of 'to get rid of', if not necessarily 'to entirely wipe out'. The Britons could either resist, risking expulsion or death, or negotiate and offer tribute. These choices conditioned the end results achieved: subjugated peoples paid tribute while those expelled enabled Æthelfrith to exercise patronage over their estates in favour of his English supporters.

At first sight it is unclear just what Bede had in mind when he deployed these concepts of tribute payment or 'extermination'. Did he intend this passage to refer to the entirety of the indigenous population or merely the military and religious elite, so the landholding classes? The matter is most easily understood in those instances where Æthelfrith obtained tribute. The term *tributarius* was used only once elsewhere by Bede, in reference to Oswiu, whom he claimed *maxima ex parte perdomuit ac tributarias fecit* ('conquered and made tributary the greater part [of the Picts and Scots]).[20] It appears, therefore, that the payment of tribute could be considered a normal consequence of military defeat. That Bede fails to refer to it in other instances does not require or even imply that it did not occur or that it was exceptional: rather it was arguably too commonplace to require specific comment. The point is made elsewhere and in slightly different language.

A similar instance occurs, for example, in the *Life of Wilfrid*, in which God's favourite son of the moment, Ecgfrith of Northumbria, is portrayed as triumphantly confronting a Mercian challenge:[21]

> For Wulfhere, king of the Mercians, with a proud spirit and insatiable heart exciting all the southern peoples against our kingship purposed not only to do battle but also to place [the Northumbrians] under tribute in a servile spirit. But he was not guided by God . . . the king fled and his kingdom was laid under tribute . . .

That Ecgfrith was later supposed by this same author to have exercised *imperium* seems to confirm his subsequent supremacy over the Mercians and the normal association of *imperium* and tribute-taking. Although it does not refer directly to tribute and its payment, the previous chapter of this same work likewise confirms contemporary attitudes towards failure in war:

> and having been reduced to servitude, even up to the day of the death of the king [Ecgfrith again], the [Pictish] peoples remained subject to the yoke of captivity.

Although Bede similarly did not actually use the term 'tribute' in the next extract (and the omission is for obvious, rhetorical purposes), it was clearly implicit in Oswiu's offer to Penda of:[22]

> an incalculable and incredible store of royal treasures and gifts as the price of peace, on condition that Penda would return home and cease to devastate, or rather utterly destroy, the kingdoms under his rule.

Tribute was, therefore, a normal facet of the settlement of royal disputes and an important indicator of unequal relationships between kings. The recognition by one king and his people of the superiority of another involved such loss of freedom that contemporaries considered this situation to be nothing short of servitude. So, for example, when the northern Britons and Irish broke free of Northumbrian hegemony following Ecgfrith's defeat and death, Bede depicted them recovering their collective *libertas*.[23] Tribute payment therefore occurred at the very highest levels of society, so between kings of various peoples, but also as a *feorm* paid by humble estate-dwellers to proprietors (see below). When Bede referred to Britons made tributary to Æthelfrith, he apparently envisaged entire British societies and territories recognising his authority and hegemony, and so paying him tribute. As he envisaged it, entire British peoples were thereby made subject to the *gens Anglorum*, whom Æthelfrith in this context was being made to represent.

When estates were transferred from one proprietor to another, it seems clear that the necessary, existing (and in parts unfree) work force remained with it.[24] When Bede imagined Æthelfrith 'exterminating' Britons and rendering their *terrae* – literally 'estates' – *habitabiles* ('habitable') by the English, it seems most unlikely that he had in mind a colonising movement comprising numerous families of poor, landless Anglian peasants but something more akin to the normal process of land transfers among the elite. Given Æthelfrith's own role as a victorious king, the recipients of such lands under his patronage were necessarily men who had access to his court and, most likely, men who had served him as warriors. It was arguably, therefore, the British landholding aristocracy who were killed or took to their heels while the local farming population could be expected to have remained, to become the typically British *vicani* of seventh- and early eighth-century Northumbria. Their renders thereafter sustained a self-consciously English landholding, warrior elite, which was careful of its own sense of a common social and ethnic identity from which the British rural population was excluded.

Further light is shed on Bede's use of the terms *tributarias* and *habitabiles* by reference to his description of the ending of Roman Britain. The elegy that he pronounced over its corpse distinguished territory south of the *vallum*, in which the Romans *habitabant* – 'dwelt' – from the further regions beyond, over which he claimed that they had 'held rule by right'.[25] These comments mirror Bede's treatment of Æthelfrith's conquests more closely than coincidence would allow and it seems probable that he envisaged the relationships which had existed between the Romans and the Britons as virtually identical to that of Æthelfrith and his *gens Anglorum* and the Britons. Bede surely never imagined that even Britain south of the *vallum* was inhabited by a preponderance of Romans, as opposed to Britons, so it was an aristocratic style of estate tenure and habitation that he had in mind when treating of the presence in Britain of the Roman imperial race of the distant past. It has already herein been established that he was in many respects modelling his vision of their activities on English (particularly Bernician) land tenure and 'lawful domination' in his own lifetime and it is that which is the better illumined by comparison of relevant sections of his text.

The Æthelfrith episode therefore sheds important light on the nature of English treatment of the Britons, at least in the early eighth century. There were two different routes this might take: either the English conquerors left the British hierarchy in control of their lands and merely exercised superior kingship over them via an unequal relationship with the British leadership, from whom they expected tribute and other appropriate services; alternatively they could displace that hierarchy and replace it as estate-holders with members of the *gens Anglorum*, so English *thegns* or *gesiths* in their own service. That Northumbrian kings had employed both these strategies in the far north is confirmed by Bede's description of the aftermath of King Ecgfrith's death at *Nechtanesmere*. The Scots *in toto* but only part of the Britons (almost certainly Strathclyde) recovered their 'liberty', so threw off the obligation to pay tribute. All the Scots and northern Britons had, therefore, hitherto been subject to the Northumbrian king and some of the Britons remained so even thereafter. The Picts, by contrast, had not been fully subdued by the Northumbrians, so Bede described them as regaining possession of those lands which the English had held in what were generally recognised as their traditional territories, and envisaged members of the *gens Anglorum* being killed, enslaved or chased out in the process. The same distinction therefore prevailed: aristocratic English households, including a bishop and clergy, had received lands during the heady days of Oswiu's triumphs but were now driven out in much the same way as the British elite which was oppressed by Æthelfrith. This has no implications for either the ethnicity or the mobility of the farming population which was arguably Pictish, Scottish or British throughout.

Another illustration of the role of the Britons at the base of Northumbrian society comes from the *Life of Wilfrid*, chapter eighteen, which describes the miraculous resurrection of a baby from the dead. The child was reputedly of 'a certain *mulier* ('woman') on a *villa* ('estate') which is called *Ontiddanufri*. Given the author's earlier use of *mulier* for 'woman of the household', the term *quaedam mulier* suggests, in this context, a woman of the estate of low status. She was later represented as having fled from *terra sua* ('her land' or 'farm') to avoid handing over her child to be raised among the clergy. However, the bishop's reeve (*praefectus*) sought and found the child 'among others of the British race, took him away by force and carried him off to the bishop'.

The boy was certainly British. Therefore his parents also were. Those with whom he and his mother took refuge were likewise. The estate is unfortunately not identified but the juxtaposition of this story with a description of the dedication of Wilfrid's great new monastic church at Ripon may imply that it should be set in Yorkshire, or at least that the author believed such a setting to be appropriate to this miracle story. Certainly, by this date (671 × 678), Wilfrid is not known to have yet received estates outside Northumbria,[26] so a location somewhere within northern England seems reasonably certain, and within western Yorkshire or Lancashire fairly probable. Wherever the precise location, the setting of this miracle tale assumes the presence of Britons on estates held by English proprietors to be unexceptional and even commonplace as late as the early eighth century, when this text was composed.

What is perhaps more instructive is the lesson in *potentia* which this tale provides. Wilfrid, as the owner of the estate, apparently enjoyed the right to determine the career of the child of one of his British tenants, implying that that tenant and his family enjoyed few basic freedoms and had no access to law on their own account. That the tenant did not himself take the child into hiding is suggestive of the weakness of his position *vis-à-vis* proprietorial authority: additionally, it may be that the father would have been better known to, so more easily recognised by, the reeve than was his wife. But even she appears not to have left the bishop's jurisdiction, taking refuge with other Britons who were likewise vulnerable to the bishop's power as exercised through his reeve. These Britons were, perhaps, characteristic of the poor *vicani* of seventh- and eighth-century Northumbria, whose world was delimited by the boundaries of the English dominated 'shire' or estate and who were subject to the comparatively unmitigated authority – *potentia* – of the landholder in control of the estate on which they lived and worked.

Hocca may himself have been British: his name probably derives from *hoc* (genitive *hocces*), meaning 'a mallow' in Old English but this is thought to have derived ultimately from Old Welsh. The child was eventually to be named Eodwald, which loosely translates as 'Lord of the flock', a delightful pun for a poor British country boy whose miraculous revival necessarily conjured up images of Lazarus and the resurrection of Jesus – the ultimate 'Lord of the Christian flock'. Wilfrid was not known for his sense of humour but this may be an instance thereof, if it were not just one more instance of his arrogance. We may, therefore, in this anecdote, be witnessing an important phase in the process of acculturation within a British community of low status which was at this point, and by the active intervention of an English proprietor, acquiring English nomenclature by various means.

In his final summary of the state of Britain, Bede reverted to precisely this issue of the subordination of the Britons to the English master race, justifying English domination by reference to the continuing failure of the Britons to accept the Roman dating of Easter:[27]

> Very many, indeed the greater part, of the Britons struggle against the *gens Anglorum* with the hatred of their race, and against the whole state of the universal church, concerning their less correct dating of Easter and depraved customs, nevertheless they cannot obtain what they want in either respect being entirely constrained by divine and human virtue in combination. Indeed, although they are in part under their own laws [or 'their own masters'] nevertheless they have in part been sold into servitude to the English.

Bede is witness, therefore, in this very generalised comment concerning the Britons in 731 to the fact that numerous of them were subject to the *gens Anglorum*. The 'greater part' who hated and struggled in vain against them were necessarily those who retained their own identity as Britons and their own preferred method of dating Easter, so their own clergy and Church. These included both those within England and those under British kings on the periphery. Those (the minority in Bede's opinion, whom he did not consider worthy of further comment) who did not so struggle were surely those who had abandoned their own Britishness, their own separate clergy, and their expectation of ultimate relief from English oppression, and begun to acculturate, so becoming ever less easy to distinguish from the English race. Bede's comments here necessarily relate in large measure to the rural proletariat on numerous estates, whose existence was a commonplace with which his northern English audience was well-acquainted, rather than the more distant British communities who lived still under their own kings in Strathclyde and Wales. It was those more distant peoples who lived under their own laws and rulers: those who were subject to English law and were as if sold into slavery to the English necessarily lived among them.

Here then is an eighth-century vision of how the British substrate of Anglo-Saxon society became such, as well as a justification of the process by recourse to the intervention of divine will. Such Britons were necessarily numerous in 731, otherwise Bede's comments would be without purpose. Yet it is likely that by this date the cultural and legal membrane separating the British farming population from their English masters was so ruptured that a considerable flow of individuals and entire communities may be envisaged, crossing from one to the other. The literary evidence for a British peasantry which has here been explored derives almost exclusively from the north of England. Since the material evidence of Anglo-Saxon culture is at its weakest in parts of the north, it might be objected that this material is exceptional and not characteristic of England as a whole. To address that issue it is necessary to turn to the early English law codes, which derive from the south.

Law and ethnicity

The distinction between free and unfree sectors of society is deeply entrenched in the laws of King Æthelberht, compiled *c.* 600.[28] Having established the relative status at law of the Church, his laws deal with various offences of interest to the king, or from the recompense of which he might expect to profit. The acts of a 'freeman' (*frigman*) were the responsibility of that individual,[29] but that a bond necessarily existed between any 'freeman' of the *provincia* and the king was recognised by the latter's additional interest in compensation for a homicide the victim of which was 'free'.[30] The 'free' community at law consisted of the Church (clearly a new addition), the king, men of the rank of *ceorl*, and an intermediate rank of *eorl*.

Gradations of free status were mirrored by the value accorded the 'protection' (*mundbyrd*) of each: that of the king was fifty shillings, that of a *ceorl* six shillings.[31] That of an *eorl* is unclear: it may have been the twelve shillings payable (presumably to him) for a homicide committed on his own premises.[32] That there was some close association between the class of *eorl* and the king is implicit in the *mund* of the widow of an *eorl*, being, at fifty shillings, equivalent to that of the king himself.[33] There is a sense in which all free men, and their widows, were considered in law to be under the protection of the king and in receipt of his bounty, and that relationship, as well as his kinship, was recognised and compensated in the event of his unlawful death.[34] As regards the *mund* of widows, four rather than three classes emerge, with the fourth carrying a compensation equivalent to that of the *ceorl*. The presence of four ranks, rather than three, may reflect the separate treatment of the *gesith* or *gesith*-born man, literally a retainer, so someone owing his position to the patronage of another man of higher rank. Compensation for a *gesith* was higher than that of a *ceorl* but this rank of *gesith* is far more distinctive in the West Saxon laws of King Ine,[35] written most of a century later, than in those of the Kentish Æthelberht, wherein it may be equivalent to the *eorl*. The scale of compensations payable throughout both codes apparently reflect the social proximity of each class to the crown, so a gradation of rank as much as personal wealth.

The interests of the king, the *eorl*, the *ceorl*, and their womenfolk, dominate Æthelberht's law code: their ownership of weapons was taken for granted and accepted, provided only that they were not misused or loaned to someone of unfree status;[36] it is they who needed access to considerable quantities of the precious metals required for (what seem to be) high compensation payments;[37] it was they who were distinguished from the remainder of society by the custom of wearing their hair long – long hair was considered such a crucial indicator of status that its seizure and damage was compensated at a wergild of fifty *sceattas*; it was only they who were protected by law against enslavement.[38]

The most senior of the king's servants – his smith and *laadrinc* (probably 'guide'), but presumably not others – were protected by a wergild equivalent to that of the *leodan*.[39] The same term was used in chapter two: 'If the king summons his *leode* to himself, and anyone shall do evil to them there, double compensation and fifty shillings to the king.' The term means 'fellow countrymen', so presumably encompasses all of free rank – the entire male community down to the level of the *ceorl*. This term, in the plural, probably approximates in meaning to Bede's *gens* (or even *gens Anglorum*),[40] at least where he used that term in the context of a specific, tribal kingship.

Another method of defining the sense of identity of this group would have been as that sector of society which claimed common descent (with the royal family) from a mythical (originally divine) and perhaps eponymous founder-father of that people or *gens*.[41] The laws serve to underline the mutual, if unequal, relationships which tied the *leodan* to the king. Despite differences in the amounts of compensation appropriate to different ranks within this free community, the protection afforded by wergild was universal and of uniform kind. The laws therefore distinguished a ranked elite, defined and protected by fundamental legal privileges, from the remainder of society. They served too to underline the social cohesion of the *leodan* around a king with whom many were likely to be personally acquainted: that assemblies summoned by the king were sufficiently frequent to require special notice in his laws suggest that these were an important arena in which personal contact between king and other ranks of free society would have been both established and sustained.[42] That the king might visit the homes of other sectors of the law-worthy community and drink or feast with them underlines this sense of a tight-knit social grouping.[43] From him the *leodan* might ordinarily expect to receive leadership, patronage, protection and high-status gifts. In return they presumably owed respect and service of various kinds. The lowest, and presumably the most numerous, rank of that elite group was of *ceorl* status, but the entire free people was, in the Kentish case, merely the dominant group and land-owning elite in a territory no larger than had been the *civitas* of the Cantii. Within that community there was scope for a wide and complex pattern of acquaintance and mutual interaction across the entire group, from kings and their close kin at the apex down to the landless sons of *ceorls* at the base.

Beneath this tribal community or *gens*, and detached from it in kinship as much as legal status, was an ill-defined sub-class of the unfree and rural proletariat who were at law dependent on masters with access to due legal process. Unless they were his own dependants or members of his own household, the king claimed no compensation in the case of the dependant of a 'freeman', payment for whom probably went to that 'freeman', with the amount determined by *his* status rather than that of the slave or *læt* (probably a peasant farmer: the term is unique in Old English texts to this passage but perhaps derives from Germanic-Latin *lætus*, a 'settler of low status'). These lesser members of society had few rights, other than those which derived from their value to the 'freemen' who were their masters or even owners. The virtue of a household woman was treated as a commodity which was the property of her master: fornication with a virgin of the king was compensated at a level commensurate with his *mund*, so presumably paid to him; if she was a servant or slave whose task it was to grind grain (literally a 'grinding slave'),[44] compensation was half the amount. A third class of female slave in the royal household, whose tasks were unstated, commanded only a twelve shilling compensation.

A similar threefold division of the servile classes was expected within the household of a *ceorl*: the king's 'maiden' was apparently equivalent to the *ceorl's birelan*, both of them being girls whose duties were 'above stairs'; a slave of the second rank was valued at only fifty *sceattas* (pennies), and one of third rank at a mere thirty. A *ceorl* might have various *hlafætan* (literally 'loafeaters' so household members who depended on him for their subsistence). These may well have included the attendant women of the household, as also found, for example, in stories concerning St. Wilfrid's birth into what seems to have been an affluent and perhaps even aristocratic household (*Life of Wilfrid*, I). In Ine's laws a *gesith*-born man was expected to have a reeve, smith and nursemaid, who were peculiarly his, as opposed to the various other (presumably agricultural) dependants who remained with the estate should that became detached from his household. A *ceorl* apparently had similar dependants but of lower status and protected by smaller sums of money at law. Given the juxtaposition of this reference in Æthelberht's laws with mention of compensations appropriate to the three ranks of *læt*, the *hlafætan* and *lætan* may have been considered of comparable rank, both being unfree and legally dependent. Although the unfree seem unable to have benefited personally from compensation, they could be liable for such payments in the event of accusations against themselves concerning homicide or theft.[45]

One of the outstanding features of the laws is the scale, affluence and high status assumed to be characteristic of the household of a *ceorl*, with its slaves of several ranks, its unfree servants, and its goods protected by a threefold compensation,[46] within a clearly defined and enclosed perimeter.[47] Despite being of the lowest free status, the *ceorl* was still expected to head a complex social hierarchy which could encompass numerous individuals for whom he had legal responsibility. His was no nuclear family farming a peasant holding: he and his family were attended by, so presumably supported primarily by surpluses generated by, subordinate members of that hierarchy, rather than by their own labour, providing in return the protection of a weapon-owning warrior with access to the assembly of the people and the court of its king and so to justice and patronage. In Ine's laws, at least, the obligations of a *ceorl* to undertake military service were specifically stated, although the compensation claimed from those neglecting this duty (thirty shillings) was only half that of a landless freeman, and a quarter that of a *gesith*-born man,[48] who presumably descended from one whom the king had already favoured with land. The *ceorl* was apparently responsible for the entire hierarchy dependent upon himself, as regards obligations to the king and the courts. He was, therefore, of at least 'quasi gentry' or 'yeoman' status in the seventh century. By the late Anglo-Saxon period, the term *ceorl* had been downgraded to the equivalent of 'farmer' or *rusticus*, but such a reading seems inappropriate to the earlier period.

The comparatively high standing of the *ceorl* in a seventh-century context may be confirmed by use of the term in the names of individuals of high status, such as King Cearl of Mercia, and later Ceorl, *ealdorman* of Devon.[49] In *Beowulf*, King Ongentheow of the Swedes was variously termed *ceorl*, *eorl* and 'king'.[50] *Ceorl* may, therefore, have been at a comparatively early date a term redolent with qualities which were considered appropriate to the naming of children of noble or even royal rank, both in fact and fiction. However, this argument is much weakened by recognition of the very large numbers of ordinary words which were used as proper names in Old English, some of which clearly derive from low-status terms. Generalisation is difficult, however: take the name Ongentheow, above, which clearly contains *theow* ('a servant') but actually means 'the opposite of a servant' (*ongegn*, 'opposite'), so 'one of the highest possible status' or 'king'.

Whatever the force of this argument, the *ceorl* was necessarily a freeman and the head of a free household of some size in the seventh century. In contrast, the *læt* of the Kentish laws was clearly of inferior status and dependent on others in law. It is this dimly perceived and uncountable group who are most often considered to have descended from the Romano-British population of Kent, being accommodated to English society in an inferior position.[51] That some groups within the lower reaches of West Saxon society were of British origin is explicit, given notice of them as *wēalas* in the *Laws of Ine*. The three classes replicate the three ranks of Kentish *læts* and, like the Romano-Gallic population in Frankia, they were accorded only a reduced wergild and status at law. Even so, Ine's law code envisaged that some Britons would have five hides of land, so be in economic terms at least members of the 'gentry' community at a level that would eventually, in late Anglo-Saxon England, be considered an appropriate threshold for the recognition of thegnly status.

The descendants of the Romano-British population were, therefore, probably still numerous, and recognisable as such, in the seventh century, in southern England, whence the surviving law codes derive, as well as the northern regions from which come almost all our literary anecdotes. Again, there is evidence that not all Britons were unfree but it is clear that the bulk were of very low status and they certainly included slaves. It is probably safe to conclude both that Britons were numerous within Anglo-Saxon society and that they were disproportionately concentrated among the peasantry and unfree dependants of the elite. The eventual convergence of the two meanings of *w(ē)alh* ('Welsh') as 'Briton' and 'slave' certainly sustains this view.

The evidence from the south, although different in kind, does seem to parallel that emanating from the north. In general terms it seems clear that Anglo-Saxon society was constructed upon a raft made up of Britons and their economic output from the land, albeit that by *c.* 731 more and more Anglo-Saxons were themselves sinking towards or being incorporated within the ranks of the 'vulgar', while the Britons were themselves increasingly exposed to anglicisation.

Another important issue relevant both to the payment of tribute (as touched on above) and the interaction between *vicani* and landowners is the nature of the hide, which is amongst the most enigmatic terms which are central to the study of early England, and it is to that subject that we shall next turn.

The hide

A second meaning of the term *ceorl* is that of 'husband', hence the verb *ceorlian*, 'to take a husband' or 'marry'. This usage has points of contact with *híd* – a 'hide', a word cognate with *híwan*, meaning 'household' or 'family'. Prior to its emergence as the basis of the royal geld in the tenth and eleventh centuries, the hide was most frequently recorded in reference to estimates of estate value but its close relationship with the household is confirmed by Bede's translation of 'hide' into Latin variously as *familia*,[52] *possessiones familiae*,[53] or *terra familiae*[54] ('family', 'possession(s) of a family' and 'land of a family'). Latin charters provide numerous alternatives, such as *mansa* or *cassatus*, meaning 'a house'. From the pattern of cognate terms, it seems clear that the 'household' element had priority over 'land' as regards the primary meaning of the term. The basic unit was an economic one: 'the resources necessary to maintain a household through time'. It was, therefore, primarily a measure of income. Given the near exclusive dependence on income deriving from land in the Early Middle Ages, however, the hide inevitably came to be used as a term which was peculiarly appropriate to the measure of land. Indeed, it was invariably in the context of a territory – be it a kingdom, an island or an estate – that Bede used his Latin equivalents. That the hide is not in origin a specific acreage has long been recognised,[55] even if many scholars have been slow to abandon entirely this conception.[56] The 'field-hide' (as occurs, for example, in Little Domesday Book) only emerges after the widespread adoption of the heavy plough in the mid- to late Anglo-Saxon period, when the fiscal and proprietorial hide became identified (in the south-east Midlands and East Anglia, at least) with a 'ploughland', the acreage which one heavy plough pulled by eight oxen could cultivate each year. This has no apparent relevance to the seventh century, when the hide (and its Latin equivalents) was generally used as a term by which to enumerate either resources or the obligations which were attached to tenure thereof.

Perhaps the most ambiguous occurrence of the term is in the laws of Ine, which refer to 'hides of the house', so renders which go directly to the focal settlement of the estate, as opposed to renders which have been granted away by the land-holder (who is envisaged as *gesithcund*, so of the rank of a *gesith* or *comes*), to his own tenants or retainers. This core of food rents which should pertain to the central household at the moment of its surrender to the king was stipulated as a specific proportion of the entire hidation of the estate.[57]

The status of the *familia* to which the hide referred is clearly a vital factor in its definition. It is generally agreed that it was that of a *ceorl*, so laying a heavy responsibility on interpretation of that status group. The common assumption that a seventh-century *ceorl* was a peasant farmer establishes a very different perception of the hide to that implicit in the definition of his rank offered above,[58] but the evolution of the hide itself provides further evidence of the comparatively elevated status of the *ceorl* at an early date: Anglo-Saxon peasants did not normally cultivate holdings approaching anywhere near the *c.* 120 acres of the 'field-hide' of the tenth and eleventh centuries (and they would arguably have been incapable of working such an area were it available) but many small manors were assessed for geld at Domesday at just one or two hides, or even fractions thereof. Then, the possessor of a one hide estate would normally be termed a 'free man' and might commonly command several tenants or servile labourers and their ploughs. The 'free' holder was at least of 'quasi gentry' status and was responsible to the king or his representatives for whatever obligations were owed on his hide. The hide had not, therefore, shared the demotion in status which the term *ceorl* had experienced during the course of the Anglo-Saxon period. Where the cognate term *híwisc* was adopted as a place-name element, it generally refers to a settlement with land in quantities far exceeding what would have been appropriate to a peasant holding, but not to a large estate or parish. The terminology appropriate to the 'one hide estate' as a large farm or small estate (which Bede on occasion referred to by the term *loca* or *locus*), does, therefore, seem to have survived in some parts (principally the West Country) even to the end of the Anglo-Saxon period.

A hide of land was not, therefore, a holding likely to have been worked by a single peasant family at any time in the Anglo-Saxon period. If it was the land sufficient to sustain a *ceorl* household in the seventh century, then that individual should only be termed a 'farmer' to the extent that a law-worthy householder in early Icelandic society, for example, should be so termed: he was a man with access to the legal system, who might own and had the right to bear weapons, and who was considered of sufficient status to approach the king. To support that status he controlled worked land and he may have taken a hand in its management and in its husbandry, but few such men are likely to have relied exclusively on their own labours, or on land under their own direct exploitation. The income of the average *ceorl* was probably less dependent on renders from tenants, and more on produce grown and harvested by demesne slaves and even his own family, than was the peripatetic household of the king, but the same mixed economy and labour force was arguably present in each instance. Only when the economic base of *ceorl* society had become eroded by partible inheritance – perhaps during a period of population growth – in the second half of the Anglo-Saxon period did the status attaching to the term *ceorl* come to approximate more closely to a peasant farmer.

The nature of the single hide estate is illumined by Bede's reference to St. Hild's first grant of land in Northumbria:[59]

> then she was called back to the fatherland by Bishop Aidan and received a place of one family [*locus unius familiae*] where for one year she lived the monastic life with a few companions.

Hild was of royal stock and, however few her companions, it is impossible to envisage her grubbing in the fields to support herself, even if this holding had a demesne farm. Her hide was, therefore, not the holding of a single peasant. The *ceorl* household which might more normally have lived off those same resources was equivalent, as regards its consumption if not its social status, to Hild and her friends. We can be reasonably certain that either or both would have been supported in large part by the work force which was a normal part of its resources and tied to it, so accompanying the estate into the tenure of its new mistress. This passage further informs us as to Bede's use of *locus* elsewhere in this text, wherein it often seems to mean a small estate, so one suitable to the landholding of a *ceorl*, as opposed to a *villa regalis* – 'royal estate', but this is far from an invariable usage. *Locus* was used in a much grander context in reference, for example, to the forty hide estate centred on a monastery, at the *locus* called Ripon (*HE*, III, 25).

The hide was not, therefore, strictly a measure of land itself but of its value to a landholder and to the king. In terms of the literary evidence which survives, the most significant expression of that value was as a specific render (or food rent) which it might normally be expected to yield as a farm (*feorm*). As such its definition does not require an excursion into the obscure subject of early English kinship rights and inheritance,[60] if only because it is not the nature of hereditary tenure to which this term is specific. On the contrary, the key to understanding the hide is recognition of its role as a unit of render. It could theoretically be obtained as easily, if not equally permanently, by inheritance, by gift or by some form of temporary grant or lease. By whatever means, the possession of a single hide's worth of income (so of course of land) was sufficient to enable a man of *ceorl* status to marry and establish a household without threat to that status; hence the *ceorl* as 'married man' and the hide as 'household'.[61] In this respect, the hide was an essential precondition of marriage among the generality of the free population. It was also the fundamental measure of that upward flow of goods and services which characterised relations between the unfree classes and their masters in early England.

The scale of the provisions which King Ine expected from ten hides was established in his laws:[62]

> ten vats of honey, 300 loaves, twelve 'ambers' of Welsh ale, thirty 'ambers' of clear ale, two grown cows or ten wethers, ten geese, twenty hens, ten cheeses, a full 'amber' of butter, five salmon, twenty poundweight of fodder, and 100 eels.

It is unclear whether this render was that normally paid by unfree tenants on estates of which the king was the landholder (so render-taker) at that time, or by men of *ceorl* status and above according to the hidation of their estates as a universal and standard obligation, or tax in kind, to the king. The relationship between this scale of renders and that which the *ceorl* might expect from a hide held as 'folkland', as opposed to the 'bookland' of a royal grant, is therefore obscure. Taking the worst case scenario, if divided by ten such an 'unearned' surplus was inadequate to support a household of any size, which may explain why the various laws envisaged that a *ceorl* would as regularly involve himself in demesne agriculture as did the lesser thegns and freemen of late Anglo-Saxon England. However, if the second possibility be entertained – and the universality of Ine's edict may encourage us to prefer it *a priori* – the renders sustaining a *ceorl* household in control of only a single hide may have been significantly greater than this passage would imply, perhaps by a margin of approximately tenfold if obligations to the crown be assumed to be in the order of one tenth of the renders supporting the landholding classes. In that scenario, the provisions appropriate to a royal render from ten hides may be approximately equivalent to the renders that the landholder might normally expect from just one, so providing a far clearer indication of the minimum income appropriate to the household of a *ceorl*. It may be, therefore, that there were two values appropriate to the hide: one being the level of the renders from an estate to the household entitled to them; the other being the level of the flow of obligations from the estate to the royal household.

It seems likely that seventh-century society expected a nobleman to have at least ten hides: hence Ine's interest in this particular unit as regards renders to the crown and as regards the estate of a *gesith* (the examples of 20, 10, and 3 hides are each explored); hence also Oswiu's granting of twelve apparently standardised blocks of land, valued at ten hides apiece, for the foundation of monasteries should he defeat Penda in 655. The initial endowment of Whitby was likewise ten hides, although this may have been one of those dozen foundations. Since a fundamental use of royal land was to grant it away in return for service, the customary unit of such dispersal may well have influenced the accounting of its renders when these were owed to the king. Similarly, this notion of a ten hide maintenance to a fully-fledged, tried and trusted warrior may have influenced the structure of hidation in the Tribal Hidage: the common occurrence of three hundred hides or multiples thereof, for example, may merely reflect the hidation necessary to sustain a force of 30 household warriors or *gesiths*, which would have formed the approximate complement of an early Anglo-Saxon ship of the type found at Nydam. Such a figure was easily memorable and had a clearcut and highly practical rationale within this social and political system.

The hide was, therefore, primarily a unit of value equivalent to that crucial unit of resource – made up variously and in any combination by a mixture of renders or rents and the product of demesne land – which was universally accepted as the minimum sufficient to sustain one free household. As such it formed the basis not only of relationships between peasant and landholder but also between kings and the free community. As James Campbell has remarked,[63] systematic services and renders underlie hidation throughout almost all England (Kent is the only obvious exception). This was, as Bede repeatedly stressed,[64] a uniquely English method of counting up resources. Excluding Kent's distinctive system, it was applied at an early date to situations which necessitated a generally accepted unit of substantial value, be that strictly economic or social in context. Once coining became a common practice, the role of the hide was more specifically confined to renders from land – whether to the possessor or as tax to the crown – but it may perhaps have been used more widely as a measure of both value and obligation in England's prehistory.

Literature which derives from the seventh and early eighth centuries spans the period during which coin began to circulate throughout England. The hide is used in four different but related contexts in that literature:

1 Hides were the units used in charters or 'books' to denote the value of royal estates granted to churchmen, or others, primarily for the purpose of constructing and supporting churches or monasteries. A minority of such grants were already being recorded in charters in the seventh and early eighth centuries,[65] and Bede and other writers provide independent but complementary evidence of this use of the term.[66]
2 Hides were used to quantify the resources of a specific people, a large sub-section thereof or the dynasty ruling over that people. Such uses occur most obviously in the *Historia Ecclesiastica*,[67] but a single example in *Beowulf* suggests that hides may have been widely used in this context.[68] Such seems to have been a rough and ready statement of the resource base of the landholders who owed service, renders and other obligations to a particular ruler, so of the value of the services by which that kingship was sustained.
3 Hides were the unit of account or audit in the only list of tribute to have survived from this period, the Tribal Hidage.[69] If the original on which this document was based was compiled in 625–26, it is the earliest written evidence available which refers to hides. That it apparently enumerates *feorm* or tribute requires that the hides of the Tribal Hidage were units expressive of value rather than acreage.
4 Hides were also used in the *Laws of Ine* as the unit appropriate to the legal weight of an oath at law. The weight of a man's oath was clearly dependent on his rank in society, so on his wergild, the basic equation of a wergild of 1,200 shillings to 60 hides being established in *cap*. XIX. This implies that a man who had a wergild of 200 shillings, which was that of an ordinary freeman (XXXIV), was enabled to defend himself by an oath weighted at ten hides. The swearing of an oath for legal purposes depended, therefore, on the individual concerned (generally the defendant in a case) assembling a group of oath-helpers

> whose collective status at law was sufficient to provide an oath equivalent to a certain hidation. This was almost certainly achieved through the recognition of the stereotyped ranking of individuals, and the equivalence in hides pertinent thereto, rather than a realistic appraisal of their actual, individual landholdings. Clearly, the aid of individuals of high rank, so highly valued oaths, were of critical importance in the instance of a *ceorl* needing to amass an oath of 60 or 120 hides (as *cap*. XLVI). The weight of an oath was clearly not standardised at the level of the minimal landholding appropriate to a specific rank – which would have left the *ceorl* with an oath of a mere one hide – but there may be an arithmetical basis to this assessment. It seems very possible that there was a ten-to-one ratio between the weight of oath and the minimum land appropriate to a particular rank. This re-emphasises the significance of the ten hide estate and the possibility of a one-tenth standard rate of taxation in West Saxon society, *c*. 700.

There is also the possibility of a fifth usage which may combine in a single valuation a large area of land and a quantity of treasure. A passage in *Beowulf* refers to '100,000 of lands and treasures'.[70] The unit was omitted for literary reasons and was presumably considered sufficiently obvious to be readily supplied by a contemporary audience. It is now generally assumed to have been *sceattas*,[71] but no other references to English coinage occur in the poem, despite mention of treasure and horses of considerable value.[72] The only unit used in *Beowulf* in a comparable context is the hide.[73] That the hide was used to express the value of tribute rather than land in the Tribal Hidage opens the possibility that the *Beowulf* poet expected his audience to assume that the lands and treasures to which he here referred were measured in hides. His use of this largest of all numbers merely emphasised the scale of the reward: like Procopius's Anglian army,[74] but unlike the Tribal Hidage's hidation of the West Saxons, the context is literary rather than historical, so its numerical system is likely to have been subject to poetic licence.

Whether or not this last interpretation is justified, it is clear that the term 'hide' was used in the seventh century as a means of measuring not the area of land but the renders deriving from it. That measurement was based on a unit which derived from the basic resource capable of sustaining a *ceorl* household throughout the year, the quantification of which was a necessary precondition of informed social interaction within the free population. Without access to that basic minimum, a young man could not marry and establish a new household without risking demotion from the status to which he had been born. Estimation of the resources available to the prospective household was of fundamental importance in marital negotiations. Among a community of 'gentry' and 'quasi gentry', there was no obvious reason to take an interest in measurement of area but a consuming need to evaluate the annual worth of an estate: the hide offered a unit which was entirely adequate for that purpose.

With that established, the unit could also be used for what were essentially governmental purposes: if the *ceorl* was weapon-bearing and weapon-owning, then a mobilisation of the full military potential of a kingdom might require the deployment of one warrior from each hide, just as King Ine's expectations of military service from the *ceorl* would imply.[75] Tenure of land valued in hides certainly placed obligations upon the holder, as is implicit both in Bede's *Letter to Ecgbert* and in the substitution of *tributarius* ('tax payer') for hide in some charters.[76] Even before the proliferation of taxation in coin, hidation does seem to have been the basis of regular obligations to the crown from which only some clerical *bocland* was, to varying degrees, exempted (or rather in reality commuted to prayer). Such obligations presumably predate the conversion. The term was equally valid as a means of assessing tribute to be paid by one king to another.

Such a definition is entirely consistent with the charter evidence. Kings, in part at least, lived off renders from estates under their immediate control and those renders were necessarily audited in hides. So too was the top-slicing of the renders of other landholders which was a form of primitive taxation in kind, supposing that to be a correct interpretation of the admittedly limited evidence available. What was required by a clerical *familia* in the seventh century was a sufficient render from an agricultural peasantry, not unpopulated land to till for themselves. What a warrior required of the king or his own kin was similarly a bundle of renders sufficient to marry and establish a household of high status, not land to clear and cultivate.[77] What kings had available to grant to both groups was worked land organised in estates from which came customary renders in known and predictable quantities. Such estates were granted as working entities with the labour force by which they were tilled (see above). Estates were clearly *ab initio* territorially fixed, so capable of measure by area, but it was the renders which derived from them which were of interest to all parties and it was in terms of renders that they were valued. The actual area of an estate was of no direct interest to king, monastery, *thegn* or *ceorl*. The estate boundaries and any outlying rights to extensive grazing, fishing or timber were, however, of considerable importance, since these defined the capacity of the estate's labour force to deliver renders and it was necessarily in the interests of any landholder, and surely also commensurate with his honour and reputation, to defend those boundaries against the dependants of his neighbours on behalf of his own workforce. Hence there was a growing tendency to define the boundaries of an estate within the *boc* or charter by which title was confirmed.

The method adopted to evaluate renders greater than the one hide/one *ceorl* household minimum was to specify that they were sufficient to sustain 'x' households of the status of a *ceorl*, and to pay the taxes in kind to the king appropriate thereto – so 'x' hides. This provided a simple method of assessing the worth of an estate to whoever had control of the renders therefrom. Seventh-century society clearly attached a fairly precise value to the term. As a unit of account the principal shortcoming of the hide lay in its indivisibility. A render of one hide would continue to be only one hide until augmented sufficiently to sustain two *ceorl* households, and so on. However, this would create problems only in commercial accounting, not for a landholding elite for whom it provided a minimum unit of resource, divisions of which were of little consequence. Resources were either sufficient to maintain two *ceorl* households, or only one. No intermediate point had much relevance in such a system. In this context, the hide was adequate as a unit by which to measure both the capital of, and income available to, a household of high status. It equates quite closely with the 'x hundred pounds per year' which was the basis of so many marriage contracts between members of the landholding classes in (for example) the eighteenth century. That the resources that sustained a *ceorl* household generally originated in a marriage settlement characterised by a commitment to it of resources from both contracting families is implicit in Ine's law code.

That seventh-century kings saw tribute as nothing more than an extension of established forms of render seems clear from the use of the same terminology in the Tribal Hidage. When King Edwin expected his neighbour, the king of Elmet, to pay him tribute of 600 hides, that value was necessarily understood in the same terms by both parties. What was required was a parcel of goods equivalent in value either to the annual renders sufficient to support 600 households of *ceorl* status, or to the share of such renders which the king might normally expect to obtain. Either solution seems possible in the light of King Ine's law code. If tribute was sometimes paid in precious goods,[78] then the hide was capable of being transposed from the measurement of estate renders in kind to an assessment of equivalent value in a high-value, single denomination coinage.

That kings were capable of making regular levies on the hides of landholders subject to themselves is implicit in the emergence of what look very much like tithes or regular alms from widely dispersed communities to support the Northumbrian bishops, concerning which Bede made disparaging remarks in his *Letter to Ecgbert*.[79] Unless this was an entirely new imposition, it was surely grafted onto existing renders or services based on a standard tax system and due to the king. The West Saxon king likewise expected the *ceorl* to undertake military service. The hide is the only candidate available which could have regulated such demands as this on the free community.

The hide was therefore the fundamental unit by which both estate renders and obligations to kings were measured. As such, they comprised at the lower level food renders paid by estate workers or tenants – the *vicani* – many of whom seem on anecdotal evidence, as well as on the basis of Bede's final, generalised comment on the current status of the Britons, to have been of indigenous stock. At a higher level of society the hide was crucial to a wide variety of interactions within the law-worthy elite, and between one elite system and another, so in the assessment of tribute.

The *gens Anglorum*

Bede's *Historia* makes repeated reference to the *gens Anglorum* – the 'people of the English' – in contexts which require that both he and his intended audience had a comparatively clear vision of the group identity of the Anglo-Saxons (however that be defined) despite their several origins, at least in his own view, as Angles, Saxons and Jutes.[80] The most recent, extended treatment of this term and its origins has concluded that the term derives from Pope Gregory's need for a single tag by which to define the peoples to whom he had dispatched Augustine, and was thence exported to Britain where it eventually prevailed over alternative terms by which the English might have chosen to describe themselves.[81] This may, however, be to overestimate the influence of Rome in this matter and to ignore more local imperatives, which may have played a more important role than so far acknowledged in the adoption of a single term for the Germanic community inside Britain.

To revert once more to Bede's comments at the close of his first book of the *Historia Ecclesiastica*, the crucial polarity in his vision of Britain was between the *gens Brittonum* – who were intrinsically heretical – and the *gens Anglorum* – who were intrinsically divinely favoured – and it is probably as much as anything his need to define these two groups that led him to adopt the phrase. It was, as has here been demonstrated, a fundamental of Bede's purposes in this work to justify the English domination of their neighbours and he adopted several means of achieving this, one of which was the widespread and recurring deployment of the analogy of the Roman Empire.

It is not, however, very likely that the favouring of the term 'Angles' over 'Saxons' or even 'Jutes' was fundamentally the responsibility of either Bede or his distant mentor, St. Gregory. The reason for this is twofold:

1 Although Pope Gregory could conceivably have learnt to refer to the Germanic immigrants to Britain as 'English' from Deiran Angles in the slave market at Rome,[82] this is the least credible facet of this well-known but surely apocryphal story. Even had he done so, the term necessarily had, thereby, an insular origin. Far more significant is Gregory's use of the term *rex Anglorum* in correspondence addressed to Æthelberht of Kent. Gregory was, by this point, in a position to know what sort of terminology would have been appropriate to the Kentish king, both from Frankish sources and insular ones; indeed his dispatch of

a mission may have been in response to Æthelberht's own initiative in the first place. We can, therefore, be reasonably sure that Æthelberht would have both recognised and approved this form of address: it may have conceded him more power than was in fact appropriate to the realities of his hegemony, but it cannot have been either obscure or irrelevant to him, let alone unwelcome. Despite the certain presence of only one significant 'Anglian' people (the East Angles) then recognising his *imperium*, therefore, and despite the inclusion within his hegemony of far more numerous groups purporting to be Saxons or Jutes, the title *rex Anglorum* was necessarily acceptable to Æthelberht. This implies that it was already in widespread use even before Gregory began its popularisation within the context of the English conversion.

2 Secondly there has been far too little attention addressed to the role of the Britons in what was, in Bede's opinion at least, a highly competitive and bitter struggle with their conquerors. English perceptions of all the very numerous British tribal kingdoms as a single *gens* is directly paralleled by British treatment of their Germanic neighbours and conquerors in similar terms. Writers of the late Empire consistently termed the Germanic intruders *Saxones* and Gildas, our only early insular source, used the same term in his only specific reference to them.[83] Other than in reference to specific tribal kingships (in particular the East Angles), the *Historia Brittonum* used the same term with some consistency. There is some evidence that the British did make use of at least one alternative to this: Bede noted that the Britons referred to the English by the generic term *Garmani*,[84] and I have sought to direct attention already elsewhere to the possibility that Gildas had, in two passages, punned on the term *Germanus*.[85] Both *Saxones* and (less certainly) *Germani* were apparently, therefore, already being used by the enemies and competitors of the English in Britain, so were essentially contaminated by their pejorative purposes.

For the purposes of this fundamental contest for the control of erstwhile Roman Britain, the English required a collective identity, whether as pagans or Christians. The contest was a very real one and not an invention of Bede's fertile mind. The extensive English military and political conquest of so much of Britain achieved in the fifth century and never thereafter reversed provides the essential backdrop to this issue. If the terms 'Saxons' and 'Germans' were already in use as pejorative terms in the mouths of their British opponents, then it was incumbent on the English to adopt an alternative and *Angli* was the obvious one available, at least to the best of our knowledge. In similar fashion did the British prefer their own terminology for themselves – *Cumbri* and its vernacular equivalents – to the derogatory English term *Wēalas* ('foreigners'), whence ultimately derived Wales and 'Welsh', with the meaning of slave.

However long the gestation of these terms, the political circumstances which called them into existence were already in being when Gildas was writing, late in the fifth century. The term 'Angles' was appropriately enough used in its generic sense by Procopius little more than a half century later, writing probably on the basis of contemporary Frankish sources. It had, therefore, presumably already then begun to take root, at least a half century or so before Gregory turned his mind to the paganism of the English. It was a deep-rooted and very long-lived Anglo-British antagonism, therefore, and the rhetoric to which that antagonism gave rise, which impelled the Germanic intruders of the fifth century, whom the world knew as *Saxones* and whom the Britons may also have thought of as *Germani* (or *Garmani*), to adopt the term *Angli* as uniformly appropriate to themselves. That this process was incomplete in 731 may be implicit in Bede's recognition of the equality of the terms *Saxones* and *Angli*.[86] Alternatively, this may be nothing more than Bede's own recognition of the use of *Saxones* by earlier providential historians with whom he wished to identify his own work. Certainly, his commoner usage is *Angli* as a generic term for the entire Germanic community in Britain, so the Old English speaking community. The vernacular term, *Englisc(ne)* was similarly used in a generic sense and specifically as a means of distinguishing the Germanic from the British population in the *Laws of Ine* (XXIV, XLVI, LIV, LXXIV). If any English community should be expected, *c.* 700, to prefer 'Saxon' to 'English', it must surely be the West Saxons: that they had adopted 'English' by this date suggests that it was already the generally accepted term throughout English-speaking Britain.

That Bede envisaged that the Britons were, *per se*, subject to the *imperium* of the *gens Anglorum* is at one and the same time a perceptive and subtle piece of casuistry and a reflection of the reality of English tenure of estates worked in large measure by unfree Britons. So were rhetoric and realism commingled in Bede's *Historia*.

Conclusions

Investigation of the literary sources available from the early eighth century suggests that the English intelligentsia expected the rural population – to which they rarely referred – to be in important respects different from their masters, even to the extent of being outside their sense of cultural and social community and kin. In several instances it is explicit that members of that rural population were British: in other instances it is either implicit or at least a reasonable interpretation. If it is inappropriate to generalise from these instances, then it must be said that the patterning of anecdotes is strange indeed.

Examination of the legal codes of the period emphasises this distinction between those who were law-worthy and those who were their dependants, or in some sense different and legally disadvantaged. While some Britons in Wessex, for example, could be of quasi-gentry status (and recall Bede's notice of British bishops there in the 660s), it is implicit in both the West Saxon and Kentish laws that the unfree were both numerous and unlikely *en masse* to be English, by any definition of that term then appropriate.

Discussion of the hide sheds further light on the structure of the rural community and the estates of which it was composed, as well as of complex interactions within the ranks of the political elite. Definition of the hide as a fundamental unit of render in reference to the maintenance of a free household once again emphasises the role of the *gens Anglorum* as a political, military and cultural elite, atop a community which remained otherwise quite visibly British even up until the early eighth century.

This survey picks up, therefore, many of the ideas and processes identified and discussed in the first of these volumes, which concentrated on Gildas's writings and examined the process of the English conquest in the fifth century. That conquest remained a reality in the seventh century, and one which was of fundamental significance to the social and political structures of Bede's own time, to the justification of which he directed as much of his own considerable rhetorical talents as had Gildas deployed of *his* own in purposing to undermine it.

If the rhetoric of Bede and his contemporaries provides a reliable indication of the social fabric of seventh-century England, then the free *gens Anglorum* – comprising kings, clergy and the warrior classes – was in a position of mastery over a larger (and probably very much larger), but rarely mentioned, unfree underclass of *servi et ancillae*, *rustici pauperes* and the *vulgus paupere*. That underclass was defined in the legal codes very largely by virtue of its exclusion from access to law. In Bede's perception, it primarily comprised the Britons who had been sold into slavery to the English – so disinherited and handed over into their dominion by God. His responsibility must be in doubt but their subordination is a matter of factual comment wherein Bede had little room for misrepresentation. His lack of interest in the conversion of this underclass – and too in so many of the minor kingships within England (such as the *W(r)ocensæte*) – perhaps reflects not so much the limitations of his knowledge but the fact that neither was in his opinion part of the *gens Anglorum*, whose glorious espousal of the true faith was the subject of his work. That many may additionally have already have been Christians is a possibility that Bede can have had little cause to publicise, for fear that it might damage his general perceptions of the relative virtues of the Britons and the English, which was such a central feature of his dialectic.

Notes

1 *HE*, V, 12; I, 19; II, 5; II, 13, respectively.

2 *HE*, III, 4, 25; IV, 27; III, 5; IV, 22, respectively, and see p. 225.

3 *HE*, II, 14; III, 30; IV, 13; I, 21; II, 14; III, 21; IV, 5, 28; V, 23; I, 22; IV, 13; V, 21, respectively.

4 *HE*, IV, 13 and see above, p. 224. See also *Life of Wilfrid*, *passim* for *servus* as a cleric, and *ibid*, II for its literal use.

5 *HE*, III, 10.

6 M. Gelling, 'The early history of western Mercia', in *The origins of Anglo-Saxon kingdoms*, ed. S. Bassett, Leicester, 1989, pp. 188–9.

7 As most recently explored by D. Kenyon, *The origins of Lancashire*, Manchester, 1991, pp. 77–8, whose opinion I followed in my own *Origins of Cheshire*, Manchester, 1993, p. 88. Identification of *Maserfelth* with Makerfield has the added advantage of enabling *Bellum Cocboy* of *AC* 644 to be identified with Wigan, Roman *Coccium*.

8 As is implicit in, but not absolutely required by, *HE*, III, 9. The rhetorical context will undoubtedly have led Bede to portray Penda as the aggressor and Oswald as the heroic, virtuous and righteous defender of the divinely sanctioned *status quo*.

9 N. J. Higham, *Kingdom of Northumbria*, Stroud, 1993, p. 122.

10 A. Meaney, *A Gazetteer of Early Anglo-Saxon Burial Sites*, London, 1964, relevant counties, *passim*; J. N. L. Myres, *Anglo-Saxon Pottery and the Settlement of England*, Oxford, 1969; P. Mayes and M. J. Dean, *An Anglo-Saxon Cemetery at Baston, Lincolnshire*, Occasional Papers in Lincolnshire History and Archaeology, III, Sleaford, 1976; C. Hills, 'The archaeology of Anglo-Saxon England in the pagan period: a review', *Anglo-Saxon England*, VIII, 1979, pp. 297–329; B. N. Eagles, *The Anglo-Saxon Settlement of Humberside*, British Archaeological Reports, British Series, LXVIII, 1979, *passim*; K. Leahy, 'The Anglo-Saxon Settlement of Lindsey', in *Pre-Viking Lindsey*, ed. A. Vince, Lincoln, 1993, pp. 29–44.

11 *HE*, V, 10.

12 *HE*, II, 14: for this use of *locus* or *loca* see above, pp. 242–3, but it may be worth noting that, in classical Latin, *locatum* can bear the meaning of 'something which is hired out'. If Bede was familiar with this usage, he may, when using *loca* in this context, have had in mind a tenanted or in some ways dependent farm. There is certainly a contrast here between the *viculi* and *locae* of the hinterland and the royal palace site at Yeavering itself and it seems likely that this disparity was as much a matter of social and tenurial status as economic and political function.

13 *HE*, IV, 13, and see above, p. 237.

14 *English Historical Documents*, II, ed. D. C. Douglas and G. W. Greenaway, London, 2nd ed. 1981, pp. 875–9.

15 *The earliest life of Gregory the Great, by an anonymous monk of Whitby*, ed. B. Colgrave, Cambridge and Kansas, 1968, XXXII: this passage is, of course, highly allegorical.

16 *Vita Sancti Cuthberti Auctore Anonymo*, in *Two Lives of St. Cuthbert*, ed. B. Colgrave, Cambridge, 1940, I, 7.

17 *HE*, IV, 22. For discussion, see E. John, *Orbis Britanniae*, Leicester, 1966, pp. 136–7.

18 *HE*, II, 12.

19 See pp. 33, 45 and note 79 above; cf. Orosius, *Histories*, VI, xx, 4–5.

20 *HE*, II, 5.

21 *Life of Wilfrid*, XX.

22 *HE*, III, 24. This is the translation of R. A. B. Mynors in *Bede: Ecclesiastical History of the English People*, Oxford, 1969, p. 291.

23 *HE*, IV, 26. For discussion, see T. Charles-Edwards, 'Early medieval kingships in the British Isles', in *Origins*, pp. 28–39.

24 As Wilfrid at Selsey: *HE*, IV, 13.

25 *HE*, I, 11. See also Bede's terminology concerning Edwin's power in *HE*, II, 9.

26 But see P. Sims-Williams, 'St Wilfrid and two charters dated 676 and 680', *Journal of Ecclesiastical History*, XXXIX, 1988, p. 181, who suggests that the *Rippel* of Ripon's foundation grant is more likely to have been Ripple in Worcs. than the Ribble valley in Lancs.

27 *HE*, V, 23. For further comment on this fundamental passage, see p. 5 above.

28 *The Laws of the Earliest English Kings*, ed. F. L. Attenborough, Cambridge, 1922, pp. 4–17; *English Historical Documents*, I, ed. D. Whitelock, London, 1955, pp. 357–9.

29 E.g. *Laws of Æthelberht*, XXI, XXII.

30 *Ibid*, VI.

31 *Ibid*, VIII, XV. For the alternative meaning of *ceorl* as husband, see *ibid*, LXXXV.

32 *Ibid*, XIII.

33 *Ibid*, LXXV.

34 *Ibid*, VI.

35 *Laws of the Earliest Kings*, pp. 36–61: the rank of *eorl* in the *Laws of Æthelberht* may equate specifically with the '*gesith* with land' of the *Laws of Ine* and the landed *comes* of the *HE*. but this identification is far from certain.

36 *Laws of Æthelberht*, XVIII, XIX, XX. That they should not be loaned to a slave is not here explicit but it is a condition of the *Laws of Ine*, XXIX.

37 *Laws of Æthelberht*, *passim*.

38 Seizure of the hair was compensated by a wergild of 50 *sceattas*: *ibid*, XXXIII. See also LXXIII for long hair as an indicator of status. See also *HE*, II, 1: English slave boys at Rome were reputedly distinguished in part by the *capillorum quoque forma egregia* – 'the unusual style (or "beauty") of their hair'. Bede was, of course, aware that the Italians were short haired and shaven. As late as Alfred's reign, to cut a man's hair could be construed as an insult: *Laws of Alfred*, XXXV.

39 *Laws of Æthelberht*, II, VII.

40 See above, pp. 250–54.

41 Hence the origin tales of the English peoples recounted in *HE*, I, 15 and various divinely descended royal genealogies.

42 *Laws of Æthelberht*, II.

43 *Ibid*, III. If ex-retainers who had been rewarded with erstwhile royal estates were numerous, then they may well have figured highly among the king's hosts.

44 *Ibid*: the compensation appropriate to the killing of a *læt* by a (free)man, detailed in XXVI, follows comment on the slaying of one of the dependants (*hlafætan*) of a *ceorl*, in XXV, and I have assumed that the possessive, *ceorlæs*, is appropriate also to this clause, following a pattern established elsewhere in the text; for female household slaves see XI.

45 *Ibid*, LXXXVI–XC.

46 *Ibid*, XVI, XXV, XXVI, XXVIII.

47 *Ibid*, XXVII, XXXII.

48 *Laws of Ine*, LI. The 'landless man' herein should almost certainly be understood to be a *gesith*, so a member of the king's military retinue in the present.

49 *HE*, II, 14; *ASC*, 850.

50 *Beowulf*, ed. C. L. Wrenn, London, 3rd ed. 1973, lines 2972, 2951, 2971.

51 E.g. H. M. Chadwick, *Studies on Anglo-Saxon Institutions*, Cambridge, 1905, pp. 112–14, who also draws attention to *ceorls* as signatories to royal documents; M. L. Faull, 'The semantic development of Old English *Wēalh*', in *Leeds Studies in English*, VIII, 1975, pp. 20–23.

52 E.g. *HE*, III, 4: *familiarum quinque*, literally 'five of families', with the noun qualified by *quinque* omitted. See also, *ibid*, I, 25; II, 9; III, 25; IV, 16.

53 *HE*, III, 24.

54 E.g. *HE*, IV, 13; V, 19.

55 E.g. W. Stubbs, *Select Charters*, Oxford, 9th ed. revised by H. W. C. Davis, 1966, p. 517; D. Whitelock, *The beginnings of English Society*, London, 1952, p. 68; F. M. Stenton, *Anglo-Saxon England*, 3rd ed. 1971, p. 279.

56 E.g. B. Yorke, *Kings and Kingdoms of Early Anglo-Saxon England*, London, 1990, p. 10.

57 *Laws of Ine*, LXIV, LXV, LXVI. The meaning of these edicts rests on interpretation of *geset(t)es*, the standard meaning of which is a 'seat' or 'house', but which is here (*ibid*, LXVIII) contrasted with *bodl*, a 'dwelling', so perhaps means the focal settlement in its totality. Given that these edicts are conditioned by the possibility expressed in LXIII that a *gesith* might choose to depart, it may be aimed primarily at restricting the sub-leasing of erstwhile royal estates by *gesiths*, so minimising the problems inherent in re-establishing control should the king resume the estate.

58 See, for example, the problem raised by this definition in relation to the oath of a *ceorl*, in the *Laws of Ine*, XIV, XIX, XXX, XLVI, LXII, LXIV: Chadwick, *Anglo-Saxon Institutions*, pp. 149–51.

59 *HE*, IV, 23.

60 J. F. McGovern, 'The hide and related land-tenure concepts in Anglo-Saxon England, AD 700–1100', *Traditio*, XXIII, 1972, p. 102, which defines the hides as: 'the concerns of kith-and-kin capitulated to territoriality'; T. M. Charles-Edwards, 'Kinship, status and the origins of the hide', *Past and Present*, LVI, 1972, pp. 1–33 is the classic study.

61 For the *ceorl* as 'husband', see *Laws of Æthelberht*, LXXXV; *Laws of Ine*, XXXVIII, LVII.

62 *Laws of Ine*, LXX.

63 J. Campbell, *The Anglo-Saxons*, London, 1982, p. 58. See also, R. H. Hodgkin, *A History of the Anglo-Saxons*, Oxford, 1935, p. 401; H. P. R. Finberg, *The Formation of England*, London, 1974, pp. 163–5; J. Morris, *The Age of Arthur*, London, 1973, p. 128; N. J. Higham, *Rome, Britain and the Anglo-Saxons*, London, 1992, pp. 144–52.

64 E.g., *HE*, II, 9: *aestimatio Anglorum*, regarding the British territories of Anglesey and Man, and III, 4, regarding Iona.

65 Campbell, *Anglo-Saxons*, p. 58; W. de Grey Birch, *Cartularium Saxonicum*, I, London, 1885, nos. 60, 78, 132, for a selection of the earliest genuine examples from Mercia and Sussex. The earliest, certainly authentic Kentish charter (Hlothhere, 675: Birch, no. 36) refers to three *aratri* ('ploughs'), which should be taken as a variant of the *iugum*.

66 E.g. *HE*, III, 25: *monasterium XL familiarum*; *Life of Wilfrid*, VIII: *terram decem tributariorum* – 'land of ten taxpayers'. The term *tributarii* recurs in Birch, no. 60.

67 E.g. *HE*, I, 25, concerning Thanet; III, 24, concerning Mercia; IV, 13, concerning the South Saxons; IV, 16, concerning the Isle of Wight. See also II, 9.

68 *Beowulf*, line 2195.

69 See above, pp. 94–6.

70 *Beowulf*, lines 2994–5; for further comment on 100,000, see p. 95 and p. 109, note 85.

71 *Beowulf*, p. 205, commentary on lines 2994–5.

72 *Beowulf*, lines 471, 1020–62, 1190–200, 1152 ff.

73 *Beowulf*, 2195: 7,000 hides in association with a *bold ond bregostōl* – 'a hall and seat of power'.

74 See note 70, above.

75 *Laws of Ine*, LI: for *fierdwite* and the nature of early military obligations, see R. P. Abels, *Lordship and Military obligation in Anglo-Saxon England*, London, 1988, pp. 11–42.

76 Bede, *Epistola ad Ecgberctum*, in *Baedae Opera Historica*, ed. C. Plummer, Oxford, 1896, I, pp. 405–23; Birch, no. 60, a Mercian charter of *c.* 681, is among the earliest relevant charters. The vernacular term was *gafolgelda*, but this could also mean 'tenant', so 'payer of rent', and the precise status of a *Wēalh gafolgelda* ('Welsh taxpayer') in *Laws of Ine*, XXIII is unclear.

77 And the needs of the king's warriors were incompatible with excessive granting of royal land to monasteries: see Bede's *Letter to Ecgbert*, note

76 above. Concerning the likely size of such grants, see p. 245 above.

78 See the argument offered on p. 96.

79 For a translation, see *English Historical Documents*, I, p. 738. For a second (earlier) comment by Bede which is relevant to this, see *HE*, IV, 29. For discussion, Charles-Edwards, 'Early medieval kingships', p. 32.

80 As in *HE*, I, 34; II, 1. Contrast with Bede's origins myth in I, 15 and his allusion to other Germanic tribes in V, 9, from whom he envisaged that the Angles and Saxons originated.

81 P. Wormald, 'Bede, the *Bretwaldas* and the origins of the *Gens Anglorum*', in *Ideal and Reality in Frankish and Anglo-Saxon Society*, ed. P. Wormald *et al.*, Oxford, 1983, particularly pp. 124–9.

82 *HE*, II, 1; *Earliest Life of Gregory the Great*, IX.

83 *DEB*, XXIII, 1.

84 *HE*, V, 9, and see footnote 1 on p. 476 of the Oxford text. For earlier notice of this point, see P. H. Blair, *The World of Bede*, London, 1970, p. 23.

85 *DEB*, XXIII, 4; XXXII, 2. See discussion, N. J. Higham, *The English Conquest*, Manchester, 1994, pp. 53, 178–9.

86 Encountered first in *HE*, I, 15: *Anglorum sive Saxonum gens*. Bede was here quite deliberately equating the 'Saxons' of existing histories with the conventional 'Angles' of his own generation as the appropriate generic term for the entire Germanic population of Britain. This treatment recurs in the context of his comment of the *DEB*, in *HE*, I, 22, but he was content, in the next chapter, to use the term 'Angles' as his preferred alternative to Gildas's 'Saxons'. See also *HE*, V, 9.

Index

Index